The Ways
of the Spirit

EVELYN UNDERHILL

The Ways
of the Spirit

Collected, edited, and with an introduction by
Grace Adolphsen Brame

CROSSROAD · NEW YORK

1994
The Crossroad Publishing Company
370 Lexington Avenue, New York, N.Y. 10017

Printed in the United States of America

Library of Congress Cataloging-in-Publication Data

Underhill, Evelyn, 1875–1941.
  The ways of the spirit / edited and with an introduction by Grace Adolphsen Brame.
    p.   cm.
  ISBN 0-8245-1008-9, 0-8245-1232-4 (pbk.)
  1. Spiritual life—Anglican authors. 2. Retreats—Anglican Communion. 3. Anglican Communion. I. Brame, Grace Adolphsen.
II. Title.
BV4501.U528   1990
248.4'83—dc20   89–48585
                                                              CIP

To
LADY LAURA EASTAUGH
generous and genuine,
original member of the
Evelyn Underhill Prayer Group
and, in later years,
coordinator for its retreats,
in gratitude
for the assistance and support
which she has given with such joy.

Contents

In Gratitude

My deepest gratitude goes to the generous people whom I name below. The continued support of my husband, Ed, has been an expression of God's grace to me. Without Sir William Wilkinson, Literary Executor of the Evelyn Underhill Trust, and his wife, Lady Katherine Wilkinson, none of my Underhill research and publication could have been accomplished. It would not even have been begun without the suggestion and encouragement of Dr. Douglas V. Steere, who has deeply admired Underhill since before he met with her in 1927. I have also received the scholarly assistance of Ms. Jane Platt of the Evelyn Underhill Archives at King's College, London. It has been warmly and carefully given.

The learning and kindliness of Canon A. M. "Donald" Allchin has supported me in Underhill research for some years. My friends, Dr. Dana Greene and Ms. Terry Coutret, have made themselves available for conversation and comment. In the summer of 1988, Lady Laura Eastaugh gathered Ms. Amaryllis Bryce, Dame Betty Ridley, and Lady Virgina Benson to listen to parts of this manuscript and answer some of my questions. Others who assisted were archivists and librarians Robert N. Smart of St. Andrews, Scotland; Patricia Methven and Evelyn Cornell of King's College, London; and Ms. Iduna Coulson and Fr. John Tyers of Underhill's favorite house of retreat at Pleshey, near Chelmsford, England.

Here in the United States, my gratitude goes to Frs. Paul Wessinger and David Allen of the Society of St. John the Evangelist; Fr. Eugene Rooney of Georgetown University; Mr. Dan Elliott of St. Charles Seminary; Sr. Christiana of All Saints Convent in Catonsville, Maryland; Ms. Louise Tabasso and Ms. Elizabeth Stack of the Newark and Wilmington Institute Libraries in Delaware; Dr. John Cavadini; Ms. Louise Green and Ms. Bente Polites of Villanova University; Ms. Betsy Brown of Haverford College; librarians Ms. Kathleen Triboletti and Ms. Janet Lafferty; and Mr. John White for advice and guidance.

Real encouragement has been given by the Bogert Fund of the Friends' World Committee for Consultation which, in two consecutive years, has financially assisted my Underhill endeavors.

Once again Underhill is right when she says: "God comes to people through people!"

Introduction

It is an exciting opportunity to share with others these four previously unpublished retreats of Evelyn Underhill (1875–1941). They increase by fifty percent the number of her retreats now available. Underhill herself published five. Her husband, Hubert Stuart Moore, and her cherished friend, Lucy Menzies, published two more posthumously in 1942 and 1945. Another followed in 1960. This means that it has been thirty years since we have had the privilege of reading original Underhill material which has not been seen before.

To add to the joy of discovering these writings is the particularly opportune time in which they will become available. 1991 is the fiftieth anniversary of Underhill's death. Many of her books which have been out of print for some years are being republished, and there are festivals of commemoration on both sides of the Atlantic in honor of her life and contributions to the field of Christian spirituality. There seems to be a reawakening to the value of this unusual person whose work was a major factor in rediscovering, explaining, and popularizing that field in early twentieth-century England and who, as a woman, broke so much ground for her sex.

It was she who was the first woman to lecture to clergy in the Church of England, the first woman to establish a position as a conductor of retreats in that church also, the first woman to forge ecumenical links between separated churches, and one of the earliest women (perhaps the first) to lecture in theology in English colleges and universities. Without a degree herself—but schooled in the classics, able in several languages, informed in current theology and philosophy, and steeped in the vast literature of Western spirituality—she became the religion editor of *The Spectator,* that esteemed journal begun by Addison and Steele in the eighteenth century and still read today.

It was she, more than any other person, who introduced to the British public in general and to Protestant Christians in particular, the forgotten writers of medieval and of Catholic spirituality. In 1965, the religious historian Horton Davies wrote of her 1936 classic book, *Worship* that no other work in the field has been as widely read or as influential among English-speaking people (DWT 157). She was named a fellow of both King's College for Women and King's College and was made a Doctor of

Divinity by Aberdeen University. Davies pairs her with William Ralph Inge and Baron Friedrich von Hügel in the field of spirituality, and the London *Times* wrote at her death that, in that field, she was "unmatched by any of the professional teachers of her day."

She spoke on radio, introduced more books of the saints and mystics than any other writer of her time in England, addressed churches of all denominations, and even spoke for church conferences on social, political, and economic issues. Three years ago, A. M. (Donald) Allchin, Honorary Canon of Canterbury Cathedral and now in Oxford, said to me: "She brought about an amazing change in the position of women in the Church, and furthermore, she was sane and balanced."[1]

The effect of Underhill's work has quietly continued. Her 1936 book, *Worship,* considered by many to be her second most important work, is used in seminaries across the country. There are people throughout the United Kingdom and America who have "walked with her" for years. There are several Anglican Bishops of her own time and today who have been deeply influenced by her. The former Archbishop of Canterbury, Arthur Michael Ramsey, wrote to me in 1987:

> I am very interested in your comments on my own books, and I think some of them were written with a good deal of influence by Evelyn Underhill, though her style never appealed to me greatly. Her influence was considerable during her lifetime. I suppose that of my own books *Sacred and Secular* was nearest to her influence.

I had first written Archbishop Ramsey about Evelyn Underhill in 1985. This manuscript would not be published now had I not been researching for a doctoral dissertation on her.[2]

During that research, in 1987, I found myself reading material I thought I had never seen before. But others had certainly had it in their hands. Obviously Underhill's husband, and perhaps her friends, had collected all the papers through which I was wading, and Jenny Telfer, of the presently inactive Evelyn Underhill Association in England, had carefully assembled them for the archives at King's College on the Strand. There the archivists and at least two or three Underhill scholars had fingered them.

Surely those individuals, like myself, must have at first supposed that the typewritten chapters and the handwritten notebooks *had* to be works already published as part of the impressive Underhill corpus of more than thirty books and almost four hundred articles and book introductions now carefully catalogued by Professor Dana Greene.[3] As it turns out, two notebooks are, but the rest are not. Why then did they remain unrecognized?

First, most of the retreat notebooks were untitled. However, it was obvious that one volume was the handwritten original of *The Light of Christ,* given in 1932 and edited posthumously by Lucy Menzies. It had been published in 1945. Another notebook, written in 1931 in beautiful, clear script, *had* been given a title: *Purgatorio: Seven Deadly Sins and Contrary Virtues.* (When published in 1960, it happily became *The Mount of Purification!*) To recognize two so clearly might well lead one to surmise that the rest were also originals of works already known.

More importantly, Underhill's script was difficult to read. Her handwriting was unique and sometimes variable, a picture of her many-sided personality. (She had at least ten ways for writing a "t"!) Furthermore, she left out words. She abbreviated constantly. Sometimes the abbreviation was only one letter such as an "r" which often meant "Reality" or "real," but *could* mean "right" and *might* mean something else. It took me two months before I learned that "Jr." was really "Fr." and so meant "Father" or "St. Francis," according to the context. Underhill drew arrows, crossed out (because of using the same material for different groups), inserted colored asterisks, and, in a few cases, wrote in now faded pencil. I was increasingly grateful that I knew her thinking and her vocabulary.

The first clues of something unusual and valuable were some typewritten pages scattered through two large archive boxes but obviously belonging together. They had been typed about the same time on the same machine and each set bore a single word as a title. One set referred to another and outlined a rather spotty order. Looking at three of the titles, I thought I might be seeing an early form of *Fruits of the Spirit,* a retreat given in 1936 and published a year after her death. There, too, Underhill had mentioned love, joy, and peace, but all the other subjects were different, and the text was not at all the same.

It was Terry Coutret of the Evelyn Underhill Association of America[4] who found those titles listed in Margaret Cropper's biography of Underhill. There the subjects named were identified as some of the sessions in her first retreat, given in 1924. Agatha Norman, then Underhill's oldest living friend, joyously concurred. And Lady Laura Eastaugh, an original member of the Evelyn Underhill Prayer Group, procured the signature list of original participants from the diocesan retreat house at Pleshey (near Chelmsford) where the retreat was given. When the handwritten notebooks were studied, one was found to be the complete 1924 retreat; thus, the missing links were found. The other three volumes turned out to be the unpublished retreats of 1925, 1927, and 1928.

What had happened to the retreat of 1926? It is evidently the basis of her book *The House of the Soul,* which both Menzies and Cropper say was based on retreat notes.[5] Since it was published in 1929 and the other retreats before that time are printed here, it would have to be the 1926 retreat.

Identification was only the beginning, of course. It remained to decipher the writing, to read and enjoy and analyze the thought, to compare the retreats to each other and to the work Underhill had already written and was writing then and thereafter, and thus to assess their value.

It turns out that Cropper, well aware of these manuscripts, had spoken of their importance in her biography. According to her, "all" of Underhill's "books in the last fifteen years of her life, except *Worship*" were based on these early retreats (CEU 118).[6]

If they eventually became so important, what function had they played in forming and coalescing Underhill's thought? What kind of spirit was emerging in her in those days? Was there any significant difference between this Underhill and the one who wrote *Mysticism* (published in 1911) and four other major books on the same subject in the fourteen years up through 1925? Where did they stand in Underhill's personal and theological evolution?

The answer is: at the crux. There is no doubt of the change that came about in Underhill from the time when she began writing *Mysticism* in 1907 until the completion of her first retreat in 1924. In those earlier days it was mysticism and mystics who met her need to be challenged by the heroic and the inspiring, yet who comforted and sustained her and gave her strength. But it must be made clear, as she so carefully explained, that mysticism meant to her nothing strange, peculiar, purely psychic, or occult in the unfortunate popular understanding of that word. Underhill increasingly described mysticism and mystics, not in terms of spiritual self-centeredness, but as its exact opposite: as sel*fless* self-*given*ness.

After the publication of *The Mystics of the Church* in 1925, her choice of language changed. She wrote about saints instead of mystics, and the spiritual life instead of mysticism, perhaps to avoid those misunderstandings mentioned above. She began to speak of life lived, not in the Mystic Way (which she charted in a book of that title in 1913), but following the Way of the Cross.

Her writings were about spiritual matters of critical importance, but she was far from being a somber individual. Her friends found her warm and bright and witty, curious and inventive. She loved good art and snow-capped mountains, sailing, bookbinding, gardening, and cats, and occasionally she went to visit a friend riding in the side car of her husband's motorcycle! She was devoted to her husband and parents, and although childless, cared for and counseled numbers of people whom her dear friend, Lucy Menzies, called her "Family."

But in 1923 and 1924 she was living through a time of intense inner turmoil of which even her best friends and family did not know. In her unpublished biography of Underhill, Lucy Menzies writes: "I had no idea of what she was going through!"

No easy answers would do for her then, no "sunshine school of piety," as she put it, no "bright, professional" approach. It was true that her theology and philosophy had cleared, largely through the guidance of her beloved spiritual director, Baron von Hügel. But she was left to deal with the *reality*, the implementation, of what she thought and believed. She had to learn to live it and to embrace it, not just believe it. Her sensitive nature—the nature of a person who felt deeply, was a perfectionist, and was highly motivated but relentlessly self-critical—truly suffered.

Reading Underhill's spiritual journal (which biographer Christopher Armstrong calls "the green notebook")[7] reveals that before this time and during it, she was having mystical experiences. She had personally experienced herself as "an almost invisible speck in the Ocean" of God's reality. She had felt all things merged together in "the interpenetration of Spirit," "we in Christ and He in us." For a moment she "saw 'the Universe that thinks and knows.'" She had felt "a divine inner peace" like "continuous music." She had heard "the Voice."

But these uplifting and extraordinary experiences not only showed her that we are surrounded and immersed in God as "our environment," but sharpened her sense of spiritual inadequacy. In those glorious times when the transcendent permeated the ordinary she saw and felt that "natural life is a sacrament of the supernatural." Yet, if that is true, it is also true that she, like each of us, had to deal with the realities of both. One does not cancel out the other. The path of life is not only *in* eternity but *toward* eternity; and the journey is not finished.

Her spiritual insight and experience had to be integrated into normal life. The process, as St. Paul and so many mystics have written, could be like "spiritual warfare."[8] And Underhill, in the green notebook, called it "war"!

It had to be interpreted too. In the same year as this first retreat, Underhill addressed the Conference on Politics, Economics, and Christianity (COPEC) on "The Will of the Voice" and quoted George Bernard Shaw as saying: "Enoch . . . has given up his will to do the will of the Voice . . . but it took Enoch two hundred years to learn to interpret the Will of the Voice" (UMP 85).

In that same year, her mother died. Evelyn, an only child, had lived across a quadrangle from her mother since her marriage, and she had had her mother to lunch almost every day. But her mother never shared Evelyn's deep spiritual concerns. Von Hügel wrote in condolence, "The very difference between you must be adding to the trial," increasing the pain of loss. With her mother's death, came the possibility of having to move from her beloved home to her parents'. About the same time, the Baron's health was failing.

In January of 1925 von Hügel died. It was an enormous loss. He had truly been her spiritual father. Although she rarely saw him and regarded him with deepest respect, and although she was a woman of great feeling but outwardly reserved, she had shared with him her deepest spiritual self, light years beyond what she could ever hope to share with her natural father or even her husband, both of whom went to church only for events such as weddings and funerals or occasions of state. She was, in one sense, very much alone.

I believe that during 1923 and 1924 this sensitive, courageous woman went through her greatest mortification. It was not simply a letting go of two people who had given her life in vastly different ways. It was a crucifixion of the ego. It was a process in which she was caught but also which she fostered. She had come to believe strongly that loss of self-centered concern was the only way to become a better tool for God. She became merciless in her attacks upon her own insufficiency and she found it difficult, sometimes impossible, to fully accept God's grace.

She fought for will instead of feeling in her faith. She struggled for constancy and certainty. She rejected spiritual consolations for sacrificial commitment. She put aside purely personal religion in favor of individual membership in the life of the Body of Christ, the Church.

It is all reflected in these four retreats. After writing a 325-page dissertation which covered her life but focused on the latter part, I am hard pressed to think of any subject I covered there which she did not mention in these first retreats.

The dissertation was based on a theme which I see as part of all Underhill writing, a theme which appears in these retreats but intensifies in her later years. It is the theme of God's grace and the response of the human will. "Which comes first?" asks Underhill. "Which is first in time and action, first in importance and excellence?" And she answers (in the 1924 retreat) with those telling words of 1 John 4:19: "We love Him because He first loved us." Indeed, "God is love," and that God, that love or grace which is the essence of God, is, in her philosphical language, "the first term."

For Underhill, God is first, not only as source of all but as the only reason for living and, therefore, as inherently deserving our allegiance, an offered and committed will. That will is, according to Underhill, "partially free," for only the divine will knows complete freedom. Thus, we who follow after the One who brought us into being, learn through the pressure of divine suggestion. Each Godly "push" is meant to help us find and surrender to our individual paths of knowing and revealing the redeeming love of God.

As I was able to explain at length in the dissertation, Underhill stated quite clearly how important this understanding had become to her. Even a small part of her landmark statement from the preface of the 1930 edition of *Mysticism* brings that out:

> Were I, then, now planning this book for the first time, its arguments would be differently stated. More emphasis would be given (a) to the concrete, richly living yet unchanging character of the Reality over against the mystic, as the first term, cause and incentive of his experience; (b) to that paradox of utter contrast yet profound relation between the Creator and the creature, God and the soul, which makes possible his development; (c) to the predominant part played in that development by the free and prevenient action of the Supernatural—in theological language, by "grace"—as against all merely evolutionary or emergent theories of spiritual transcendence. I feel more and more that no psychological or evolutionary treatment of man's spiritual history can be adequate which ignores the element of "givenness." (p. viii)

Underhill continues her introduction by embracing critical realism as her philosophic preference. What she has said above has already explained it. God is not only an immanent "force" but an awesomely transcendent "Reality" without which no other reality would exist. While we are meant to be vessels of the divine, as all life is meant to be, we are not the source of that divinity, but only its channels. The Creative Spirit made and sustains all created spirits.[9] We are derivative and dependent. Each life, as St. Paul said, is "hidden in God," and *in* God "we live and move and have our being."

I inevitably find that many of those who write about Underhill say that she did not have this point of view before she came under von Hügel's direction. I also read that before that time she was a vitalist (who says there is no life force outside of nature), a monist (who says that there is but one non-differentiated fundamental reality which pervades all things in what Underhill describes as a "sameness"), and a pantheist (a monist who says that each thing is divinity). I simply do not agree, although there is no doubt that her sense of the transcendence, the perfection, and the awesomeness of God was a continuously growing thing, and was greatly fostered by her relationship with von Hügel. Nevertheless, although she made the above statement about critical realism in 1930, the essentials of that point of view are found, but not emphasized, in *Mysticism* as originally published in 1911.[10]

Underhill, of course, cannot be divorced from her time any more than anyone else. She spoke of God as "He." Were she living today, I am certain she would have made quite clear, probably in a quite humorous way, that since she would not have the affrontery to limit God, she would most certainly not limit God's attributes except for the constraints of language.

Looking through these retreats, we of course are seeing the major themes of Underhill's thought from the mid-twenties to the end of her life. At the beginning of her list is always the transcendent but pervasive God whose essence is love, but who makes demands, and to whom the first response is adoration. That adoration, "caring for God above all else," is "the supreme duty and delight" of the creature, and "the central service asked by God of human souls" (UEM 138, 180).

The human being is a "little half-made creature," comparatively insignificant, yet derived from and indissolubly linked with its parent as we are to our human parents, regardless of our goodness or waywardness. Our response to God is of our own election, our own choice. To the call of God, which is offered to everyone, each child has the awesome privilege of saying "Yes" or "No," of growing up toward God and in God or of moving farther and farther away as did the Prodigal Son. Indeed, "the whole of religion, sanctity, and undeveloped spiritual life hinges on the incredible power to say 'Yes' or 'No' to God" (UCG 214).

When the child says "Yes," its growth, transformation, or sanctification is aided by the inspiration of those heroic souls who have gone before and walk beside it, the Communion of Saints, on earth and in heaven, for death, says Underhill, makes no difference here. The saints are, for her, incredibly important, and sustainingly real.

Prayer is the essential ingredient for life in God and for that "unselfing" which is sanctification. And prayer is two-sided for Underhill. It is passive and active. As passive prayer, it is adoring, attentive, contemplative, and receptive of God's grace. As active prayer, it is intercessory and so a means to follow in the work of Christ, the work of loving redemption of the world. After all, "redemption," Underhill explains, "does not mean you and me made safe and popped into heaven. It means that each soul, redeemed from self-interest by the revelation of Divine Love, is taken and used again for the spread of that redeeming work" (USP 68).

Underhill is always aware that grace given to an individual soul is to be shared through some outward reach. She is quite clear that to know and delight in God and to become a tool for God's redeeming work is the only reason to be alive. "We exist for nothing else," she writes (UIG 176).[11] The members of Christ, then, as parts of His Body, are here to bring the Kingdom "on earth as in heaven." But it will be possible only when heaven is already in their souls. The road to the Kingdom *always* includes the Way of the Cross, and the Cross means cost, perhaps even giving up that which matters most, even one's own spiritual good, for the sake of another. Yet as children of God, we are the heirs, and the inheritance, which is living in the full presence of our parent, awaits and is offered to us.

Most of these basic themes are found in all the retreats. In those of 1924 and 1925, the relationship of God and the soul, election and the influence of the saints, adoring prayer and growth are all emphasized. Both dwell on love that serves, or "charity" as it is called in the Authorized or "King James" Version of the scriptures which Underhill employed. Of course, the 1924 retreat dwells on love, joy, and peace as well: love as the inescapable presence of God and the human response of devotion, joy as the humility of childlikeness, and peace as the harmony of the human will with the divine.

Underhill felt that her "mission" was to laity in particular. But the second two retreats were also given to priests, wives of clergy, and social workers as well as volunteers in the program of the church. She refers to one of these groups as the BVM. This was the Community of the Blessed Virgin Mary, a group of lay women banded together to serve the church and provide homes for homeless children, women, and the elderly.[12] It is interesting to see that, among the 1927 registrants at Pleshey was Olive Wyon who, herself, became a well-known writer in the field of Christian spirituality.

By knowing who was listening to her in these years, her choice of subject matter becomes more understandable. In the 1927 retreat, she deals with courage, generosity, and patience, the three virtues she sees as most necessary in a life of service to God. She follows that with the means of attaining and sustaining such a life through adoration, communion, and cooperation with God. In the last retreat, she focuses on vocation as the pesonal call of God, repentance upon seeing the vision of God, and consecration as the response. Then she balances the personal with the corporate aspect, the meaning of being a member of Christ's living Body and one of God's children. The final chapter is about the common struggle and ambivalence in accepting what is finally found to be our natural inheritance and home, the very presence of God.

As noted above, Underhill had not titled the retreats which are in this book. Those titles were chosen by reading what she had to say and encapsulating it in a short phrase for each retreat. The paragraphs on each title page are those which seem to sum up the purpose and theme of each retreat.

Sanctity: The Perfection of Love (1924)

It was an exciting experience to find Underhill summarizing her view of sanctity so briefly that her own words could be used for the title of the first retreat, *Sanctity: The Perfection of Love*. The theme of "sanctity" or "holiness" runs through her writing, and Dana Greene makes a point of saying that "Underhill's search was for the holy" (GQH 2). There are ample statements by Underhill to substantiate Greene's point. In Underhill's lectures to clergy entitled *Concerning the Inner Life* (1926), she wrote very simply and clearly: "Sanctity after all is the religious goal." In a 1932 address entitled "The Need of Retreat" she stated that the object of the retreat movement was "the same as the object of the Christian life— sanctity—the production, fostering, and maintenance of holiness" (ULC 106).

And yet, that is not the end of the story. What good is holiness? What is it for? Underhill answers: sanctity is for the sake of love. Indeed sanctity is the perfection of love, an unselfing that enables us to truly give. Underhill's view of sanctity is not of a perfected state which is attained just because God requires it, or to make one good enough for heaven, or for the sake of one's own hidden spiritual pride. It is *not*, in this sense, the final goal. It is not final at all. It is potential. It is dynamic. It has power, a power to be used to bless the world, to increase the awareness of Reality, to bring in the Kingdom.

In the address to the clergy mentioned above, she quoted her beloved von Hügel, writing on holiness and the soul: "The soul is a Force or an Energy; and Holiness is the *growth* of that energy in love, in full Being, in creative, spiritual Personality." That transfiguring growth which is called "sanctification" is for a purpose, and that is to become a tool of God.

So holiness is not a state to be gained by going away from life but by entering into it in the most vital way, especially through prayer—the prayer of adoration, the prayer of communion that we share unseen with others, intercessory prayer, and life lived as a prayer of love. Although some are truly called to a contemplative vocation, all are called to prayer in the midst of ordinary life.

In this first retreat, Underhill begins by preparing her listeners for full use of the hours ahead. Still remembering the temerity with which she went to her own first retreat in 1907, she consciously works to make plain the most important things they need to know. For several pages we read her beautiful words about silence: "Without silence, the inward stillness in which God educates and molds us is impossible." "Our deepest contacts with God are so gentle because this is all that we can bear." She cautions against conversation unless truly helpful, and urges each person to let themselves be led by God, not by the leader of the retreat, saying: "I am no more the authority over your real journey than the conductor of a bus."

Turning to the subject of sanctity, she embraces Christ's statement in His High Priestly Prayer found in John 17: "For their sakes I sanctify myself." It is a prayer appropriate to all who would seek to help others.

But then she cautions that we cannot give what we do not have. "It is impossible to bring Christ to others until He has been revealed *in* us." Therefore she gives each a second aim: to discover themselves in God's presence and God's presence in themselves.

Underhill's second session is based on a problem which was always with her, and which plagued her particularly at the time: excessive self-criticism. She passed on her new understanding, not because she had conquered her problem (for she evidently never did) but because she could see it so clearly. We go on retreat, she said, not for exhausting, microscopic self-scrutiny, but to open our souls in order to drink in God. It is a discourtesy to God not to receive what He is giving, just as it is "a mean, self-centered attitude towards perfection" to go to a magnificent concert and think only of how badly one plays his or her own instrument. "First to last," she states, "put all emphasis on God. Attend to Him. Forget yourselves if you can. Bathe in His light."

Underhill's idea of love, which she next presents, is not at all a sentimental one. She adopts Teresa of Avila's view that the object of life is "to love, work, and suffer" but admits that it is impossible unless we grow in a realization of the love of God. Then we can love God back and, in so doing, learn to love all weak and imperfect things. "The bread of life seldom has any butter on it," writes Underhill, and the consolations of religion are merely its "chocolate creams"! If we want a model in loving and living, we might look to the devoted and steady sheepdog who seldom comes back for strokes, but when it comes time for rest, is generally found beside the shepherd.

There is a lightness in Underhill's next words on joy. Sanctity is the perfection of love, but when we look at sanctity, we see joy. And the root of adoring joy is the realization of our own insignificance in comparison to God's perfection. Why? Because then we *realize* that we are God's *child*. In the recognition of our true status, we find ourselves "in a magical and most exciting world . . . the Kingdom of Heaven which Christ *promised* to the child." Then, if our love can move away from anxious effort and lose its self-consciousness, an extraordinary burden falls away. Thus detached from the ups and downs of the world, our joy becomes "the greatest missionary instrument" of all.

(When readers of Underhill are put off by her terminology as a Victorian woman who speaks of us as "naughty children in the nursery," it is helpful to refer back to this section on joy and to notice that it is because God is so magnificent that Underhill sees humans as so very insignificant or small.)

The following section on peace was evidently a favorite of Underhill's since she used it more than once, adding it to the end of her 1927 retreat as well. It will be found, in this volume, only in its original place here.

Underhill, like many of the Christians of her day, read and loved *The Imitation of Christ* usually accredited to Thomas à Kempis. It was, of course, for some time the most read book other than the Bible in the Christian world. Underhill begins her section on peace with a quotation from that work and midway quotes again from Thomas his words of utter dedication: "If Thou wilt that I be in the light . . . (or) in the darkness, blessed be Thou."

Perhaps Underhill's simplest definition of peace is "the harmony of our will with God's." We are mistaken if we think it is "basking in the divine sunshine like comfortable pussycats" or being satisfied with a "copy-cat sort of holiness." (Underhill had several beloved cats who furnished her with metaphors.) Peace is, instead, a *profound* giving of ourselves to God, tested in our own Gethsemane, and sometimes better realized in the darkness than in the light. Underhill's wry humor explains this trusting peace with a smile: "It is a very poor sort of faith and love that will not face a dark passage until it knows where the switch is." Later she adds much more seriously: "It is not in our comprehension, but in God's will" (as Augustine had written) "that our peace abides."

According to Underhill, it takes both God's grace and our will to create prayer. She reminds us of Christ's commands to "ask," "seek," and "knock," and she begins with Teresa of Avila's example: the water for which we thirst is God's grace, but God gives us the job of hauling it with our own buckets! To ask should make us ready to receive. To seek is to meditate and to think without strain and in confidence in the presence of God; thus we discover His call within our souls. To knock is to find God opening the door and sharing that world beyond the door and so giving us a new and overruling consciousness. She cautions, however, that as we train ourselves in the habit of attention to God, we need to learn it in our own natural and simple way, for each person's best way of praying is his or her own way.

Underhill's next subject is the Communion of Saints. In 1907, when she stopped herself from joining the Catholic Church to which she had given her heart, and remained outside because of Pius X's pronouncements against Modernism in theology,[13] it was the saints who gave her courage, comfort, and inspiration. She devoured their stories and their writings. I am convinced that what appeared at first to be an enormous tragedy to her was turned into a blessing that lasted throughout her life and deeply affected her gift to the world. Stories of the saints and quotes from them are threaded through almost everything she wrote. Their importance to her is obvious when she says that "spiritual reading is second only to prayer as a support of the inner life." Her awareness of the saints (and not just the "official" ones) brought about "a horizontal growth" in her soul and underscored von Hügel's teaching that all of us are "literally members of one another." When, in the next session, she turns to the subject of growth, Underhill tells us that the saints are simply people like ourselves whose souls have fully grown up and so are able to fully serve.

When Underhill talks about growth, we cannot help but notice the times in which she lived. Henri Bergson and Rudolf Eucken held a compelling fascination for her in the early years of the century, yet she had disagreements with both. Although not Darwinian, Bergson spoke of evolution in psychological terms and Eucken wrote of spiritual evolution, ideas which Underhill related to sanctification. But many will be surprised to read in this section: "Most of us now accept the theory of evolution. We recognize the growth of conscious mind from the humblest animal origins as consistent with the divine creative will, but . . . we have not seen the extent of this will." It fits with her statements about human beings being "half-made" and "half-animal." Contemporary language puts it succinctly too: "God isn't finished with me yet!"

It is obvious that Underhill stood in direct opposition to Charles Darwin's "My deity is Nature" (see UM 8–11) and to secular humanism which has developed from Darwinism and knows no deity other than the human being. Underhill's use of the term "evolution" refers to the natural fruition of God's plan for humanity, based on a path providing for growth in consciousness and commitment, selflessness and outreaching love.

"He created us for Himself," she writes, quoting her favorite, Augustine, "to continue His line of creation beyond nature to *more*." Evolution is to be from natural self-regarding individualism to becoming a fellow worker with God. That is accomplished only in dependence upon a single source, as a plant grows toward the light by reaching deep into its "invisible foundation" for its food, accepting whatever nourishment is provided. She cautions against striving to match another: "What is demanded . . . is the perfection of our own inherent powers and not conformity to a pattern."

For the last address Underhill reaffirms the object of growth as service, the redemptive life. "In choosing God, we take sides with . . . a holiness that pours itself out to sinfulness" and loves the unlovely into loveableness. We discover the connection between the holy and the ordinary. Then we realize that "sanctity comes right down to and through all the simplicities of human life, and indeed would be of no use to us unless it did so." Yet the demands of such a life are impossible without receiving the gifts which God provides. When we have learned to do this, we have learned "the whole secret of the saints."

Underhill finished the retreat with a service of meditation, based on her major themes. We will discuss how she did this when we speak of retreat devotions. For now, let us turn to her second retreat.

The End for Which We Were Made (1925)

The most surprising thing about *The End for Which We Were Made* is that it is based on the sayings of Ignatius of Loyola, the founder of the Society of Jesus. Underhill mentions him here and there in her various books, but he never gets more than a few lines in any case. Yet here she challenges her retreatants with three sets of the most penetrating questions and the most meaningful statements she can find—all from Ignatius and restated here on the opening page.

For some time, Underhill made a yearly private retreat. One cannot help but wonder if, on some of those occasions, she used the *Spiritual Exercises* of Ignatius. There is no doubt she was familiar with them and probably knew them by experience. In her short address entitled, "The Need of Retreat," published with *The Light of Christ*, she states that most people should not make a practice of making regular retreats in the Ignatian form because it can be too "shattering." Its effect is long-term for most people. Evidently it was for her. To introduce all three of the retreats for 1925, 1927, and 1928 she uses meditative suggestions derived from those *Exercises*. Throughout those retreats, she speaks in picture language, setting a scene, as did Ignatius, and asking her listeners to put themselves in it, there to see themselves in the light of God's presence and accept His revelation. But she never approaches the extremes that Ignatius sometimes touched upon.

In October of 1926, Underhill wrote an article for *The Spectator* on Paul Van Dyke's *Ignatius Loyola*. She marked in her own copy of that book (now in Dr. Williams's Library in London) the aim of the *Exercises* as given by Ignatius: "To conquer self and order life without . . . exaggerated affection." In her article she commends Ignatius as one who: "Like the Oxford Methodists . . . wove together his intellectual, practical, and spiritual capacities. . . . [in a] supple and selfless life . . . unsparing in its demands . . . , yet free from rigidity . . . [which is] the ideal of the *Spiritual Exercises*."

Yet it may have been partially the example of Ignatius which caused her to be so self-critical. On the margin of another page she noted "the particular examination of conscience" which recommends working on a specific sin by remembering it upon arising, noting after both lunch and supper how many times one has yielded to it, and comparing the record of every day with several weeks.[14] There is no indication that Underhill ever went this far, but the advice may well have influenced the way she consistently reported specific personal inadequacies to von Hügel. None of this, however, seems to be in any of her retreats or letters except for one line almost hidden in *The Call of God* where she tucks in six words: "Then make little lists of sins" (UCG II).

This retreat affected two other projects which Underhill took on in the next two years. Evidently Underhill felt that what she had said here was valuable because she took several pages from it for her addresses to clergy the following year. Thus those who know those talks, published as *Concerning the Inner Life,* will notice some similarities in chapters II, VI, and VII of this retreat. Some will also see that Underhill used part of the section on prayer in this retreat for her chapter on adoration in *Inner Grace and Outward Sign.*

Underhill begins this second retreat by reminding us that our lives have meaning only as they relate to God's eternal reality, the great wholeness within which our lives are lived and which we come to remember in retreat. Again she urges quiet, not so we can speak to God, but in order to hear God's whisper, the quiet voice of "One who has everything to tell us and nothing to learn from us."

"Deliberate meditation should be a chief act of retreat," says Underhill. She gives two paragraphs of direction about how to meditate by reading a passage from the New Testament and imagining oneself within the scene, looking at Christ and hearing, in the present, what He says. Then she offers the advice of Mother Janet Stuart to "think glorious thoughts of God."[15]

"What matters first and last is God," writes Underhill in chapter II. The principle which Ignatius made the foundation of his exercises was that the very reason for human life is "to praise, reverence, and serve God." But we miss the point, says Underhill. We think God is here to serve *us,* rather than the other way around. Our prayers show it. "God becomes merely the source of energy for carrying on our activities," rather than the One whom we seek. Furthermore, we think we can serve God without attention to or a relationship with God, and that is impossible. "If God is real, it is the most important fact in our lives," and whether God is real to us or not is not a matter of His true presence or absence, but of our own awareness. When He is real to us, God lives and works in us.

But what, in comparison with the magnificence of God, is the little human soul? The third chapter answers with another Ignatian axiom: "I come from God. I belong to God. I am destined for God." We begin as embryonic spiritual personalities who are called to growth in the image of God, that sanctification which Teresa described so well when she spoke of "the seven mansions of the soul." And the test of our growth is not special experiences in prayer, but the result of those experiences outside prayer, the things we do because we have forgotten ourselves. "Pride is . . . more stupidity than . . . sin," Underhill states with disarming directness. "It is an inability to grasp the facts," to realize our utter helplessness without God. Even Jesus knew that as He faced the three great temptations, all of them testing His pride. And He deliberately chose to depend only on God through "homely," that is "ordinary," ways.

Now Underhill comes to the subject of election. But here she is not speaking of God's choice of some of us for eternal salvation (as that term frequently signifies), but of our own choice regarding "the end for which we were created." She presents the three probing questions which Ignatius includes in the final *colloquy* of his first exercise: "What have I done for Christ? What am I doing? What ought I to do?" Our path of life will depend upon our answer.

Three paths are possible: the paths of respectability, sanctity, or sin. If we dare to choose the path of sanctity, a life of love and prayer, it will mean enough detachment from the world so that we may truly put our attention on God, but sufficient attachment to the world to work for God within it. It will mean the discipline of a disciple and the yoke of surrender. It will mean courage and initiative on one hand and gentleness and mercy on the other.

"When we elect for God," writes Underhill in the next chapter (V), "we envisage the end which is called . . . 'the fullness of the stature of Christ,' . . . . the creative spiritual personality." Yet Christ's own stature was not attained in vague, fluffy, heady experiences, but "in the naturalness of the supernatural," in ways we would never have invented, which could never have come in humbler disguise! The life of Christ is *realism*, proclaims Underhill, and then explains:

> Redemption was not worked out in temple worship. It was worked out in ordinary life among the ruck of the sinful, sick, maimed, stupid, and self-interested. It was accomplished through sharing the suffering and injustice of life. There was a temple ritual all ready, but Reality reached and won its creatures by contact through personality, a contact that then and now evades nothing and leaves nothing out.

God's action on human beings is through a human being. Therefore, Christ's life is the pattern for our growth. Perhaps we shall see that saints are not people of aloof, uninvolved calmness, but individuals who are willing to be wounded for someone else's sin. And we, when we are fully awake, will realize that "we *can* accept redemptive suffering for one another," just as the saints really *do*.

The saints, says Underhill, are heroic and tender people of prayer. And prayer is not just a holy electrical energy provided by God to do our jobs. It has something to do with God's purposes and something to do with our whole life. Indeed prayer is life. As such, we should not expect it to be always joyous or peaceful or the same from one time to the next any more than we expect the weather, the geography, and the associations of life to be identical from day to day. And although we pray *to* God and *for* others, " 'Thou shalt love the Lord thy God' comes first."

Underhill then returns to the subject of receptivity, emphasizing that it is impossible to do anything for God without receiving the gifts that God offers. "We forget," she writes, "that our primary need is to receive in order to nourish our adoring love." "We must receive before we can transmit." Indeed, to pray in a receiving way affects the very destiny of the soul. Our destiny is to be a receiver and transmitter of grace. It is only when our hearts are full of God that we can share what has been given.

The influence of Teresa of Avila is threaded through Underhill's writing, and it appears again in the last section of this retreat. It is Teresa's advice that Underhill passes on for testing all spiritual experience, including prayer: has it left us more humble, more loving, and with "a keen sense of the holy character of our daily work?"

The main thrust of this last chapter, however, is Teresa's second test, the challenge to charity, "the outward swing of prayer toward the world"—in a word, "intercession." Underhill puts it quite clearly: "We have to grasp that if we are really members of the Body of Christ, His redeeming work in this world will be done through us and largely through our prayer." In life and in prayer we are God's tools, and there is a cost. Underhill has come to realize, by this time in her life, that intercession involves sacrifice. She may puncture many a spiritual balloon when she makes clear that union with God, the aim of countless numbers on the spiritual path, is not all bliss, nor divorced from the sin and pain of the world. "Union of the soul with God," she states, "is in the Cross." "We can't help to redeem what we don't love."

Inner Grace and Outward Sign (1927)

As Underhill moves to her 1927 retreat, *Inner Grace and Outward Sign,* her message seems to become more challenging and more passionate. It is almost as though it were written to follow the subject which we have just left. She is stronger within herself, and she has been fully embraced by the Anglican Church, being a member of the committee for the revision of the Book of Common Prayer, a matter of enormous importance to both the Church and the country.

In this retreat we find her pushing to the limit the subjects of which she speaks. Her goal is perfect servanthood through perfect courage, generosity, patience, and so on. She can be daunting. When a retreatant told her once that she felt overwhelmed, even "shattered," Menzies says that Underhill explained that the perfection which she counseled was "an ideal to be striven after rather than attained in this world" (ULC 11). It probably would have helped many if she had written or said those words in public. Christ did ask us to be perfect, but even of Himself, He said: "Why do you call me good? Only God is good" (Matt. 19:17).

This was the first retreat that Underhill was asked to give in Canterbury Cathedral. In October of that year she shared it in the crypt of that beloved church. The influence of the surroundings can be felt particularly in her introduction: "We have come together in this wonderful place to think of . . . the life of prayer and consecration."

The Ignatian influence is still there. "What am I for?" she asks. And her response comes: "to translate something of [God's] spiritual reality into the terms of human life," "to be a temple of the Holy Spirit." And "how am I doing my job?" Such a question must have an individual response.

She suggests that such personal questions be answered by using two processes. The first is meditation where each individual lovingly gazes at the Mysteries, the events of the life of Christ, and bathes in their light. The second is self-examination in that same light and the realization of utter contrast between the finite and the Infinite. Her point is that the answers to life's major questions cannot be found by reason alone but in the primary experience of relationship with God. "We have come," she states, "not to get information . . . from addresses [but] . . . to look." Underhill offers her own simplified version of the *Spiritual Exercises*. Then she comments: "Such a sort of mental prayer is the most searching and purifying of all religious exercises if we use it correctly. It forces the soul . . . to realize that the full grandeur of religion is not in the consolations it gives us but in all which it demands and evokes from us."[16]

The second chapter reminds us that the Christian church was founded where the blood of the martyrs fell. It was founded by supernatural courage, a courage whose very essence is summed up in Christ's journey to Jerusalem. Underhill puts before us a picture of Christ setting his face deliberately, not toward ecstatic communion, but to the accomplishment of the Father's will. When she moves to the scene in Gethsemane one begins to feel that now she is talking personally, that what she is describing is her own experience of meditation when she came to "the first true realization of the Cross," "the shrinking horror," "the entire pure act of resignation," "the uncalculable surrender." The next question is unavoidable. What then does Gethsemane mean now? It means that "each time we go to commune, we really accept that cup too." It means that "the Way of the Cross goes from the contemplative joys of the Transfiguration to the lonely trials of Gethsemane, and then on." It means that "our souls are not made over to God by one mechanical act of conversion, but by the long, unremitting, courageous effort that conversion begins." Then Underhill's humor enters in: "The Holy Spirit isn't like one of those patented cleansers that does our washing while we are asleep!"

The toughness of the chapter on courage is softened by the next one on generosity. Underhill begins with a sense of the light and warmth of the givenness of God, and then sets before us one picture after another. There is the Good Shepherd who both lives and dies just for His sheep, the "loving sacrifice of infinite worth for the apparently worthless." What a terrible waste! But no, says Underhill, it is God's normal, non-commercial approach: uncalculated and unfailing generosity. From this scene she takes us to the washing of the Disciples' feet, then to Christ responding to the weeping Peter, to the daughters of Jerusalem, and to the thief on the cross. Generosity means longing to bring all that is good to everyone and anyone, whether "tiresome, embittered, selfish, degraded" or "twisted out of shape." Nothing but a "generous love will help them or release them: no justice, no good advice, no teaching or reforming. Nothing but indulgent, uncritical, sacrificial love." Why else do we go to Communion, but to join ourselves with others offering themselves to and for a love like that?

Finally Underhill comes to patience. The strength of this piece is in the recognition that, although we often have little choice of what happens *to* us, we surely have some choice as to what happens *in* us. There is a "letting go," an appropriate relinquishment of needs and wants that the growing soul must learn. There is a forgiving and a dying to self-centeredness that is as important as the affirmation of life. Patience is, for Underhill, "that aspect of our love that bears evenly the uneven," and impatience is ultimately a form of self-love which keeps us from putting God first. Underhill speaks of patience toward God, toward others, and toward ourselves. To her that means accepting life as it is, "to simply and generously forget what goes wrong" in the actions of others toward us, allowing the knowledge of our weakness to "purify us from the last crumbs of self-esteem." At the end of life it may well be not the impressive religious persons but the quiet heroic people who will be found to have best accomplished the work given them by God.

I feel, however, that in this section, Underhill may unintentionally mislead people who, like herself, desire complete commitment to God. She cannot speak to all people when she says, "Strain is always our own fault. It is always a failure to accept . . . events." Unless one believes in the Hindu doctrine of karma over several lifetimes, it is appropriate to ask, "Is the strain of starvation in Ethiopia, or political imprisonment by tyranical governments, or suffering the prejudice of others the fault of the victim?" Do we sometimes add more strain when we require the acceptance of intolerable conditions from someone already burdened? Furthermore, those who choose the uphill, narrow, rocky path that leads to the Cross are knowingly assuming strain. It is not their *fault*, but the accepted challenge of their vocation. Facing the Cross is a strain. Luke says that Christ's sweat was "like great drops of blood" before He was able to say, "Not my will but Thine be done!"

Underhill speaks of God testing us through "people He puts in our way," and asks us to surrender to His chipping and shaping of our souls through such individuals. Yet the Bible tells us that God is not the author of disorder (1 Cor. 14:33). Would it not clarify things if Underhill were to say that God can and does offer grace within such situations, but is not responsible for creating them? Surely we must not confuse surrender to God with surrender to anything that happens to us or to someone else. There is injustice in the world, and when Christ was here, his anger blazed against it. He who came to give abundant life suffered at the enforced patience of those who bore the pain of tyranny. It is because Christians have misunderstood the theology of patience that liberation theology has been born. The danger of patience is in accepting whatever situation we are in as "God's will." The danger of patience is the danger of hiding our talent in the field and refusing to claim it. The danger of patience is in not fighting for justice for others or in allowing the meaning and value of our own lives to slip away. It is the problem of taking any virtue to its extreme. It becomes a stumbling block.

When Underhill turns to the themes of adoration, communion, and cooperation as the components of the life of prayer, she attributes the schema to Jean-Jacques Olier. Those who know *The Spiritual Life*, which originated as broadcast talks ten years later, will remember that there she used Cardinal de Bérulle's schema of adoration, adherence, and coopera-tion. Her treatment here is more extended. It is impressive to see Under-hill write on similar subjects throughout her life but always with unique freshness and added insight. She does, however, repeat a portion here from her section on adoration in her 1925 retreat.

Underhill is a writer of metaphors, and Olier must have reached her imagination when he described adoration as "Christ before our eyes," communion as "Christ within our hearts," and cooperation as "Christ in our hands." Underhill describes these three as the soul looking up to God, then discovering that very source of joy and power within, and responding by offering itself as an instrument of God's creative, redemptive work.

We already know that adoration is the heart of prayer for Underhill. It is refreshing to hear her say that it is not repentance, but adoration that is "putting first things first." So she writes: "The 'Te Deum' and 'Sanctus' are . . . far more profound expressions of humility than any prayer of contrition can ever be because . . . the self is entirely left out." To adore is to open wide our souls to God who is already there. That is also the beginning of communion.

There is communion between God and the individual soul, communion within the Body of Christ as the Communion of Saints, and communion with Christ through the sharing of His Spirit. Underhill notes how we look forward to the spiritual joys and solace of communion, but clearly states that communion also means acceptance of suffering and the Way of the Cross. Yet she reminds us that we are never alone. We are supported by a "vast, interpenetrated society of loving spirits 'in Christ.'" And when we pray, we are surrounded by a boundless "invisible society, ceaselessly loving and praising God." We lose our little, narrow, individual lives to find ourselves as cells within the Body of Christ, "called upon to be channels of His mystical self-imparting," to share in outward signs His inward spiritual grace.

"Communion alone can be almost passive and almost individual; cooperation can't." Underhill, in the last chapter, becomes quite plain about self-regarding spirituality. She is even searing: "The devotee who is content to be shut up inside his or her own enjoyable, pious practice . . . is the mongrel of the spiritual world. One of his parents may be Spirit, but the other is Self." What, then, is cooperation? She explains:

It is complete, active, practical self-giving to God for the purposes of His *redemptive love,* whatever those purposes may be. It is taking the Cross into the very heart of the life of prayer and thus the necessary fulfillment of all *true* communion with Christ.

Underhill finds the essence of Christianity and Christian vocation in redemptive love. Finding its perfection in the life of Christ, she finds the reason as well, for there human nature cooperated so willingly with the Father that the line between human and divine was melted.

The Call of God (1928)

Now we turn to the last of the four retreats, *The Call of God.* Those who are familiar with Rudolf Otto's classic work, *The Idea of the Holy,* may well be reminded of it as they begin to read Underhill's response to the vision of Isaiah. Here, in her writing, we find the same overwhelming sense of the holy and apophatic which Otto called the "numinous," the overpowering awe and fascination before God's mystery, and the inescapable feeling of unworthiness and of being daunted by the One experienced as "wholly Other." It is interesting that Otto's book was published in English in 1923 and that in 1927, one year before Underhill gave this retreat, Otto presented several lectures on mysticism at King's College, London.

But Underhill does not stop with the themes with which Otto dealt so magnificently. She wants to deal with vocation, consecration, sacrifice, and abandonment to God as part of a redeemed community. Every human soul comes into the world to do some particular work for God, writes Underhill. Each is called to a vocation. For Isaiah, just at the beginning of his adult life, and for St. Francis, in the midst of a full life of service, there were remarkable visions.

Visions enable us to see the awesome Reality which constantly surrounds and pervades all life, says Underhill. To "know" that Reality, that is, to become conscious of its presence, is to adore. There are always the same results: "a tremendous sense of our own contrasting frailties, the cleansing power of love responding to our penitence, and finally the impulse to serve." The problems and puzzles of life are not solved, but they become transcended.

Such a rift in the veil between eternal and temporal reality may bring an almost unbearable mystery and wonder as it did to Isaiah. Thus, from Underhill's point of view, such a true vision brings "the utter death of self-assurance." But the experience of Francis on Mt. La Verna included a new dimension appropriate to Christianity: the approach of an angel, bearing the image of a crucified human being. To Underhill the vision reveals that "the supreme revelation of the love of God is in heroic suffering and generous sacrifice for others." Therefore, "the crucifixion of the self is essential to full knowledge and service of God."

Someone might well say to her: "But the self is all we really have to give back to God!" and she would agree. Her aim would never be the kind of self-destruction such as so many ascetics have worked for and accomplished. Her goal is rather to relinquish anything that stands in the way of one's most far-reaching commitment. But she was not always clear about this, and many saints who preceded her (such as her beloved Julian and Teresa) wanted to suffer or die for God before they had fully lived for Him. She is quite clear elsewhere that if God gives life, our first job is to receive and then to share it. One would hope that, if she were preparing this text for a publisher, she might say that we are called upon for crucifixion, not of the self, but of self-centeredness, of self-importance and self-sufficiency in order to be true and effective channels for God. Surely it is in "losing life" in *this* sense, that we find it.

Underhill is one of the most balanced writers one can find in her field. Eternity and time, contemplation and action, grace and will are always connected. At this point she pleads again for perspective and proportion. For her the holiness of the Eternal and the holiness of incarnate Love are everywhere, even in the most wretched circumstances. She is convinced that it is the purpose of our lives and the glory of our calling to reveal their interconnection and to share their transforming presence. It is worth any sacrifice.

The chapter on penitence points to Isaiah's cry during the vision: "Woe is me, for I am a man of unclean lips!" How similar that is to the response of Francis: "What am I, face to face with Thee, my God and All!" It is inevitable, says Underhill, that one's first reaction to such glorious revelation might be self-contempt. But the only healthy response to such self-contempt is self-abandonment. It seems to her that most people come to this second response only by way of the first, acknowledging that something greater than their ordinary selves must save them from themselves.

Underhill encourages her listeners. She claims that there is always the possibility of a fresh start. She writes: "The fire of love from the altar of the Sacred can touch you and stir you to life again, however dead you feel." But, she adds, there is no need to go to some special place for celestial surgery. There is plenty of opportunity for purification in any ordinary life! Of course it is true that, for Isaiah, the cleansing was done through an extreme and dramatic method. A burning coal brought from the altar by an angel touched his lips. But in the New Testament story, when Peter asked to be cleansed, Christ simply knelt before him, and gently washed his feet.

Consecration is Underhill's third subject. In her version of the Isaiah story, the probing question is put before Isaiah: "Who will go for us?" and Isaiah cries, "I'll go! What else is worth doing in comparison?" The young prophet-to-be was not commanded as a slave, but offered a choice as a son would be. There is, says Underhill, "something in us which [is] not subject to determination." The human will "cannot be used fully except insofar as we offer it." The will of God includes giving us the privilege of initiative, and our human freedom is to make ourselves God's willing tool. The workers in the vineyard were rewarded, not for their work, but for their willingness and their love.

The Christian story begins with the statement: "Behold, the handmaid of the Lord." Closer to the end come the words: "Thy will be done." Consecration is self-oblivious zest, unconditional response, a complete absence of self-chosen aims or concern for our failure or success. It is unquestioning acceptance of a necessary job, regardless of that fear of failure (sometimes called humility) which is "a fundamental want of trust." And it is giving all. It is not: "I am going that way anyhow. Is there anything I can do for you?" When one of us says, "Send me," we "accept the route along with the errand." But regardless of the challenges of either, we will never travel alone.

From the three great moments in the awakening of the soul, Underhill turns to the threefold aspect of the Communion of Saints in which we are members of Christ, children of God, and inheritors of the kingdom of heaven. Again she intends her words to be words of strength.

She writes: "Christian humiliation is not groveling in despair, but joyful . . . for it is literally true that 'when I am weak, then I am strong' " (2 Cor. 12:10). A Christian is part of a redeemed community whose interests and work transcend those of any individual. That community, as the Body of Christ, the Church, is "the actual organ of Christ's action on earth," and its significance lies in God's movement within it, using it as a sacramental channel. Because it is a body with many members, as Paul described, each must depend upon the other. Those who are ordinarily in positions of leadership are challenged to learn gratefulness toward persons who seem inadequate. And those who move at such great erratic bursts of speed need to learn to maintain the pace and rhythm which is necessary for health and longevity. Underhill notes that it is erratic cells which cause cancer, and it is sometimes the quiet and unnoticed parts of the body which turn out to be most essential.

Turning to the story of the Vine in the Fourth Gospel, Underhill reminds her listeners that the life which flows to and through the branches is for one purpose: to bear fruit. "Yet the grapes, to become wine, must be sacrificed and crushed, devoted without reserve to an end beyond themselves." We are called, says Julian of Norwich, to "the possibility of sharing in the eternal redemptive act." "I live," cried Paul, "yet not I, but Christ who lives in me." And that is to be true for us as well. We exist to express the loving purpose of the Creator.

As part of Christ's mystical Body, each of us is a cell, but, says the next chapter, as an individual child of God, each of us has a unique and personal relationship to our Father. Since we are derived from Him, "we are not wholly unlike Him." And we are bound to Him by a link that no feeling, belief, or conduct can destroy. A child's knowledge of its parent is intimate, but it is incomplete and inexact. God "far exceeds what we can think about Him."[17]

Although the child is never left alone, it will never grow to true maturity unless its parent takes risks and allows the child to do the same. Only a free soul can grow. As growth proceeds, difficulties increase. The child learns by making choices, even in times when it seems to "get no guidance." But it could grow in no other way. The perfection which the Father asks of it is never really *gained*, but *given* by the "uncalculating eager generosity" of the parent to the child.

The last chapter of the retreat is a charming story about learning to swim. What Underhill is really talking about is learning mental prayer or "meditation" so as to live in the presence of God where we truly belong.

"When I was a child," she says, "we used to be taught to swim by lying across a chair . . . and exercising our arms and legs in a corresponding way." Jumping into the water, although somewhat similar, is very different. Just so, real mental prayer is not something one can learn as a routine or from a book, away from the water. Real prayer, says Underhill, is the experience of plunging into the ocean where we belong, the ocean of God's love. Like a frog on the edge of a pond, we may spend a great deal of time on land, but there is no way to be revitalized, or live more than half our lives, without jumping into the water, that is, by using mental prayer. "We are children of a double order and ought to expect as both natural and spiritual creatures, another life to live here and now."

That other life is our inheritance. Sadly, says Underhill, there are those of us who know we have been offered such a legacy, but whose lives are too full of our other riches to find room for this special gift. We do not realize that we will receive as much of the kingdom of heaven as suits our souls. Furthermore, it is an inheritance given not hereafter, but now, and what we receive and live in now will become our home for eternity. Underhill is echoing a verse by John Donne which she once posted for a retreat:

> Since I am coming to that Holy Room
> Where with the choir of saints forevermore
> I shall be made Thy music—as I come
> I tune the instrument here at the door,
> And what I must do then, think here before. (ULC 13)

It is the presence of God which is our true home, the country of the soul. It is there that we belong. It is that which we may claim.

On Retreat with Evelyn Underhill

At the end of her first retreat in 1924, Underhill wrote in her spiritual journal: "The object of my life toward God is not . . . any personal achievement or ecstasy at all but just to make one able to do this kind of work." In her mature years, in spite of lectures and other writing, nothing else was closer to her heart and nothing more important than conducting retreats and giving spiritual direction to those who had attended. Menzies and Cropper call it her "real" and "most distinctive" work. Five years before her death she gave an address entitled "The Life of Prayer in the Parish" to a clergy convention at Oxford. There she said:

The guidance and support of a soul seeking closer communion with God [is], I suppose, . . . the most delicate and responsible work with which anyone can be entrusted. (UCP 154)

She responded to that trust with a kind of awe, a humility and responsibility that recognized that she was dealing with something fragile and precious: the critical relationship of a soul with God.

It was in retreat that she most often saw the awakening and growth of that relationship. Thus, in her address entitled "The Need of Retreat" (published with *The Light of Christ*) she stressed that the making of at least one retreat a year should be "an absolute obligation" of the priesthood. Her own private yearly retreat was to her an essential.

The way she prepared for conducting a retreat showed her regard for its importance. According to her dear friend, Lucy Menzies, Underhill's little black notebooks were ubiquitous. They traveled with her, were read and written in during quiet moments. Thus the retreats came out of her everyday life. The mental and spiritual preparation began long before they were to be given (ULC 10).

What would it have been like to have been at a retreat which Evelyn Underhill conducted?

We would arrive to find that she had preceded us, perhaps by so much as a day. Already there would be Bible readings, prayers, and selected thoughts for private meditation posted where people could see them best. Sometimes there would be a picture too. There would always be a list of hymns which we would soon discover were to be practiced early in order to be most effectively used in worship. Perhaps, if Lucy Menzies were present, she would laughingly warn: "Woe betide the organist if the hymns lag!"[18] We would begin to realize that we had a conductor who was sensitive to every detail.

The retreat begins. It is about 8:30 on a Friday night. Evelyn Underhill, slight of body and wearing a little white lace Dutch cap,[19] has greeted everyone in her cheerful, quiet way and introduced herself to newcomers, pronouncing her first name as *E*velyn, with an initial long *e*. We practice the hymns up to time! Then the preparatory service begins. There is a psalm or maybe two, several hymns, and a number of prayers. The prayers seem to come from a collection she has made in a rather worn-looking notebook. When it is time for the address, Underhill reads from another notebook in which she has written her text by hand. Her voice is calm, but has a charming, bell-like quality. Here and there it lifts with a touch of humor or a pointed question. As she speaks, she sets the theme for our time together and makes a point of asking for silence through the next two days. We go out into the quietness and to our rooms carrying a sheet on which there are thoughts and prayers and Bible readings for times alone with God.

In the morning, we see her going to the chapel to prepare the altar, a task that seems to give her a special joy. There will be worship and an address at 10 A.M., 5 P.M., and 8:30 P.M. each day. In the quiet hours between gatherings, time will be set aside for interviews with those of us who wish spiritual direction, the schedule for that having been posted as well. Sometimes the day will end with Compline, and Underhill will lead it. One day there will be a service of intercession. But most important, there will be at least one Communion service for which a priest, of course, will serve. It will be a high point of the retreat, having been given added depth by the thoughts of the preceding addresses (CDC 93–94; CEU 157–63).

About midday on Saturday or Sunday, there is a very special time of guided meditation which Underhill has very carefully prepared. She explains what she is going to do and something of what to expect:

> We take . . . a passage or event in Scripture, and by dwelling on it, make it the material of a prayer. . . . We must of course begin by a few moments of quiet before God, proceed by reading the passage we have chosen or . . . thinking of the subject, [and] by picturing it as vividly as we can. . . . Having done that we stay quietly and gaze at the picture and watch and listen—realizing that what is said, is being said to us and has a direct message and direct relation with our own lives.
>
> We shall presently find ourselves . . . talking quite simply from our hearts to God, [then] entering more and more deeply . . . into communion with God . . . confessing the faults we have been shown and asking for the things we need . . . at the end, we sum it all up in a prayer of confidence, thanksgiving and love, and a resolution for the future. (UM&P 85)

Underhill's voice is gentle but clear. She reads slowly, pausing after each sentence, allowing silence to do its work. She sets the scene vividly. It is as though we are actually there. Then she begins to respond for us all with a prayer. The scene changes. The location is now our own hearts, and the words which we hear are spoken to each of us individually.

(Only six of these meditations have survived. They have been printed singly as well as in combination with *The Mount of Purification*. No one who reads *The Ways of the Spirit* or gives a retreat based on its contents should miss reading the meditations and making use of them. They give a depth of perspective and experience which would otherwise be impossible.)

As at the end of any session, when Underhill is finished, many remain in the chapel in silence. Underhill stays too and, as often happens, seems to be the last to leave.

On the last evening, as we gather together, the thoughts and aims of our retreat are the focus of our meditation. Then Underhill tells us that once a year she sends out a list of her upcoming retreats to some treasured friends who faithfully support us all in their prayers. She reads each of their names, and we, in our turn, offer our own thanksgiving for them.

Once again we are aware of the Communion of Saints which surrounds us and of the Ocean of God in which all of us "live, move, and have our being." So we depart, remembering, as we have so often been reminded, that "no one ever goes alone."

Underhill's spiritual journal mentions how much it meant to her for the retreat to be held in prayer by this "tremendous circle" of people who cared. For her first retreat in 1924, one of that circle was von Hügel who not only interceded for the retreat but gently counseled her "to concentrate on knowing and entering into each individual soul and its needs, even while giving addresses." That was very much in her mind. As she began, she even forgot her own prayer and, simply opening to grace, experienced what I call "receptive prayer."[20] She wrote:

> As soon as I began . . . I was surrounded and supported by *something* which carried me steadily right through . . . told me what to say in interviews—how to do the prayers with effect. . . . [I] ceased to count as an individual [and] felt completely a tool used by this strong unwavering power. (USJ)

That retreat was the beginning of a new direction.

Preparing the Retreats for Publication

Underhill had enormous spiritual drive, but limited physical energy. Since she lived to the utmost her strength allowed, she prepared only one retreat a year, and that was usually given five to eight times. Often she would be asked to give "a quiet day." For these she might choose three sessions from the retreat she was using for the year.

Perhaps one of the most fascinating things in preparing this material for publication was to study the notes which Underhill had made for devotions. Only in the 1924 and 1925 notebooks were complete worship notes included, but they were enough to tell a great deal. Obviously Underhill liked hymns, and it is easy to see that she knew quite a few. But the perplexing problem was to discover which prayers she meant when she gave only a name or an abbreviation and a page number!

Of course, anyone could find the Collects for Trinity VI or for All Saints. With the names "Teresa" or "Ignatius" or "Gertrude More," it was possible to look at the subject for the session and search for the most appropriate prayer. When she wrote "Newman—fervour," it was quite clear which prayer was meant. But where are the prayers which she called

"Everlasting Clearness" or "The True Pilot?" And where is her "Purity" book with prayers?

There are many prayers listed which may always cause perplexity. Should anyone reading this know the answer to the puzzle, I would like to have that person pass it on. Underhill wrote "P.B." and then a number. Did that mean "Prayer Book," and if so, did she mean *The Book of Common Prayer* (which it wasn't) or her own collection of prayers (which can no longer be found)? Then there was "P.P.B.": surely a "Priest's Prayer Book" such as *The Priest's Book of Private Devotions* compiled by Oldknow in 1911 or some Protestant book of prayer! But at this point, the answer is that "none of these fits."

Apparently one of those abbreviations refers to that little book of prayers which Underhill had made for herself, one single copy of hand-written prayers which she loved. Cropper says that there was such a volume which went with her to every retreat. If that is ever found, it will be a treasure.

But one book, whose author was listed over and over, *was* found after weeks of searching! It is *Mysteries of the Mass in Reasoned Prayers* written by William Roche, S. J., and published by Longmans, Green & Company in 1915. It was discovered too late to include any of its prayers in this volume, but if it is ever republished, the words and imagery will be clearly seen for their effect on Underhill.

Since her cryptic notes were only for herself, I have "worked with" Underhill on the devotions, knowing that some of the prayers were exactly what she wanted, others were probably her choice, and the rest might have been!

Were Underhill alive, she would have carefully gone over her retreat notes to make them as clear and as effective as possible for the 1990s. I have tried to do this for her, changing a few Victorian expressions and omitting some capitalizations, but leaving her message intact. I have worked as carefully as I can in deciphering what was sometimes a very difficult text, to present what was her true intent. To those who have helped along the way, I am particularly grateful, especially to my English friends and librarians here and abroad.

At first I prepared this entire book using the original English spelling. But my friends in England convinced me that, since it was to be published in America and therefore read by larger numbers of Americans, it should be presented with American usage. That was finally the publisher's decision, made with the thought that if there would ever be an English edition in the future, there should be no problem in adapting English usage where necessary. I hope that this will be understandable and acceptable to the many whom I honor in the United Kingdom.

I hope that this volume can be used in many practical ways. Of course it can be the basis for both private and group study and devotions. However, one of the reasons for providing Underhill's own suggestions for worship and including her method of preparing for and giving retreats was to make it easier for conductors to use the material just as it is for retreats. From my own experience in giving retreats, I believe that many of the essentials are here.

The experience of bringing this book to publication has sometimes been most challenging, but the blessing far outweighs the effort. My prayer is that the work begun by God through Underhill shall continue, by means of these pages, in and through many other people. Perhaps each of us can be, as Donne says "God's music" where we are.

Grace Adolphsen Brame

Notes

1. A. M. Allchin, formerly Canon Residentiary and now Honorary Canon of Canterbury Cathedral, is the founder and director of St. Theosevia Center for Spirituality, Oxford, England.

2. Grace Adolphsen Brame, "Divine Grace and Human Will in the Writing of Evelyn Underhill," Ph.D. diss., Temple University, 1988; available from UMI Dissertation Information Service, Ann Arbor, MI 48106.

3. *Evelyn Underhill: Modern Guide to the Ancient Quest for the Holy*, ed. and intro. by Dana Greene (Albany: State University of New York Press, 1988), pp. 224–56.

4. Evelyn Underhill Association of America, 1209 Tulane Dr., Alexandria, VA 22307.

5. Lucy Menzies, "Evelyn Underhill," *Chelmsford Diocesan Chronicle*, July (?), 1941, pp. 93–94, and Margaret Cropper, *Evelyn Underhill* (London: Longmans, Green & Co., 1958), p. 153.

6. *Man and the Supernatural* (1927), Underhill's religious philosophy, included all her basic themes but was of very different style. *Mixed Pasture* (1933) is, of course, a collection of essays and addresses. *The Spiritual Life* (1937) came from a series of broadcast talks but includes two themes from the 1927 retreat. *Eucharistic Prayers from Ancient Liturgies* (1933) was a collection of prayers which she edited and introduced.

7. Christopher Armstrong, *Evelyn Underhill: An Introduction to Her Life and Writings* (London: Mowbrays, 1975). The notebook to which he refers is in the Underhill archives at King's College.

8. St. Paul discusses the subject in Romans 7:13–21. Lorenzo Scupoli wrote one of the famous books on the subject. His was entitled *Unseen Warfare*.

9. See especially *The Golden Sequence* (London: Methuen & Co., 1932), probably Underhill's best treatment of the subject (and her favorite book). It is interesting to compare Underhill's thought regarding God as the "Wholly Other" and the "Great Reality" with that of Rudolf Otto, Karl Barth, and Emil Brunner, all writing about the "Wholly Other" at that time. Underhill, however, points out the inbuilt or ontological link between the human and the divine here and on p. 229, for instance.

10. Brame, "Divine Grace and Human Will in the Writing of Evelyn Underhill," pp. 40–46.

11. As this book goes to press, I have learned of Terry Tastard's *The Spark of the Soul* (London: Darton, Longman & Todd, 1988). Tastard shows the relationship between the inner life of the soul and its outward compassionate expression. He chooses as his examples: Eckhart, St. Francis, Evelyn Underhill, and Thomas Merton.

12. Peter Anson's *Call of the Cloister* (London: SPCK, 1964) identifies the Community of the Blessed Virgin as a "quasi-community" of lay women begun in 1855, during the Crimean War, and still in existence, housing and serving women, children, and the elderly.

13. "Modernism" was a term employed by Pius X when speaking against the tendency toward biblical historical criticism and the authority of personal spiritual experience, tendencies especially strong at the beginning of the twentieth century. His decree against it, *Lamentabile Sane Exitu* and his encyclical, *Pascendi Dominici Gregis,* were both published in 1907 when Underhill was preparing to join the Roman Catholic Church. See Brame, "Divine Grace and Human Will in the Writing of Evelyn Underhill," pp. 25–32.

14. Such examination of conscience was a common medieval spiritual exercise among those committed to a particular religious vocation. This was not the only time Underhill had come across it. The letters between von Hügel and her show great attention to such detail, yet he and others of her spiritual directors suggested that she not take such exercises too far.

15. See Maud Monahan, *Life and Letters of Janet Erskine Stuart, Superior General of the Society of the Sacred Heart, 1857–1914* (London: Longmans, Green & Co., 1922).

16. Mental prayer is defined by Underhill beginning on page 43 of her article "The Degrees of Prayer," first published by the Guild for Health in 1922 and reprinted in *Collected Papers of Evelyn Underhill* (London: Longmans, Green & Co., 1946). She says it is unspoken prayer without set forms, but elaborates: "We think in some way of the subject of our meditation. We feel the emotion, whether of love, penitence or joy, which it suggests to us. And finally, the aim of all meditative prayer is a resolution, or a renewal of our surrender to God; and this is an act of the will" (p. 44). It may well lead to contemplation and absorption in the presence of God. Here she notes that Ignatius calls mental prayer "contemplation."

17. Underhill loved this phrase and always credited it to Aquinas since that is where she read it. Aquinas, of course, was quoting Anselm's famous argument for

the existence of God written in *Proslogium*. See the note in chapter VI of *The Call of God*.

18. See Menzies' introduction in *The Light of Christ*, p. 13.

19. Cropper tells us that in later years the little lace cap was replaced by a larger piece of her mother's lace which she draped over her head and tied in front. See Cropper, *Evelyn Underhill*, page facing page 89.

20. This is explained in my book, *Receptive Prayer: A Christian Approach to Meditation* (St. Louis: CBP Press, 1985).

Key to References

AEU   Armstrong, Christopher J. R. *Evelyn Underhill: Her Life and Writings*. London, Mowbrays, 1975.

BGW   Brame, Grace Adolphsen. "Divine Grace and Human Will in the Writing of Evelyn Underhill." Ph.D. diss., Temple University, 1988.

CDC   Menzies, Lucy. *Chelmsford Diocesan Chronicle*. Chelmsford, July (?), 1941.

CEU   Cropper, Margaret. *Evelyn Underhill*. London: Longmans, Green & Co., 1958.

DWT   Davies, Horton. *Worship and Theology in England*. Princeton: Princeton University Press, 1965.

MEU   Menzies, Lucy. Unfinished biography of Evelyn Underhill, TS, Underhill Collection, St. Andrews University Archives, St. Andrews, Fife, Scotland.

UCG   Underhill, Evelyn. *The Call of God*. Published in this volume.

UM   ———. *Mysticism: A Study in the Nature and Development of Man's Spiritual Consciousness*. New York: E. P. Dutton & Co., 1961; first pub., 1911.

UEM   ———. *The End for Which We Were Made*. Published in this volume.

UIG   ———. *Inner Grace and Outward Sign*. Published in this volume.

UMP   ———. *Mixed Pastures*. London: Methuen & Co., 1933.

UM&P   ———. *Meditations and Prayers* in *The Mount of Purification*. London: Longmans, Green & Co., 1960.

UQH   *Evelyn Underhill: Modern Guide to the Ancient Quest for the Holy*. Ed. with intro. by Dana Greene. Albany: State University of New York Press, 1988.

USJ   Underhill, Evelyn. The untitled and unpublished spiritual journal of Evelyn Underhill, 1923–29. Referred to by Christopher Armstrong as "the green notebook."

USP   ———. *Sanctity: The Perfection of Love*. Published in this volume.

Retreats of Evelyn Underhill in the Order in Which They Were Given

Most of Underhill's work published in book form began as retreats. They are listed here, not in the usual order based upon publication dates, but in the order in which they were given, thus giving a truer sense of historical continuity.

	given in	published in
Sanctity: The Perfection of Love	1924	1990
The End for Which We Were Made	1925	1990
The House of the Soul (probable date)	1926	1929
Inner Grace and Outward Sign	1927	1990
The Call of God	1928	1990
No subject known, but retreat given	1929	——
The Golden Sequence	1930	1932
The Mount of Purification	1931	1960
The Light of Christ	1932	1944
The School of Charity	1933	1934
Abba	1934	1940
The Mystery of Sacrifice	1935	1938
The Fruits of the Spirit	1936	1942

Evelyn Underhill in her Dutch cap while giving a retreat at Pleshey, her favorite retreat center.

SANCTITY:
THE PERFECTION OF LOVE

*The first retreat given by Evelyn Underhill
at the Diocesan House of Retreat, Pleshey
March 15–18, 1924**

What is sanctity? Just the perfection of our love—its growth towards God and others. The more we love, the better is our work. Even if we are only doorkeepers in the House of God, the more likely we are to attract others to the door.

Chapter I: "Preparation for Retreat"

Pure love or charity, that utter self-giving of the creature which is the human reply to the Love of God, that is the same as sanctity.

Chapter III: "Love"

The mark of a saint is a burning interest in and love for other souls.

Chapter VII: "The Communion of Saints"

---

*Underhill gave this retreat for the Time and Talent Settlement, a community of some professional social workers and many volunteers doing charitable work in Dockland, London.

I

Preparation for Retreat

Preparatory Worship

Psalm 19: "The Heavens Declare the Glory of God"

Hymns: "Come Thou, Holy Paraclete"
"The King of Love My Shepherd Is"

Prayers asking for the presence of the Holy Spirit and any or all of the
following:

Lord God Almighty, who hast safely brought us to the beginning of this
day, defend us in the same by Thy mighty power, that this day we may fall
into no sin, but that all our words may so proceed, and all our thoughts and
actions may be so directed as to do always that which is just in Thy sight.
Through Christ our Lord. *(The Roman Breviary)*

In the evening, and in the morning, and at noonday we praise thee, we
bless thee, we give thanks unto thee, and we pray unto thee, O Lord of all:
Direct thou our prayer before thee as incense, and incline not our hearts unto
words or thoughts of wickedness; but deliver us from all who seek after our
souls. For unto thee, Lord, O Lord, lift we up our eyes, and in thee have we
trusted. Put us not to shame, O our God. (The Great Vespers of the All Night
Vigil, Orthodox Church)

O Master Christ: Thou hast loved us with an everlasting love:
Thou hast forgiven us, trained us, disciplined us:
Thou hast broken us loose and laid Thy commandments upon us:
Thou hast set us in the thick of things and deigned to use us:
Thou hast shown Thyself to us, fed us, guided us:
Be graciously pleased to accept and forgive our efforts,
And help us, Thy free bondslaves, forever.
(Thomas à Kempis, *The Imitation of Christ*, iv, 8)

Shine into our hearts, O loving Master, by the pure light of the knowledge
of Thyself and open the eyes of our minds to Thy teaching: that in all things

we may both think and act according to Thy good pleasure, and meditating on those things that are holy, may continually live in Thy Light. (The Dawn Office, Eastern and Leonine Churches)

A few hours ago, we were in the midst of our bristling lives, reacting all the time to the outside world. Now we enter the silence in which we will try to readjust our balance and attend to all that we usually leave out.

We come into retreat because our lives are busy and hurried and we feel the need of getting beneath the surface, of being for a time alone with God in that inner world where we discover His presence and reality. Two priceless days have been cleared, and it is essential that we not waste them. We have this lovely place, soaked in love and prayer, where everything we see and hear is calculated to lead us deeply into God—where nothing is meant to be done except for His service. We want to make the most of its influences.

The way we enter a retreat is very important. Often, we waste the first day getting our bearings. I want to speak especially to those at their first retreat. I remember my own first retreat and the apprehension and vagueness with which I entered it. But what a wonderful revelation it was! I remember my alarm at the idea of silence, the mysterious peace and light distilled from it, and my absolute distress when it ended and the clatter began.

Silence is the very heart of a retreat. We get away from the distractions of talking, interchange, and action. We sink into our souls where God's voice is heard. Without silence around us, the inward stillness in which God educates and molds us is impossible. We come to rest before God, to find space for brooding and recollection in which we possess our souls and learn His will.

It is an *elected silence*. We cannot find it in the world. We must come together in a special place, protected by our own rule from distractions, interests, and surface demands. We have for our examples, Enoch who silently listened for the voice of God in order to discern the divine will, and Teresa, quiet and alone in her watchtower. The silence of this house is full of God's voice. Treasure that silence. It will do far more for your souls than anything heard at our services. These times together are only meant to keep you pointing in the right way and to help you to best use your silence.

Remember, silence is more than non-talking. It is a complete change in the way we use our minds. We lead very active lives. One thing swiftly succeeds another. Our mental machinery is so made that the more active our work, the more incessant the whirr of wheels, the harder it is to be quiet in the divine presence. Yet *nothing* so improves that active work as such quietude, the sense of eternity, and the restful reception of the Holy Spirit, ceasing all introspection and all altruistic fidgets. Only in such a silence can we look out of our workshop window and see the horizons of the spiritual world.

A most wonderful description of spiritual silence is given by St. Augustine in the *Confessions*. This great saint tells us what the hushing of outer life can come to mean, and what silence can do.

> If the tumult of the flesh were hushed; hushed these shadows of earth, sea, sky; hushed the heavens and the soul itself, so that it should pass beyond itself and not think of itself; if all dreams were hushed, and all sensuous revelations, and every tongue and every symbol; if all that comes and goes were hushed—They all proclaim to him that hath an ear: 'We made not ourselves: he made us who abideth for ever'—But suppose that, having delivered their message, they held their peace, turning their ear to Him who made them, and that He alone spoke, not by them but for Himself, and we heard His word, not by any fleshly tongue, nor by an angel's voice, nor in the thunder, nor in any similitude, but His voice whom we love in these His creatures—Suppose we heard Him without any intermediary at all—Just now we reached out, and with one flash of thought touched the Eternal Wisdom that abides above all—Suppose this endured, and all other far inferior modes of vision were taken away, and this alone were to ravish the beholder, and absorb him, and plunge him in mystic joy, might not eternal life be like this moment of comprehension for which we sighed? Is not this the meaning of 'Enter thou into the joy of thy Lord?' Ah, when shall this be? Shall it be when 'we all rise, but shall not all be changed'?*

Our deepest contacts with God are so gentle because they are all we can bear. We need quiet to experience them. They do not come as an earthquake of mental upheaval or in the scorching fire or rushing wind of emotion. In the silence, there is nothing devastating or sensational, but only a still small voice.

Let us not break this holy silence. Those who preserve it unbroken, use the retreat best. It can become quite easy and natural to be at home in the silence. The atmosphere itself helps you. If you take walks in the afternoon, it is far better that you go alone and think over what we have received. To be silent with nature is to witness to God.

There is no rule about this except to avoid strain and any imprisoned feeling. If talking with a friend *really* helps, of course, feel free to do it. But remember how short our time is, and the purpose for which you have come. It is not unfriendly to preserve the solitude and to give quiet

The Confessions of St. Augustine, trans. C. Bigg ([1897] London: Methuen & Co., 1929), x. 10.

attention to God alone for two days, to open our souls to His love and light and to commune with Him. The stream of talk will all too soon smother us. Let us use this time to the utmost in the way that is best for each.

Next, let us remember that this is your personal retreat. It is not a joint undertaking in which we all do the same thing. Each of us is at a different stage in defining our needs and problems.

Don't think that the main thing is to learn from the addresses. They are the least part. Take what helps your meditation, and leave the rest. Your objective is to attend to God, to Christ, to learn His love and what He wants of you. I am here simply as your servant to do all I can for each of you, to help, to suggest, to listen, and, perhaps, if you want, to talk of difficulties. I will not press you in special paths. There are one thousand ways to God.

I am no more the authority over your real journey than the conductor of a bus. Disregard what doesn't suit you. Let yourselves be led by God.

A retreat is your time *with Him,* for facing realities in His light, for thinking in His presence. It is an opportunity to be like the simple but devoted old man who was once asked how he prayed, and quietly replied: "We look at one another." The rest of us would have to say: "O sight to be wished, desired, and longed for!" Make *that* your aim. Don't be nervous or self-conscious. We are all on the same quest, and we do it by forgetting ourselves.

In meditations be simple, natural. Sit or kneel. Use books or not. Make notes or forget them. Take devotions very slowly as meditations. After the addresses we shall just remain here quietly as long as it seems good to us, each quietly leaving when we like. Some think and pray best in a chapel; some—alone. It is said of our ordinary lives, with great truth, "God is at home. *We* are in a far country." But here we are at home with God, so we behave as if we are at home!

It is a good plan to enter retreat with some ruling thought on which we can return from time to time. There are two thoughts with which I suggest we live for these two days. First, the wonderful words of Christ in the High Priestly Prayer: *"For their sakes I sanctify myself"* [John 17:9]. Such an attitude is so deeply true, for it redeems personal religion from its self-regarding taint. Such a purpose is appropriate to all who seek to help others.

Yet we cannot give to anyone what we don't ourselves possess. Service depends on personality. It is impossible to bring Christ to others until He has been revealed *in* us, as Paul said [Gal. 1:15–16]. That is a solitary experience.

Such a retreat as this is a genuine bit of social service. The more we deepen our lives in God, the more we perfect our surrender and learn to realize His presence, the more use we will be to those whom we serve. Don't we sometimes feel how thin and poverty-stricken our lives are? They seem, don't they, to need something added? We don't always have something to give those who appeal to us. Therefore, for *their* sakes, we deepen our interior resources through prayer, adoration, joy, and confidence in God.

What is sanctity? Just the perfection of our love—its growth towards God and others. The more we love, the better is our work. Even if we are only doorkeepers in the House of God, the more likely we are to attract others to the door.

Our second thought that we will take with us is from St. Catherine of Sienna. She once said: "I have not seen Thee in myself, nor myself in Thee, Eternal God!" Yet this is the only kind of self-knowledge worth having. If a saint could so reproach herself, what about us? In the rush of life, the attainment of such knowledge can seem hopeless. But our retreat should bring us nearer this double vision where *we see ourselves in the atmosphere of reality and discover the reality of God's presence in our souls.*

No training and no industry makes up for a lack of sanctity in social service. But the sanctified outlook is hard to keep up. It is impossible without a vision of our work in God and the vision of His Spirit in us and in all others too. Our task as children of God is to grow more and more up into this. If this retreat we now begin is to be fruitful for us and for all whom our lives touch, it will be so because it draws us a little bit nearer to this outlook which is that of our Lord and His saints.

II

Objects of Retreat

Preparatory Worship

Psalm 8 or 42

Hymns: "Dear Lord and Father of Mankind"
"Love Divine, All Loves Excelling"

Prayers of dedication and requests for guidance, including the well known "Prayer of Humble Access," ordinarily used at Communion:

We do not presume to come to this Thy table, O merciful Lord, trusting in our own righteousness, but in Thy manifold and great mercies. We are not worthy so much as to gather up the crumbs under Thy table. But Thou art the same Lord, whose property is always to have mercy. Grant us therefore, gracious Lord, so to eat the flesh of Thy dear son, Jesus Christ, and to drink His blood, that our sinful bodies may be made clean by His body, and our souls washed through His most precious blood, and that we may ever more dwell in Him, and He in us. (Thomas Cranmer in first edition of *The Book of Common Prayer*).

Teach us O God, that silent language which says all things. Teach our souls to remain silent in Thy Presence: that we may adore Thee in the depths of our being and await all things from Thee, whilst asking of Thee nothing but the accomplishment of Thy will. Teach us to remain quiet under Thine action and produce in our souls that deep and simple prayer which says nothing and expresses everything, which specifies nothing and expresses everything.

Do thou pray in us, that our prayer may ever tend to Thy glory, and our desires and intentions may not be fixed on ourselves, but wholly directed to Thee. (J. N. Grou)*

*Underhill also suggests prayers from pages 29 and 57 of *Mysteries of the Mass in Reasoned Prayers* by William Roche, S.J. (Longmans, Green & Co., 1915).

The French mystic, Lucie-Christine, who died a few years ago and led the ordinary life of a Christian woman, said, describing her prayer:

> My soul opened and drank in God,
> and He was to me Light, Attraction, and Power.

To me, this is the description of the perfect retreat. Let us keep it before us as an ideal for these days, as an ideal answer for our profoundest needs. Lucie-Christine's mind was enlightened, her heart attracted, and her will given new power. It is an example of the whole nature responding to God, not just one bit intensified.

How solid, sane, and far away from all feverishness this is! The soul comes from such experience more fit to deal with daily life, more able to link up all practical duties with God. His sustaining Spirit of love is felt right through these common experiences, giving light, incentive, and strength.

"Blessed," says à Kempis, "are those who listen to God's whisper and hear not the murmurs of the world." That blessed opportunity is ours now for two days. This is your opportunity to open wide your souls and drink in God—to obtain the food that helps your growth.

Again—for this, silence is imperative. Thus we can feel the molding act of God in His deepest and most gentle touchings of our spirits. The Holy Spirit educates us in inward stillness. Prayer should be attention, waiting on God.

Too many people come to a retreat possessed of the idea that most of the time is to be spent exploring, examining themselves. Very often, going in with this idea, they come out in the exhausted state of women who have been to a remnant sale. They are weary and distracted with overhauling rubbish and things that don't matter: considering a particular fault and whether it's been substantially reduced, wondering whether a certain achievement is quite worth the price put on it. What does all this matter?

Remember what our Lord said to Julian of Norwich when she was inclined to be fussy: "Take it generally!" That's the voice of wisdom— quietly ignoring the importance we attach to our little selves. Once for all, tonight, let us turn our backs on our niggling self-scrutiny. Let us look at God, at Christ. That will bring us to a state of mind more humbling, more really contrite than any penitence based only on introspection. It will condemn every failure in love. "My soul *opened*" said Lucie-Christine, not "my soul turned *inwards* and began to look at itself through a microscope"!

Now I don't mean to discredit all self-examination. It must have a place in the soul's life. But do take it generally, in a broad spirit. Let it be examination of motive rather than of act. Let it be swift, all 'round stock taking: review of needs, weaknesses, habits, and difficulties here in the quiet before God. And do it with gratitude to Him, not with horror. Remember, our difficulties of character, our unspiritual instincts, are material given us for sanctification.

Be patient. It is wrong to speak of "our dreadful nature." It is the nature that Christ took. The sight of faults and deficiencies are a grace; they are shown us by God. We can't find them alone. (Psalm 73)

So, in communion tomorrow, let us ask such degree and kind of self-knowledge as Christ has in His purpose for us as His workers. Then, this bit of work once honestly done, *don't* continue to dwell on it. We waste time brooding on these discoveries. That is discourtesy to God who has brought us here and offers us joy and peace. That joy and peace will bring more and more impulses and interests that will crowd out selfish and wrong impulses and interests; and it's far better and more satisfying to crowd them out than to kick them out!

"Look forward, let go of the past!" is another sentence we might well take into retreat.

Suppose you were at a concert where divine music was played. Would you profit most by meditating on how badly you play yourselves? That's a mean, self-centered attitude towards perfection. It is not humility but stupidity. We come here to open ourselves to the beauty and harmony offered us by God in Christ, to learn more surrender and adoration, *not* just to scrape and sandpaper ourselves. When we have been quiet in God's Presence for a little—especially if we catch notes of the music—we shall feel quite small and humble. It is far more important to feel humble than to feel scraped and raw. Our Lord never makes people feel raw. Often our inverted egotism or the injudicious attention of others does. God's mercy and gentleness are the most humbling and bracing influences which can come into the spiritual life.

So the first recommendation tonight is: don't let us waste much time gazing at ourselves. A deepened and enriched sense of God is far more important than increased and detailed knowledge of the self. *God,* our redeemer and sustainer, is all and does all, and is the one Reality. Life comes with such thoughts. Plunging more deeply in Him with faith and love will do more than self-concerned efforts. We can do nothing of ourselves but depress ourselves and get fussy.

Don't behave like the inexperienced motorist who goes for a drive and spends all day lying in the road under the machine examining the works. The soul is a delicate and intricate machine. When it needs pulling to pieces, it is best to leave it to God. Our prayer should be that of St.

Augustine: "The house of my soul is narrow. O enlarge it, that Thou mayest enter in! It is ruinous. Do *thou* repair it!"

First to last, put all emphasis on God. Attend to Him. Forget yourselves if you can. Bathe in His light. Respond to the unmatched attraction. Be energized by His power. Try to realize a little of the perpetual molding action of His Spirit on your souls.

Have you ever seen the popular experiment of iron filings in the field of a magnet? Those little specks of matter are nothing in themselves, but when they are placed in the field of the magnet, each becomes a centre of energy, instantly influenced by an invisible power. They align themselves parallel to the lines of the magnet's force.

I think we are rather like that. Our mysterious nature, of which we know so little, is controlled by forces flowing through us from God, the Magnet of the Universe. We find ourselves by resting each in our own place, in His field of power. Though we can't see it, we are part of the pattern. The great spiritual scheme is controlled by His energy. It pulses through conditions and arranges us.

In silence we realize something of this. It takes us away from fussing over our individual lives or aiming at self-chosen results. The work of Christ in us is to improve and use us for God as the sort of persons we *are,* not to try to make us turn into the sort of persons we aren't. God's world shows that he likes variety and, put in a homely way, if He means us to be monkeys, sticking feathers in our tails won't turn us into parrots. We are all different, have different angles and vocations, but *every vocation, if real, is God's call.*

In religion some are more active, some contemplative. We come to try to develope and consecrate *our* right attitude, to increase the energy of our souls. We can only do that by opening ourselves to the energy of God and taking from Him the food by which we grow. It is offered us. Our access is free, open, and direct. Our religious experience, in essence, is just the same as that which gave its thrilling joy and beauty, strength, and self-sacrifice to the saints.

Let us think of that when we make our communion tomorrow, joining with the heroes of Christianity. It is the sacrament of fellowship not only with other souls here and now, but with all heroic lovers of Christ since the beginning.

The Christian altar is the only real democracy. There we are with all our degrees of weakness, littleness, and imperfection admitted to an act which was, for Catherine or Teresa, means of the most sacred intimacy and awstruck delight beyond our range.

More than that! When we associate ourselves with angels, archangels, and all the company of heaven, what miraculous opening up of the world's horizon, what opportunity to realize and enjoy our supernatural inheritance in a way made easy and possible to our childishness.

To lift our hearts from the ceaseless drive of life—the heart-breaking poverty, squalor, pain, and hopelessness of human lives gone wrong— perhaps the difficulties of our own lives—to turn from all that to join for a moment the love and adoration of Beauty, Wisdom, and Power, "evermore praising . . . Holy, Holy, Holy." When we do that, we just vanish as individuals, but we find ourselves again in God as persons, growing and deepening more and more through our adoring communion in His Reality, and bringing back new strength and light for our service of other souls.

III

Love

Preparatory Worship

Psalm 139: "Oh Lord, Thou Hast Searched Me"

Hymns: "Most Glorious Lord of Life"
        "Immortal Love, Forever Full"

Prayers:

O God who hast prepared for them that love Thee such good things as pass man's understanding, pour into our hearts such love toward Thee, that we, loving Thee above all things, may obtain Thy promises, which exceed all that we can desire; through Jesus Christ our Lord. (Collect for Trinity VI)

O *my* God, let me walk in the way of love which knoweth not how to seek self in anything whatsoever. Oh! that thy pure love were so grounded . . . in my heart that I might . . . be able . . . to live without all comfort and consolation, human or divine. O sight to be wished, desired, and longed for, because once to have seen Thee is to have learned all things! Nothing can bring us to this sight but love. But what love must it be? . . . It must be an ardent love, a pure love, a courageous love, a love of charity, a humble love, and a constant love, not worn out with labours, nor daunted with any difficulties. O Lord, give this love into my soul, that I may never more live nor breathe but out of a most pure love of Thee, my All and only Good. Let me love Thee for Thy self, and nothing else but in and for Thee. Let me love nothing instead of Thee, for to give all for love is a most sweet bargain. . . . Let Thy love work in me. (Dame Gertrude More)

Today we are to group our meditations 'round the three outstanding necessary characteristics of the spiritual life. Perhaps it would seem more natural to consider faith, hope, and charity, but instead of these we will think about what St. Paul called "the three firstfruits of the Spirit"—love, joy, and peace. The three heavenly virtues are really included in these, for

59

we do not begin to know what love really is, we cannot be inwardly joyous and peaceful unless we have already begun to grow in faith, hope and charity.

You might perhaps think that a meditation on harder and more practical virtues would be more suitable to the vocation of active workers for God, but it is just because you are active workers that I want you to dwell upon these qualities. They are the signature of the Spirit of Christ in the soul and the originating cause of all other spiritual fruits: long-suffering, gentleness, goodness, faith, meekness, and temperance [Gal. 5:22]. No really good work of any kind is ever really done unless it is done in love, joy, and peace, so that unless these characteristics are established in our souls, and nourished by prayer and adoration, it is not likely that they will ever fully come to us in the pressure and difficulties of active life.

Now we do not want to think of the spiritual life as colored right through by pleasant devotional feelings. It never has been so understood by those who entered into it most deeply. A modern saint has said, with the directness and simplicity of the saints, that the bread of life seldom has any butter on it. And this is so just because it is life and not a lovely dream or a heavenly vision: a life which is full of tension and of difficulty, and full of opportunities for heroic choice and for sacrifice in spiritual as well as in material things.

St. Teresa said that the object of this life was to love, to work, and to suffer on ever higher levels of self-devotion. Such an aim as that is surely worthwhile and gives us something real to do. It brings together and unites our deepest vision of God with our craving to serve others.

Love, work, and suffer: the work must be done in joy, and the suffering must be accepted in peace, and this cannot and will not happen unless both are rooted and grounded in love—the one absolute essential of the inner life and the one guarantee of the growth of the soul towards God.

There is another reason why it is good to meditate on love at the beginning of a retreat. Love is the complete answer to and the complete cure of sin. We have just said together the marvelous 139th Psalm. Now in that psalm it is Perfect Love that we address, a Love that is ceaselessly present with us, ceaselessly molding us, and inviting us to grow up into greater love, and so into greater reality.

O Lord, Thou has searched me and known me.
Thou, Holy Love, art about my path.
There is not a word on my tongue but Thou, Perfect Love, knowest it
    altogether.
Whither shall I go from Thy Spirit or whither shall I flee from Thy
    presence?

We cannot go away from it because that presence is in our souls, the very spirit of our life.

As we become more and more fully conscious of this, so sin must become more and more impossible to us. Therefore the only real cure of sin lies in an ever more vivid realization of God's love. This purifies at the root. All other devices merely deal with results. Pride, envy, anger, laziness—all of them different kinds of failure to accept the obligations of love which alone is the fulfillment of the law—all these are forms of half aliveness, to be cured by a more complete entrance into the Absolute Life. Therefore we dwell first upon this quality to remind ourselves, as we cannot do too often, that only those who have love or strive after love, have any part in God whatever, or any capacity for serving Him.

"We love Him because He first loved us" truly means that what awes, humbles, and entrances us, when once we realize it, is the fact that we, poor little half-real creatures are objects on which Perfect Holiness and Beauty pours out a love of which we are unable to conceive at all. This is the cause of our own poor little efforts to love God, and when we really feel it, it drives us in our turn to love for Him all weak, imperfect things.

This is why the old mystics always insist that love and humility are sisters. As we learn about love, we seem to get smaller and smaller and the wonder of God to get greater and greater. The more we realize the fact of this love pouring out from the heart of God to draw all things, without exception, to their place in Him, the greater and the deeper grows the love which is demanded of us in return.

Christ's idea of love is not a sentimental one. It requires the consecration of all our intelligence and all our energy as well as our feeling, for it involves the gift of the whole personality to God. It means turning in prayer to God Himself, attending to Him, entering by self-forgetfulness into His very life. This is not an easy thing to do, nor is it an especially emotional thing to do. There is nothing effusive about it, but it is the essence of full life.

Religious emotion and sanctity are not the same thing. Sometimes they appear to be mutually exclusive. But pure love or charity, that utter self-giving of the creature which is the human reply to the love of God, that *is* the same as sanctity.

What is pure love? It is that which gives and gives and never demands. It is steady, orderly, and without feverishness. In the words of Gertrude More, it is courageous, humble, constant, not worn out with labors, not daunted with difficulties. That is the line along which we must try to respond to the love of God which passes knowledge.

It is plain, isn't it, that we need not be afraid that this won't be a practical business? It does not mean pious effervescence. It means bravely sticking things out when we are tired, disheartened, and worried; and it means doing this because we look beyond it all, because we are trying to respond to the love of God, seeking and serving Christ in our fellow human beings.

Now if we do that faithfully, if we so give ourselves to God's purposes, we will develop such depths of devoted and peaceful love as passes beyond the need of being fed by mere feeling, beyond what are called the consolations of religion. They are merely the chocolate creams of the Christian life. It is by no means always the perfect lovers who have such feelings. Do not make the mistake of thinking, if you sometimes feel cold and dead, that you do not know how to love.

Consider it like this. You have offered yourselves, one way or another, to try to work for God. You want, as it were, to be one among the sheepdogs employed by the Good Shepherd. Now have you ever watched a good sheepdog at his work? He is not at all an emotional animal. He just goes on with his job quite steadily, takes no notice of bad weather, rough ground, or his own comfort. He seldom or never comes back to be stroked. Yet his faithfulness, his intimate understanding with his master, is one of the loveliest things in the world. Now and then he just looks at the shepherd. When the time comes for rest they can generally be found together. Let this be the model of our love.

A love like that will really help us in our work, work in which it is often very difficult to maintain a clear outlook upon spiritual things. It may be full of tiresome and harassing details, may abound in petty discouragements and disappointments. But remember, it is a mark of true greatness in love to develop the power of being interested in tiny nothings for love's sake.

Real love is homely and gentle as well as lofty. It does not merely put up with the petty details but enters into them. Where the treasure is, there the heart is also. We take the keenest interest in every detail, however humble, which is connected with our treasure and its life. Stupidity, weakness, and disappointing narrowness are things that we must sometimes bear from those whom we must work amongst, but God bears them from us the whole time!

How often grace and love reach us through and in spite of our narrow ideas of Him, our cowardice and our refusals. Just think of the wonderful divine loving kindness, never despising or refusing any vessel in which we try to catch and hand on the Living Water. After that, can we dare to be critical or impatient of the smallness, weakness, and absurdity of those to whom we are sent? Love teaches us that it is above all by admiration and generosity of spirit that we shall help and win them.

Admiration is so much more humbling to receive and so much more ennobling to give than any criticism can be. Christ never criticized any-body but the respectable and the pious. With everybody else His thought went like a shaft of delight straight to something that He could admire. The love shown by the prostitute, the meekness shown by the publican, the faith of the centurion, the confidence of the penitent thief—all the things that irradiate and save humanity—love looks for these first, and one reason why Christ gives rest to the soul is that in His presence we are bound to love and not to criticize.

We should feel the same too towards the humble beauties of human character, all the things that Christ appeared to in love and which leapt out in response to Him, and still do. How deeply He loved and admired the children, the birds, and the flowers! He entered by sympathy into every type of soul. What a passport that love and sympathy was to the very heart of the world!

That sense which is now called brotherhood, that vivid consciousness that God is present to us in the souls of our fellow men and women—this is a discovery of the very essence of love. The souls of the fallen and the degraded and of the helpless people who wear us out because they simply won't be helped, the slatternly, the irresponsible, the indifferent, the bigoted, and the silly—all these various sorts of intractable human mate-rial—God is with them as well as with us. His unguessed molding influence is working in, on, and all 'round every soul in ways beyond our conceiving and with apparent results that sometimes puzzle us.

This is why, *if we love and desire to give ourselves to Him, we are bound to give ourselves also to the whole world.* Otherwise we should divide off our personal experience of God from His greatness and Infinite Presence, and so turn what ought to be a dedication into a private enjoyment.

It is one of the holy miracles of love that once fairly started on that path of dedication, it cannot stop. It spreads and spreads in ever-widening circles until it embraces the whole world in God. If we begin by loving our nearest, we shall end by loving those who seemed furthest. And as this love expands, so our whole personality will grow slowly but truly, for every fresh soul that we touch in love is going to teach us something fresh about God.

One of the mystics said that God cannot lodge in a narrow heart, and our hearts are as great as our love. Let us take that thought into our meditation, measuring our prayer and service against the unmeasured generosity of God.

IV

Joy

Preparatory Worship

Psalm 84: "How Lovely Are Thy Dwellings"

Magnificat

Hymns: "Let Us with a Gladsome Mind"
"Praise, My Soul, the King of Heaven"
"Oh Jesus, King Most Wonderful"
"When Spring Unlocks Its Flowers"

Prayers of joy and gratitude which may include:

> Thou hast given so much to me
> Give one thing more—a grateful heart:
> Not thankful when it pleaseth me,
> As if Thy blessings had spare days,
> But such a heart whose pulse may be
> Thy praise.
> (George Herbert)

O everlasting Light, surpassing all created luminaries, flash forth Thy lightning from above, piercing all the most inward parts of my heart. Make clean, make glad, make bright and make alive my spirit, with all the powers thereof, that I may cleave unto Thee in ecstasies of joy. (Thomas à Kempis)

This morning we thought about love as the governing characteristic of all spiritual life, and when we consider all that it is and means, it seems as though those who possessed it truly would need nothing else. Love is of God. Love *is* God. Such words are easy to say, yet it is impossible for us to touch more than the fringe of their meaning, uniting as they do the lives of our comparatively insignificant souls with God's supernatural life.

Paul goes on to point out some of the immediate results and characteristics of this love. Remember, Paul was the first and the greatest of the practical Christian mystics, and in this letter from which we quote, he was not writing lovely religious prose but trying to tell his converts how they could know for certain that they were living as the children of God. They were to know it by their possession of joy.

Paul himself had so lived, in one of the hardest and most driven careers to which perhaps a servant of Christ has ever been called. In journeys, in illness, in persecutions, in disappointments, he held fast to the principle of joy as the first quality of Christian love. Love, joy, and peace—within this threefold atmosphere, the ceaseless activities of his life went on. St. Paul never believed in grim and dismal Christians. He would have supported Francis who wished his brothers to be like larks with hearts that were always full of song.

As his life drew towards its close, Paul seems to have felt more and more the holy character of joy. Philippians, his last epistle, is full of joy. It drenches every line of that glorious little letter, written from prison in the shadow of death. And ever since Paul's day, joy, which is the very color of holiness, has been the one quality which the Church has always demanded and gotten from her saints. This is inevitable, for it is the mark of perfect consecration, the mysterious result of that complete surrender and death of self which is sanctity. Joy is not a luxury, it is a duty of the soul.

What is the root of the adoring joy which is felt by all great Christians? It is the sense of our own comparative insignificance as against God's transcendent greatness and perfection. When St. Augustine has gotten to the end of all he can say of his gratitude, his rapture, and his awe, he can only exclaim, "What shall I say my God, my holy Joy, what should any man say when he speaks of Thee?" When we realize even a hint of that infinite, unwavering Love which enfolds, supports, and penetrates—which comes to us in Christ—then adoration made up of joy and abasement is surely our only possible attitude.

Love makes us humble, and humility makes us joyful. Perhaps the greatest of all God's mercies is His humbling of us. When men humiliate us we feel sore and angry, but when God does it, it is the loveliest thing in the world. You remember the story of Alice in Wonderland and the mushroom: when she ate along one side she got smaller and smaller, and when she ate along the other side, she got taller and taller. We too are always nibbling one side or the other of that mushroom. If we want to know the meaning of joy, we must stick to the side that makes us get smaller and smaller, for as we get tinier and tinier, everything else gets more majestic and awesome. All sorts of simple things take on a new interest and radiance.

Only the very humble can see "the world in a grain of sand and heaven in a wild flower," but when they do see that, they are swept by heavenly joy. When we thus become as little children, we find ourselves in a magical and most exciting world. It is the Kingdom of Heaven which Christ *promised* to the little child.

Our love must move right away from the region of anxious effort, must entirely forget itself, and expand into delight if it is to be really fruitful for God. When it becomes joyful, then it is quite certain to be fruitful, for joy is the greatest missionary instrument which God has put into the hands of men.

It has been said that joy is the reward of creation, the sign that we are spiritually alive and at work, and no doubt it is true that unless we do have joy in our work, we shall never do anything really well. But I think that Christian joy goes far deeper than this. It is a grace that comes from God, a grace that irradiates us when we cease to resist in any way His action upon our souls.

You remember the wonderful chapter in the *Little Flowers* which describes how Francis discoursed to Brother Leo on the nature of perfect joy. We shall all agree that Francis was the most joyous of all the saints, and here he shows us something of his secret. Real joy, he said, did not come from anything that one did. It was not the result of being able to do work for God. That sort of feeling might get a little self-sufficient and priggish, and I suppose there is nothing in the world that equals priggishness in the power of keeping us out of heaven. The Pharisee was a perfect prig—that is what Christ disliked in him so much—and we can hardly imagine the Pharisee feeling perfect joy!

But for Francis, and indeed for all the saints, perfect joy is never the result of anything that they have done themselves. It comes indeed from the annihilation of self. Its very essence is an absolute acquiescence in the purposes of God, gently and serenely, without murmur or disquiet, meeting all humiliations, trials, and practical annoyances. When Francis had catalogued all possible sources of vexation, the rudeness of other people, the fatigue of long journeys, the wet and the cold—everything in fact that can possibly contribute to a thoroughly rotten time—it is at the end of this that he comes to his triumphant conclusion: "If we suffer these things with patience and with gladness and with love, Oh Brother Leo, write that herein is Perfect Joy."

Now what does that really mean? It means a self-abandonment so genial and so complete that the ups and downs of life cease to hurt us. It means the transference of our centre of interest from ourselves to God. Joy is simply the result of loving Him in that way. An extraordinary release comes then from three-quarters of the burdens which we habitually tie on our own backs, a release too from worry in every form. Worry cannot live in the presence of that sweet eagerness and delight which comes to those who give themselves without reserve and no longer care what happens to their own interest or comfort.

Now that state of joyful self abandonment is the state of the true child of God, not merely of the servant of God, but of the child. To live as a child of God does not necessarily mean a frantic moral correctness; even the nicest children sometimes misbehave, and we from time to time are absolutely certain to fall far short too, perhaps to the very end. But it will not prevent us from being children of God. The tax collector was a child of God but the Pharisee was not. Living as a child of God does mean living in self-abandonment and joy. It involves a sort of gay detachment from the ups and downs of the world, a detachment which carries us wonderfully through all our work with its pressures, its failures, and its problems.

There is a marvellous letter which Fénelon wrote to Madame de Maintenon because he was not entirely satisfied with the way in which that very austere and pious lady was going on. After a little general advice about common sense, he suddenly says to her, "I do wish you would love more and suffer less." Then he goes on to describe that airy, sunny freedom of the spirit in which we never hunt deliberately for crosses, but accept, without hesitation, those that come to us. And here, at the end of his letter, is the ideal which he wished to put before that very solemn Christian:

> Be free, gay, simple and childlike, but a plucky child that fears nothing and says everything frankly, that lets itself be led, that can be picked up and carried—in one word, a real child, a child that knows nothing and cannot do anything, that does not anticipate things or try to make them fit, but has a freedom and a courage unknown to the grown-up. This is that child-likeness that confounds the wise, and God Himself speaks by the mouths of such children.

Now we know that our active lives are not and cannot be perpetually easy or gay. How then are we to keep that serene temper of happiness which is the only Christian temper? We must feed it, and to feed it rightly is one of the great functions of prayer. The very heart and foundation of our joy is the way we think and feel about God, and all the various practices of our religious life—prayer, meditations, communions, glances of love and confidence during the work of the day—all these are meant to help to build up, to preserve that sort of thought and that sort of feeling.

Such joy has always been recognized as a governing characteristic of the saints. You remember how Ruysbroeck, one of the greatest of all contemplatives, exclaimed, "I must rejoice without ceasing although the world shudder at my joy!" And Pascal, that great scholar and tortured soul, suddenly experiencing the presence of God, could only exclaim: "Joy! Joy! Tears of Joy!"

Now anything short of that joyous awe and self-abandonment does not fully answer the demands of religion on the soul. But if God becomes to us everything and we ourselves nothing except, we hope, His tools, then we cannot fail to know both the joy of surrender and the joy of creation. An exultant sense will come to us of belonging to a larger, fuller life, of actually being allowed to take some tiny part in the great movement of the spiritual world.

Isn't it when we find ourselves being used by God, when through and with us He reaches out to touch other souls, that we first realize the full miracle of Christianity? Nothing so much abuses yet entrances us, so makes us feel our own abject weakness and imperfection and the immensity and power of the Love that can work with such tools to create and to save. That is what redemption really means.

Redemption does not mean you and me made safe and popped into heaven. It means that each soul, redeemed from self interest by the revelation of Divine Love, is taken and used again for the spread of that redeeming work. It gives us a sort of measure of our own spiritual state, the degree of our real effectiveness, if we consider what, plunged in the real world of spirit, our first instinctive action would be. Should we want to exert power and love for the redemption of others, or should we ask and need those gifts for ourselves? Should we first remember our own helplessness and dependence, or should we be so deeply at one with the Divine Love that all we care about is to spend and redeem?

The Catholic Church has lately added to the list of her official saints a young girl whose pure life was without any conspicuous incidents but was completely filled with love and radiated love. She died when she was twenty-four, and her last words were "I shall spend my heaven in doing kind things for those upon earth" [Thérèse of Lisieux].

Now in choosing that girl as a model and helper, Christian feeling went straight to the point. Only that joyous self-spending in and with God is full sanctity, full salvation, full living out of eternal life. Only this could fill us to the brim with joy, and only this implicit aim can make our difficulties, sorrows, renunciations, and fatigue full of a secret happiness, because in all these there is material for fresh consecration.

Now that joy is the best of all Christian evidences and, more than anything else, guarantees to others the realness and solid value of our faith. Winning people for God has got to be done one by one, and one of the very best ways of doing it is through joy.

If, in the next life, we could feel sure of being met by even one soul who said to us, "Through you, God found me," I think that would be sufficient for our beatitude. And I don't think that, if it happens, the soul will be one that we consciously tried to instruct in Christian doctrine. It will be someone who noticed our certitude and our joy.

One loving spirit does set another spirit on fire. So, even in the narrowest sphere, there should be no room for discouragement, but always room for hope and joy. God comes to men and women through other men and women, but He cannot do it through us until we have in some degree entered into His joy. It is this transformation into channels of His Life and Joy which is the essential character of the spiritual life. Therefore open yourselves widely and gladly towards the divine joy whenever you can. Store up the supernatural sunshine so that you can spend it again on others.

Richard Rolle says, "What is grace but the beginning of joy, and what is perfection of joy but grace complete?" That saying reminds us that entering into the joy of the Lord is a part of our duty as Christian workers, a fruit of the Spirit without which we cannot become the Spirit's effective tools.

This does not mean that dreadful thing, the professional bright woman, nor any other easy heartless sort of cheerfulness. It is those saints who have, like St. Francis, most fully accepted the mystery of the Cross and therefore have drawn nearest to God, who know most about this heavenly joy. You will remember how Dante, the type of every pilgrim soul who has sounded the depths of sin and of suffering and has endured the utmost purifications, at last draws near the heart of God and gazes upon the secret of the universe, and there he finds not earnestness but laughter, not frozen awe but joy!

V

Peace

Preparatory Worship

Psalm 116: "I Love the Lord Because He Has Heard"

Hymns: "Love of the Father"
    "Jesus, These Eyes Have Never Seen"

Prayers for peace and receptive of peace such as:

O God who art peace everlasting and whose chosen reward is the gift of peace, and hast taught us that the peacemakers are Thy children; make us, we beseech Thee, children of quietness and heirs of Thy peace, that all discords may vanish from among us and Thy tranquility be about us evermore. This we ask for Jesus Christ's sake. *(The Mozarabic Sacramentary)*

O Lord, if only my will may remain right and firm towards Thee, do with me whatsoever it shall please Thee. For it cannot be anything but good, whatsoever Thou shalt do with me. If it be Thou wilt that I should be in the light, blessed be Thou. And if Thou wilt that I be in the darkness, blessed be Thou. Light and darkness, life and death, praise ye the Lord. (Thomas à Kempis, *The Imitation of Christ)**

Son, now shall I teach thee the way of peace and of very liberty.
Lord, do as Thou sayest, for that is agreeable to me to hear.
Study, son, rather to do the will of another than thine own. Choose evermore rather to have less than more. Seek ever the lower place and to be under all. Desire ever to pray that the will of God be all and wholly done. Lo, such a man entereth into the coasts of peace and quiet.

*Underhill suggests here the prayer on p. 71 of *Mysteries of the Mass in Reasoned Prayers* by William Roche, S.J.

70

These words are from the twenty-third chapter of the *Imitation of Christ* which is called "Of Four Things Bringing Great Peace," and when we consider what those four things are, we see that Christian happiness and tranquility is built upon hard and rocky ground and not upon vague and shining sands.

What are the four things in their essence? They are obedience, self-denial, humbleness, and surrender. From these, says Thomas à Kempis, comes great peace. That deep tranquility which we mean by peace of soul is the surest of all signs of spiritual health. Its calm atmosphere must enwrap our love and our joy if that love and joy are to become and remain spiritual things and to work God's will. A peacefulness which persists through success and through suffering alike is the real mark of the Christian soul. Without it love and joy may easily become mere emotional effervescence.

Peace is, above all things, a state of the will. It is a calm, willed acceptance of all the conditions which God imposes upon us and which deepens with our deepening realization of Him. The things which work against it are four forms of wanting our own way, four kinds of disharmony between our will and the will of God. And that which conquers these four kinds of self-will for us is the fourth suggestion made by à Kempis: that we "desire ever and pray that the will of God be all and wholly done." When we thus completely transfer the center of interest from our ideas to His ideas, then we indeed enter the coasts of peace and quiet.

This peace, which St. Paul says must crown our love and our joy if they are genuine, is not merely a nice religious feeling that comes to us in times of prayer. It does not mean basking in the divine sunshine like comfortable pussycats. It is a peace that needs and indeed produces a courageous and yet humble kind of love. It means such a profound giving of ourselves to God, such an utter neglect of our own opinions, preferences, and rights, as keeps the deeps of our souls within His atmosphere in all the surface rush, the ups and downs, demands and disappointments, joy and suffering of daily life. We cease to matter. Only God and His work matters.

He demands an unmeasured love, and His response is an unmeasured peace. "My peace I give unto you." Think what that peace really is!—a peace tested in Gethsemane, in mockery, in insult, misunderstanding, apparent failure, the extremity of pain, yet so radical that it could be given from the Cross to the dying thief. "Not as the world giveth . . ." but as the Crucified giveth, at His own cost, now from beyond the world. If we are really growing towards God, we are growing toward that ideal.

And it is only in such a state of peace as this that our best work can be done. We don't do it in a state of tension and anxiety. We don't hear God's voice then. Worry is one of the most ungodly things in the whole world. We shall do our best work in a deepening spirit of earnestness, responsibility, and a sense of obligation. We shall do our best when we are inspired by that loving longing of the soul to do the last bit we can for God, being wholly swayed by the Spirit that molds and uses us. But we shall not work in agitation or strain. So too with our mental obligations, problems, and difficulties. We are called upon to deal with those problems up to the limit of our understanding, but always in the atmosphere of "the peace that passes understanding."

Again à Kempis says, "Seek ever the lower place." Humbleness, a necessary condition of our love and our joy, is the very substance of our peace. The more our sense of God's infinite reality, His steady mysterious action on life, deepens, the less important we and our little efforts and failures grow, and the greater our peace grows. You see it as the golden thread of humility which links together the three great gifts made to us by the Spirit of God: love, joy, and peace.

If we are not to let our hearts be troubled about our work and its difficulties, even about the sin, failure, and need with which we may be trying to deal, still less are we to let them be troubled about our own souls. Self-occupation of that sort is not so much wrong as idiotic, but it is the kind of idiocy which soon brings decay into the spiritual life. Softening of the soul, which is worse than softening of the brain, sets in. We become religious invalids, always wondering what we can venture to eat, drink, do, or risk—and that sort of personality is miserable stuff to offer God.

Some people are always wondering what is the best thing for their souls, and if you told them that really it did not much matter, they would be shocked. But the best way to manage the soul is much the same as the best way to manage the body. First look at its real needs, real weak points, and real obligations squarely in the face. Prescribe for them if necessary, or get someone else to do it for you. Find out the rule of life that suits you, the work to which you are called, the right way to manage yourself so that you can do this work, and then, having found this out, stick to it.

One of the things which can well be done in retreat is something which everyone who takes spiritual life seriously should do. It is to decide on the balance of prayer, spiritual reading, work, recollection, recreation, and rest which will make us most effective instruments of God's will and help us to live, work, and endure on higher levels. That is the real point, not our particular devotional preferences or daintinesses. That is the road to peace.

Here too an ever deepening and more loving vision of God's greatness and our immaturity will help us to see things in proportion, to realize ourselves, as it were, as seedlings growing in an infinite garden. It will check what St. John of the Cross called "spiritual gluttony." We might call it "spiritual ambition," that fussy envy of people who are doing better than ourselves: all the copy-cat sort of holiness. If we can see things in proportion, it will make us very willing, even in the things of the Spirit, to have less rather than more, and take the lower place. And we shall grow, expand, and deepen in proportion to the extent to which we achieve this peaceful forgetfulness of ourselves.

Such forgetfulness of self means peace too in the necessary ups and downs of our own spiritual course, accepting here, as elsewhere, that which comes from God. When we can say with no sense of unreality, "If Thou wilt that I be in the light, blessed be Thou. And if Thou wilt that I be in the darkness, blessed be Thou. Light and darkness, life and death, praise ye the Lord," as à Kempis says—if we can really say that, it means that in the deeps of our souls our wills are indeed peacefully united to the holy will and love that guides this little world and gave us the model of the Cross. Merging ourselves in that will, we find our peace.

We think it is rather immature to be upset about the weather, yet very few souls tranquilly pursue the spiritual course without minding the spiritual weather. Here too we must expect fog, cold, persistant cloudiness, gales, and sudden stinging hail, as well as the sun.

We ought not to mind the fact that there are dim, flat, and obscure patches in our religious life. When we come to them, joy may seem to go, but if our love is really a courageous love, peace will remain. Peace can be there even when it seems to us that we are not getting on in the least because we are not seeking our own profit. And we can have peaceful belief in the infinite patience and generosity of God who knows how to wait.

Perfect clearness in religion often really means just shallowness, for, being what we are, we cannot expect to get eternal life into sharp focus. Often indeed God and His peace are more surely present with us in darkness than in light. We ought to be equally ready for both. It is a very poor sort of faith and love that will not face a dark passage until it knows where the switch is.

It is also true that there are moments in the life of communion when the soul doesn't *wish* to see, to fully comprehend. The gift is made so subtly because we can't endure the full daylight glare. It is not in our comprehension, but in God's will, that our peace abides.

Often we hear complete surrender to God spoken of as something that very religious people may possibly attain, but we hardly realize how exceedingly absurd the opposite is. We do not see the hopelessness of setting up our tiny, half-real, half-animal, and altogether infantile wills, swayed by all sorts of silly longings and primitive impulses, against the mighty process of His perfect will. Nor do we recognize the folly of trying to make little whirlpools in the great, steady stream of that creative will and love. How utterly impossible to be happy or harmonised if we do that! His service is perfect freedom, and service means doing things in your master's way and not your own. No service is possible without humility and obedience.

Now you see we have gotten down to the very foundations of love and joy. It is the same law as the law of Paradise which Dante learned and which we have quoted from Augustine: "In His Will is our peace." This is the law which turns the whole world into the Kingdom of Heaven, for peace is a state of the will, and the will, as the old mystics liked to say, is the king of the soul. "Heaven in our souls" then, simply consists in the harmony of our will with God's will. If then, "Heaven is a temper of mind and not a place," heaven is that temper of peaceful surrender which places our wills in perfect harmony with God's.

We have perpetual opportunities, both little and great, of entrance into that heaven. We have chances offered to us of doing hard and boring and self-forgetful things, of accepting the rebuff, the misunderstanding, the sudden disarrangement of plan which comes to us. We have opportunities of going on quietly with our job without recognition, taking all the ruffles of the surface of life just as they come. The result of that is peace, peace even if our outward life does seem a continuous rush, or even a continuous discouragement.

St. Augustine said that we are nothing else but wills: our inner life, that is, is always aiming at something, intending something. Generally it is a self-interested something which attracts and keeps our attention. The result—since God made us for Himself and is the only adequate object of our will—is that we are restless. Different and really incompatible things are pulling at our will and our attention, and the result of this is an interior conflict that saps our strength.

Now it is right and wholesome that we should have varieties of interest, but it must be variety in unity. Yet the unity within which all our differing interests, occupations, and desires are enclosed must be the overruling peace of a will that has been given to God. In the rush of our daily lives, to absent ourselves for a moment, to turn to Him, and to reaffirm that consecration is to recover peace. We all know too well how easily we turn in odd moments to our worries and preoccupations. We should use the same method to pacify, instead of exasperate, our souls.

You remember how the *Pax Romana* embraced and gave security and tranquility to many different nations by freeing them from the burden and exhaustion of war among themselves? They remained different and distinct nations. They kept their own customs, industries, and ideas, but they were harmonized under one steady rule.

So, within the peace of God, we retain our personal and diverse interests and powers, our full variety of life and vocation, but redeemed from conflict. Thus we are able to use the whole of our strength for creation and for service.

It is just as St. Paul, before his conversion, wasted his splendid energy kicking against the pricks. But after his conversion, that stream of power flowed into one channel of creation given to Christ, and he lived in perfect peace one of the hardest lives that a Christian has ever lived. The vision of Christ which he met on the road to Damascus did not reproach Paul with wickedness but with silliness. How hard it is to kick against the goad. What a foolish, wasteful thing to do!

The Spirit of God is always pressing our souls to fulfill His mysterious purpose for each one of us, and our peace consists in obedience to the pressure. Misery and discord come from kicking against it. After his conversion, Paul was always talking about peace, although he seemed to be living a life that most people would consider unpeaceful to the last degree. He begins every letter by wishing his correspondents peace—grace and peace. He wishes them God's presence in their lives, and the tranquility which follows. A sense of power and of quietude comes to us when we read his words.

We have spent a great deal of time today in dwelling upon three qualities, the three firstfruits of the Spirit when it quickens the Christian soul and makes it grow: love, joy, and peace. It is right to call these qualities virtues, for virtue means strength; and love, joy, and peace are no mere personal comforts. They strengthen the soul, brace, and deepen it, redeem it from pettiness, and make it able to do better work for God. Therefore it is good to meditate upon these qualities.

It is also good because of that law of our mental life by which we tend to become that which we behold.* In the long run we shall find that we grow best, not by direct conflict with our difficulties and bad qualities, but by turning to and gazing upon the love and joy and peace of the saints, by trying to learn the secret of their harmony with God, by contemplating and learning from them, setting our own will that way. It is then that we become most capable of dealing with evil in ourselves and in the world. Then we become strong and quiet, and are able to meet life with gay courage and deep serenity, opposing to its half-real demands and temptations, the full and solid realities of the spiritual world.

---

*This is actually a quote from Plotinus whom Underhill read in her early days. Jesus spoke of the same thing in the Sermon on the Mount: "The eye is the lamp of the body. So, if your eye is sound, your whole body will be full of light" (Matt. 6:22–23).

VI

Prayer

Preparatory Worship

Psalm 63: "O God, . . . Early Will I Seek Thee"

Hymns: "Holy, Holy, Holy"
      "O Thou in All Thy Might So Far"
      "Teach Me, My God and King"

Prayers of dedication, petition, and receptivity:

O Lord Jesus Christ, who hast said: Ask and ye shall receive, seek and ye shall find, knock and it shall be opened unto you; mercifully attend to our supplications, and grant us the gift of Thy divine charity, that we may ever love Thee with our whole heart and with all our words and deeds, and may never cease from praising Thee. *(The Raccolta)*

Suffer us, O Father, to come to Thee. Lay Thy hands on us and bless us. Take away from us forever our own spirit and replace it by the instinct of Thy divine grace. Take away from us our own will and leave us only the desire of doing Thy will. Give us that beautiful, that lovable, that sublime simplicity which is the first and greatest of Thy gifts. (J. N. Grou)

Yesterday we meditated on the three outstanding marks of the Christian soul: the love, joy, and peace it receives bit by bit from God as it grows. These are the gifts which must be poured out again on all the need and misery of this poor muddled world in which the soul is trying to work for Christ.

Today we have to think of the channel by which we get and feed those things which religion calls the "means of grace." We must consider how to enrich our souls, how to breathe, grow, and stretch. And the answer is that there are two ways: loving encounter with God Himself as well as with His other children. We are to stretch up to Him and out to them. Intercourse with God is prayer. This is the subject of our morning meditation.

To merely stay in such a house as this is to learn something about prayer, for this place is full of its spirit. It makes us begin to realize that *the Christian life is prayer* right through. It can be nothing else, really. If our souls were deeper, stronger, and more real, we might maintain the spirit of prayer all the while.

Our formal prayer and times of silence are not the whole of our prayer or shouldn't be. The old definition of prayer was that it is lifting our minds up into God. That can and should be our constant habit. There are always the set times, the services, the "drill" of the devotional life which are largely intended to tune us up and gradually educate us for this. It has always been the Christian view that every bit of work done toward God is a prayer.

There is a story of a humble Czechoslovakian woman who is believed to have lived close to God. She declared: "I can't say prayers for you—but I'll boil the potatoes for you!" It takes a long education to get to that point!

Prayer looks out all the time towards God and stretches towards him with desire. Jeremy Taylor describes it wonderfully when he says: "Prayer is only the body of the bird. Desires are its wings!"

Prayer is our soul's response to God's immense attraction, and this response begins in the activity of the *will*. Will and desire are the heart of the mental life turned to God. This is not mere pious reverie. As Saint Teresa says, at the beginning of our prayer life, we have to draw the living water out of the well. It is hard work. We can't leave it to chance. God requires our communion with Him to be an act, an effort, and to *cost* something. Think of the trouble we give ourselves to get time to be with those whom we love. Is it not ever so much more important to make a way to commune with God?

We are spiritual creatures with the power of communion with God, breathing the air of eternity. We can't keep this power unless we exercise it. Nor can we fully get it unless we train ourselves to it. We must accustom our attention, that wanders over all other interests, to fix itself on Him. Such deliberate attention to God is the beginning of real prayer. Prayer is never to be judged by feeling that goes with it: it is the willed intercourse of our tiny spirits with the Infinite Spirit of Love.

In the life of prayer, our wills and God's grace act together. When we consider what prayer is and what it can become, how *wonderful* that little half-grown creatures like us can have communion with God! We realize that we couldn't do it by our own strength alone. But this doesn't excuse us from using our strength. Teresa got to haul the bucket up. Going limp or having a nice all-overish religious feeling is not prayer; it is not interchange with God. Prayer covers all ways in which our will and love reaches out to one Reality and Love in adoration, longing, penitence, confidence, and joy.

Consider Christ's three *promises* of prayer [Matt. 7:7–8]. Note how all of them are attached to something done by us. The question of whether we will commune with God is left to *us,* to the freedom of our wills. God gives out of His treasury what we *really* ask, seek, and long for. His supply is infinite; it is our demands which are shallow, mistrustful, and vague. The saints were so sure about the extent in which human life is a spiritual thing and Spirit-fed that they asked and received *much*.

"Ask," "seek," and "knock;" there is something very definite about that. Those words represent three very real stages in the life of prayer corresponding to a steady growth and enrichment of the soul's encounter with God. When we begin real prayer, all of us feel very helpless. We are filled with craving, with longing. We are asking for God. We want assurance, light, spiritual food, strength to carry on and deal with our difficulties and sins. We are met by grief and temptations which we cannot face alone. We begin the terrible struggle up from a mere animal selfish life, and we *must* be helped. We want something to be added to our human nature from the supernatural world if we are to grow up to be children of God. And opening our souls to the spiritual world in prayer, *asking, we do receive*—although perhaps not instantly or sensationally. Perhaps the answer is not exactly what we expect. Still a gift is made, and prayer in the spiritual life becomes possible to us. A response comes from the dim world which surrounds and penetrates us.

The second promise is that if we will seek, we will find. That meditation which is a deep brooding exploration and thinking in God's presence is a way to the real discovery of the spiritual life. Some people are helped by formal meditation. Others can't do it. But there is always some way in which all can seek to know more of God and their own souls. The utmost that we can achieve is only a tiny bit of full reality but more than enough of happiness. Yielding ourselves to God in prayer, gradually discovering bit by bit, often not in big disclosures, is His call to our souls.

We may not be specialists in our vocation to one definite kind of sacrifice or redemptive work in action or in prayer. The Church is not a society of specialists, but of living, loving, ever-growing souls which must stretch up to God in adoration and out to one's companions in active love, doing or not doing ever in accord with God's will and God's voice. One of the great functions of prayer is to train us to this attitude of soul. Seeking His will requires courage, patience, and trust. The deep things of prayer are first given in response to these.

Seeking God in prayer means we have realized that we want Him more than any of His gifts. In seeking in this single-minded way, we discover enroute a good deal about ourselves. The woman with the lost piece of silver had to have a complete spring cleaning. She found much dust, but forgot the rubbish and perhaps forgot the treasure too.

That seeking in prayer, like all spiritual processes, must be gentle, not feverish, and unstrained. A method of patience and confidence marks good explorers. In seeking ourselves, there should be no uproar or wild hunting. We need to clean the windows and let in the light. Then like a householder, we find the new and old appropriate to our souls, which help us to slowly deepen and widen our life in Him. Thus acting, at last we *find* ourselves as truly living the life of the Spirit, truly supplied by Love.

We also find our own vocation in this life of prayer. Our vocations vary. Some specialists are appointed for intercession. We develop our power, as the souls of others open, to embrace their lives and needs. Yet not all can do this. Others are drawn to adoration or loving absorption in God. Both types find more and more the homeliness and naturalness of this life with God. Julian said this was the deepest of her discoveries about Him. It was the inward gentleness and humbleness of God's approach to our souls in prayer that St. Teresa referred to as "gentle rain."

For the third promise we are asked to knock. Now comes the time in our prayer when we seem brought up short by a closed door. Generally, we experience the other side of that door, the riches of the house of God. But this is the real life at which all our education in prayer has been gently aiming, life lived in the atmosphere of God beyond entreaty and search. We leave those off when we are at home.

Home—When we realize all that that image implies, don't prayers merely *asking* for help or comfort seem a bit mean and ungenerous? True, they are answered out of the boundless generosity of God, but our aim ought to lie beyond, in a life lived in Him. As we began we sang "Holy, Holy, Holy"! All that matters is God, not ourselves. This is the attitude to which the life of prayer should bring us. It is St. Paul's attitude of adoration, of delighted surrender.

Knock. Nothing is said about what happens when the door opens. Christ's silence is more eloquent than speech. We needn't suppose that other sorts of prayer are then shut to us. St. John said that the sheep come in and out of the door and find pasture. Adoration brings us to a door, but it is life in the world beyond the door that then overrules all.

Now to some, these thoughts I know will be commonplace. To others, there will be those which are new and strange. We are all in a different class in the school of prayer. It is important not to try to force ourselves to practice one kind of praying when God is teaching us another. Children don't try to do sums in the middle of a music lesson. Nevertheless, it is not uncommon for people whose attraction is to silent communion to struggle to do formal meditation or get through intercession or vocal prayer which they've taken on as a discipline. Do be simple and natural!

To be truly silent before God is one of the loveliest things in the world. It is much like the story to which we referred in our first meeting together, the story of the old man whose prayer was simply looking at God and letting God look at him.

Silence comes of itself. Mechanical silence, the silence for which one struggles, is one of the most sterile of silences. This is why some find corporate silence difficult. They don't know what to do with it. But if each person *attends to God in the way we attend to anyone we deeply love,* instead of attending to the silence or what others are doing—if we just open our souls to God, the result will be all right.

Everyone's contribution is not required to be the same! Get real about it. Live, breathe, open your souls and feed them. Turn to God. You will find Christ offering Himself just in the way *you* can bear it. He will teach you best. And remember Teresa's advice: when you start to pray, get yourself some company as quickly as you can!

Remember also, fixed times of prayer have as their object the building up of a constant state of prayer in which we live and work in God's presence. That alone is a full Christian life. It is hard at first to acquire and keep such a state. Do you recall how Brother Lawrence said that for a long time it brought great difficulty to him? We have to realize that our souls need a long education in prayer. We must expect it and be patient with ourselves.

Much of our prayer is at first a sort of training and most of us need frequent tuning-up and the help of ideas and phrases that keep us pointed in the right way. If anyone says that this is self-suggestion, I agree. Some of it is. But we ought to suggest to ourselves spiritual ideas. That is a method God has given us. We needn't be afraid of doing what always has been done when we do it under a new name.

Formal prayer makes a direct suggestion to our souls and reminds us of what we always tend to forget. If this were grasped, then the supposed unreality would cease to trouble us. If that proposal is used, it will train us to a sense of God's presence.

Writings on prayer refer to acts and aspirations, little phrases by which, from time to time, we lift up our minds and hearts to God. They are seen as among the most valuable forms of prayer. We should try to accustom ourselves to use them frequently during the day. For example, we can use the Psalms, the Prayer Book, or the *Imitation of Christ.* They are full of aspirations.

These phrases of aspiration and thousands like them slip past us easily. If we stop, dwell, brood, and make food of them, we will find that thus used, they will open to us paths to mental prayer. They bring about levels of devotion wonderful in their claim and demand. They give the mind something to hold onto. They quiet it, but they stir us to feel the love, humility, and adoration which they suggest. In trains and at odd moments, they can lift our hearts to God. Hymns, too, lull distressing thoughts and so gradually educate our thoughts and feeling to run more and more in their channels. Such habits furnish an immediate source of peace and security.

Some individuals have what we would call an aptitude for contemplation. This attitude of mind comes almost naturally. But all of us must feed it and renew it if we wish to keep it fresh and real. We must have the skeleton of a habit. A *rule* of prayer is essential to the life of prayer just as for the sacraments there must be a definite rule of Holy Communion. The rule is not to be forsaken because we feel cold and dead. It is no use to say that our work shall be our prayer. It won't be unless we train our souls and get the color of prayer into it; and this means regular times of total attention to God as well as frequent aspirations.

A Christianity which is only active is not a complete Christianity at all. Christ's times of retirement for communion with his Father prove that. There is a lovely and even homely intimacy of spirit in God, in Christ, which lights up for us not only what we call good works but every sort of creative work. Thus we learn to weave together this world and the Eternal World; and we fill all we do with gentle loveliness which is of God.

VII

The Communion of Saints

Preparatory Worship

Te Deum

Psalm 90: "Lord, Thou Hast Been Our Dwelling Place"

Hymns: "Holy, Holy, Holy"
      "Who Are These Like Stars Appearing?"
      "Let Saints on Earth in Concert Sing"
      "Ye Watchers and Ye Holy Ones"
      "For All the Saints"

Prayers:

O Almighty God, who hast knit together Thine elect in one communion and fellowship, in the mystical body of Thy Son, Christ our Lord: grant us grace so to follow Thy blessed saints in all virtuous and godly living, that we may come to those unspeakable joys which Thou has prepared for them that unfeignedly love Thee. Through Jesus Christ our Lord. (Collect for the Festival of All Saints)

O King, eternal, immortal, invisible, before whom stand the spirits of the living and the dead, who in the righteousness of Thy saints has given us an example of godly life, and in their blessedness a glorious pledge of the hope of our calling, we beseech Thee that, being compassed about by so great a cloud of witnesses, we may run with patience the race that is set before us, and with them receive the crown of glory that fadeth not away; through Jesus Christ our Lord. *(Acts of Devotion)* *

We have been thinking today of the way in which we might hope to build up a solid and vivid spiritual life. We have talked about prayer, the

*Underhill suggests here the prayers on pages 55, 34, and 50 of *Mysteries of the Mass in Reasoned Prayers* by William Roche, S.J.

chief source of power through which comes this communion with God. We have spoken of this lifting up of our minds to Him, of the development of that which has been called the soul's vertical movement to God in adoration, in simple contemplation, and in a more and more continuous intercourse with Him.

But we cannot either achieve or maintain this intercourse by ourselves. To suppose that we can is an illusion, the favorite illusion of the Quietist and the false mystic. We are creatures of earth; we are immersed in history; we are members of society. So, having just thought of the eternal world that enfolds us, now we think of the physical world in which we are placed and its inhabitants, for the Christian religion has its visible and its invisible sides.

God comes to us in part through history and through society, that is to say, through other men and women. He is wholly revealed to us in Christ and partly revealed to us through all great loving and heroic souls. The history of our religion is the history of the Holy Spirit in the world. It shines out and transfigures other souls; we see its radiance in them and learn from them. And the more we thus stretch out in love towards them, the greater the horizontal growth of our soul's life, the richer the soul's life will become. Their loving spirits will set our spirits on fire.

Thus the fellowship of the saints is a very important aspect of the complete Christian life, for the saints are fully grown spiritual personalities. They are simply the men and women who have responded fully to God's demands upon them. He gives Himself to all. The saints differ from us in the generosity of their response to the gift, and because of this generosity of response they have become His intimate friends.

It is a mistake to think of the saints as dead examples. They are, like ourselves, members of the mystical Body of Christ, living, real and ardent spirits; and it is often through them that His life reaches us. Therefore we ought to think about them and love them far more than we do. It is a part of our life in Christian fellowship.

Now when I speak thus of the saints, I do not just merely mean the official saints, though these include some of the loveliest flowers of the human spirit, the most perfect expressions of love, joy, and peace. But beyond this, I mean the simple, homely, and splendid examples of supernatural heroism and love wherever found. I mean all those who have grown up, as St. Paul wants every one of us to grow up, to the fullness of the stature of Christ, those for whom He is a real and living presence.

Our Christian social duty and privilege includes communion with all these. We are literally members one of another, and physical death makes no difference to this. Therefore do not let us forget it in any scheme of life which we may form. Even at the lowest, it helps us all to have examples to look up to, and for this alone we might well make friends with the saints and see what, at its best, Christianity can be and do.

The easiest way to find God in all men is first to see Him shining in His infinitely various friends. You may say that we have Christ's example and that is enough, but we cannot always raise our eyes to that height. It helps us to realize the power of Christianity and what it can do for us when we see it producing, from ordinary material, such human beings as Benedict, Francis, Catherine, Ignatius, Teresa, Fox, Wesley, and Elizabeth Fry. All these were people who began as throughly willful and sometimes even sinful men and women but were picked up, utterly remade by Christ, and used as His tools because they responded with courage to the demands of God. They are our spiritual brothers and sisters, and to dwell on their lives, sufferings, and joys is a humbling, but adequate cure for low spirits and general fed-upness.

Just consider the variety of these lives which were completed and transfigured in God. Think of St. Ignatius. He began as a worldly and self-indulgent young soldier, and he was turned right 'round and compelled to begin living in a new way by reading, during an illness, the lives of the saints. In his last years, Ignatius was described as "something all love" and as never making any decision without resorting to God.

Look at Francis of Assisi. He too was a self-indulgent and pleasure loving boy feeling the human loathing we all feel for hideous sights and squalor. He began his new life by bravely conquering his disgust and making it a stepping stone to God.

Think of Angela of Foligno: a worldly, vain, hypocritical, perhaps actually sinful woman. She ended her life as a master theologian because of the vigor and reality of her life in God.

Think of St. Teresa, a high-spirited, romantic, passionate creature who confessed that the devil often sent her such a spirit of bad temper that she wanted to eat everybody up! Here was a person who could exclaim, in a way so delightfully unlike the truly pious, "May the Lord keep us from silly devotions!" And she privately alluded to the mitigated nuns as "the pussycats." St. Teresa reached the very heights of the spiritual life and, in middle age, with broken physical health, was able in the power of the Spirit to reform the life of the religious in Spain.

Think of Augustine Baker who forsook the spiritual path for nine years out of mere slackness and discouragement, yet returned and, through the fullness of his surrender, became one of its highest, deepest, and gentlest guides.

People like these show us what the common stuff of human nature can do, and their presence stimulates us and helps us. They have all our half-animal instincts and desires, all the complexes and cravings by which we try to reduce responsibility, yet see what they make of them! They are the true Cloud of Witnesses. They witness to the solid reality and power of the spiritual life. Therefore we ought to be friends with them, to seek them in the books that they have left behind, to realize their human and vivid aliveness; and because in these books they speak to us and are willing to share their secret with us if we can understand it, spiritual reading is second only to prayer as a support of the inner life.

Such spiritual reading is a social act. It gives us real intercourse with those great souls who are the honor and glory of the family, and we gradually discover them to be people who were originally very much like ourselves. They can tell us more and more as we learn to love more and more. We enter into their lives by sympathy and hear them speak. St. Augustine's *Confessions*, St. Catherine of Sienna's *Dialogue*, Julian's *Revelations of Love*, or St. Teresa's *Life*: such books immensely enlarge our social environment and are one of the ways in which the Communion of Saints can be most directly felt by us.

We all know what a help it is to live amongst and be intimate with keen Christians. How much we owe in our own lives to contact with them! We seem to catch something from them and obtain from them a secret and invisible support. We know too how hard it is to struggle on alone in a non-Christian atmosphere. In the saints we always have the society of inspiring Christians, are always in touch with the classic standard. Their personal influence still radiates centuries after their physical presence has left the earth, reminding us of the way in which God acts on people through people, reminding us too of our own awful personal responsibility in this matter.

Remember that as Christians we belong to a religion which is rooted in personality and works in and through personality. God is brought to us in the person of Christ, and news about God, bringing a deeper, richer, and lovelier understanding of Him, comes through personal contact with the vision of other and greater souls. The saints are the great experimental Christians who, because of their unreserved self-dedication, made discoveries about God which are impossible to us. They teach us that Christian holiness is never monotonous, that the household of faith is full of variety and action, and that we find in it the ups and downs of real family life.

The saints range from Lawrence in the kitchen to Aquinas in the philosopher's chair; but whatever their position, whatever their mental attainments, we notice in all the best of them the easiness, the sweetness, the lack of rigorousness which comes from dying to self and its limitations. We learn from their friendship not only to keep our sense of God's immediate presence alive and vivid, but also to share His gentle, patient tolerance of those amongst whom we work.

Most of us at one time or the other have had the holy privilege of contact with saints of our own day, and we know how humbling and how stimulating that contact was, how real it made God to us, how awed we felt, and how utterly unconscious of it all the saints felt. We realized then with shame and joy what Christians really could be. There are few things that help us more than thus to live for a little bit with those who have a deeper, richer sense of God than ourselves; yet, at least in our reading and meditation, we can all do this every day.

It sometimes seems as though we had almost lost now the beautiful old sense that the visible and invisible Church is really one: that all Christian souls, living and dead, are truly woven into one Body, and so the saints are still part of our community and are concerned with it. The medieval habit of asking for their help once kept this sense of actual touch alive and enormously enlarged the bounds of the individual Christian's life. So too the ancient form of the General Confession made each Christian confess his or her sins, first to God, and then to the saints, those fellow members of the invisible Church whose standard of purity has been sullied by his or her own act: "I confess to the Virgin Mary, to St. Peter, St. Paul and all the saints. To every soul in Christ, I confess that I have tarnished the family record."

The saints, after all, are as much concerned with us as we are with our fellow Christians, and at least as much interested. "Do not mourn for me," said St. Dominic when he was dying. "I shall do much more for you where I am going."

As we get to know them in all their variousness, we gradually learn that there is no such thing as a saintly type. What is called the saintly type is often an objectionable and showy form of pietistic character. But there is a steady sanctification of every sort of character once it has been given to God and died to self. Indeed the idea of the Communion of Saints as a society of persons all wearing the same patterned white robe, stiffened with the same starch, is a very depressing one. Their variousness, like our own, is the variousness of real life, but all are irradiated with love and joy and peace. All have killed the poison of self interest and know what it is to be fed and used by God. They teach us that what we have got to do is to irradiate that which we already have and are with the Divine Love, not turn away from it and seek some different and perhaps imaginary type of perfection.

True saintliness is found to fulfill itself in scholarship, in art, and in science, in lives of prayer and lives of action. Some of the saints were pure contemplatives; some were organizers of genius; some of the very greatest were both. St. Ignatius, according to one of his early biographers, "combined a supreme knowledge of the things of God with great good sense in matters of business." Claudel says that God chose St. Teresa for her courage and common sense, qualities that we all want now in social service. They are the same qualities which God has always required for His service.

"Who are these like stars appearing?" Well, they are just people who accepted the whole obligation of Christianity as a real and concrete fact—the new creation that Christ prayed for and Paul realized so keenly. They are people who always, every time and in every relation, put God first and stuck to it, people who could fully actualize the promise of their baptism and who really behaved like members of Christ, children of God, and inheritors of the Kingdom of Heaven.

Now there is no reason why everyone of us should not be that kind of person if we make it our real objective, if we keep an eye on it all the time and are willing to face drudgery and pain for it. If we were like that it would mean a new and regenerate world. The Church and the State would then be one thing; and the saints, in their intense humanity and variousness, keep on reminding us that, as Christians, this and nothing else is our call. They show us the great work they accomplished and remind us that only their steadfast union with God in Christ made these works possible. Their strength was "made perfect in weakness," and our poor little efforts are redeemed by association with them.

Finally, they can also teach us something of their outlook. They can give us a share, as it were, in the family point of view. We learn through them to recognize everywhere, often in the most unexpected places, touching hints of this aptitude of the soul for God. They show us His presence and his action all 'round us here and now, often exhibited in circumstances of heart-piercing humbleness and simplicity. We see the patient, unselfish, and heroic slum mother, carrying on against hopeless odds. And there are the thousands of acts of quiet renunciation performed by inconspicuous persons, often in the interests of an apparently unworthy cause done—why? We hardly know why. They show themselves again in gay courage and suffering and in steady, noble, burden-bearing love. They are revealed in every kind of devotedness, often quite unconscious of itself and its own beauty. Such selfless devotion cannot but feed our faith, hope, and love. The world is full of these things.

Often those who show these qualities never accept the doctrines of Christianity at all, but are they not just the persons who reveal most clearly our miraculous capacity for God? Would not Christ's joyous recognition rush out to them? When we read of the saints in the Apocalypse ("These are they who follow the Lamb wherever He goeth"), we picture to ourselves those in white garments who walk through the flowery fields of Paradise. But I like to think that the vision of the poet went further than that. These are truly the close followers of Christ, those who go wherever He goes and do whatever He does: saving, healing, and redeeming work. We find their spirits present in the poorest and roughest places and most hopeless situations. They are present with sick souls; they enter profoundly into all innocent suffering; they exercise unfettered love. These are the agents of the Spirit, completely loyal and devoted servants of God, who have chosen the heroic career.

Whoever desires to spend himself completely in God's service has already set his face towards sanctity, however far the goal may seem, and belongs to a communion of life-giving spirits. Those spirits are truly present where a struggle is going on in the heart of a sinner or wherever a soul in weakness or in grief prays for help.

The mark of a saint is a burning interest in and love for other souls, and it does not matter at all whether they belong to what we call the living or the dead. All these are "pure, lovely, and of good report," and it is good for us to think of them and to commune with them. In so doing we balance our upward movement of adoration towards God in His eternity by our widely sretching movement of love and sympathy towards humanity, that wonderful humanity in which He can be revealed in the world of time. It is under this double influence that our souls will grow most quickly in reality, in love, and in power.

VIII

Growth

Preparatory Worship

Psalm (not noted)

Magnificat

Hymns: "The God of Love My Shepherd Is"
"Dear Lord and Father of Mankind"

Prayers for growth in love and service such as:

O Lord, Thou who teacheth us to grow in purity, simplicity, and self-control, lead us on: "ministering, in the world without, . . . in love and mercy; . . . inwardly abiding in simplicity, and stillness, and in utter peace . . . turning from all things of self into the freedom of the Will of God." (Ruysbroeck)

We Know, O God, that we must change if we are to see Thy face: none but the holy can see Thee. O support us as we proceed in this great, awful, happy change, with the grace of Thine unchangeableness. Let us day by day be molded by Thee and be changed from glory to glory by ever looking towards Thee and ever leaning on Thy Strength. (John Henry Newman)

Come! Spirit of Love! Penetrate and transform us by the action of Your purifying life. May Your constant, brooding love, bring forth in us more love and all the graces and works of love. Give us grace to remain still under its action, and may that humble stillness be our prayer. (Evelyn Underhill, *Meditations and Prayers*)

We spent our last meeting together in the atmosphere of the saints considering the qualities which crown their perfection. These set our standard. The main business of life consists in the effort to achieve that standard. Saints are simply human beings like ourselves whose souls have grown up to their full stature by full response to their environment which is God. The seed of this possible growth is in us all. Perhaps the best of all descriptions of the saints is that which calls them "great souls"—souls so great that they can receive God.

Now, in retreat, it is good to consider this spiritual growth, for those who have been in the silence in a place like this begin to feel somewhat crude and undeveloped. In these conditions they recognize that there *is* a deeper and bigger life possible to us and a more wonderful contact to be had with the mysteries of the universe. Going back to the saying with which we began our retreat, we realize that Lucie-Christine's soul was able, as she said, to "drink in God" because a soul is as great as its love.

Most of us now accept the theory of evolution. We recognize the growth of conscious mind from the humblest animal origins as consistent with the divine creative will, but we do not always remember that we have not seen the extent of this will. In the saints, we receive a hint of it. They are the advance guard of spiritual humanity, and the main difference between them and us is maturity and depth of soul. We see in them a finished product, a genuine and achieved work of God. They set the standard at which we are to look and represent our assigned end toward which we must grow, each in our own way.

Of each of us God demands full sanctification—that is to say, our full spiritual growth—as the only way in which we can become capable of full and perfect service and take our place in the economy of the spiritual universe. He desires and invites all souls to become saints by the perfect flowering of love. He created us for *Himself*, that is, to continue His line of creation beyond nature to *more*. And the line of this growth must be from a narrow and self-regarding individualism, swayed by the primitive impulses to self-preservation and self-satisfaction, to a full, rich, warm, self-forgetful personality, capable of God and able to share His creative work. Receiving the divine life, love, and joy, we are invited to become, in fact, as St. Paul said, "fellow workers together with God" [2 Cor. 6:1].

What a thought! That ideal, fully received, steadily expands the soul and increases its energy. The alternative is a steady shrinking of the soul which comes from turning inwards and concentrating on self-love, self-will, and self-interest, even—and perhaps even especially—religious self-interest. Real growth means the death of all these and is the equivalent of what the old writers meant by mortification.

We do not, however, grow by thinking about it, by measuring ourselves, by pulling up our roots and having a look; and that conception must be put away from the first. Christ never showed the slightest interest in self-analysis, but much in self-giving and service and the feeding and development of souls. We may be sure the injunction to Peter to "Feed My sheep" was quite as good for Peter as for those he was to feed. Saints are notoriously not interested in themselves, but passionately interested in God and other souls. They represent the perfect flowering of personality within an atmosphere of all-demanding love. The mere external incidents of life do not really matter to them except in so far as they contribute to this development. Their contributions can be made anywhere and on any level. The true miracle of human experience is that every bit of it can feed the growth of that soul which always and everywhere puts God first.

Once a soul has definitely chosen God, everything is changed for it, though it may not realize this at first. Everything that happens now matters to it because God is in everything and is working through everything on that soul. Everything now gives it a chance. All things work together for it since it has become sensitive to the spiritual energies in which it is bathed. Such a soul may not be better or nicer than others, but its attitude towards and experience of life is changed. These now find their meaning beyond themselves. This is why election, choosing God and great spiritual realities as against all passing aims and satisfactions, is of such cardinal importance and the thought of election should be present to us now in retreat.

As the natural world is a sacrament of the supernatural, we can by looking at it learn a good deal about growth. We see that healthy growth needs food, light, and air, and is so gentle as to be almost imperceptible. We see that it is two-dimensional. Plants push up towards the light and expand, but this upward and outward growth depends for its perfection upon the downward push deep into the invisible foundations for food. And such a deepening of the soul's spiritual attachments must keep pace with its expansion up and out to the surrounding world if its growth is to be wholesome and robust. Thus a balanced enlargement of life towards God *and* towards our fellows alone fulfills our full human destiny.

We have to make ourselves fit to do that which love makes us want to do, and therefore the deepening of the inner life of prayer is central to our growth. The particular form which this takes in each case is of less importance so long as it helps us to throw roots into the spiritual world where we seek out and assimilate the food there given to us, and so long as the result of such feeding is to strengthen, humble, stretch, and brace the soul.

Look at all this in a large, vital way. Consider what mere crumbs we really are. Our true status in the spiritual universe is not likely to be greater than it is in the physical universe. How tiny and shallow is our best knowledge and our widest outlook, and yet how abasing is even that small vision to which we can attain. The greatest of the saints have been those who most keenly felt the inadequacy of their vision of God. It is easy enough to say words like "unsearchable" and "transcendent" in reference to God, but very hard to realize all that they imply of the divine self-giving. There is so much more there than we can possibly hope to take in or assimilate. The best we *can* hope to do is to act like the plant, to take from the rich and generous soil in which we grow the food that we need and *can* use, not that which we can't. It is by doing this that we grow: by feeding, not by forcing. Thus growing, we become able to assimilate more and more.

No gardener who knows his or her job ever gives seedlings rich soil, and God does not either. A step by step response to that which is given is the way to prepare for more. The simple food comes first, and there is lots of it to be found in religious institutions and traditions which modernists are too apt to despise. All the hoarded spiritual food of the race is there, all that it has found out about God. It is silly and arrogant not to accept it.

It is quite true that it is not the same thing as direct experience, just as jam is not the same thing as fresh fruit; still, it is made of fruit and will feed the soul and make it capable of more. Such variety of nourishment is better than fastidious concentration on one kind of food. We are a multiplicity in unity with mind, sense, heart, and spirit—all, possible channels of grace.

The plant does not know, or need to know, all the resources of the world it feeds on. We can make good roses without teaching them chemistry. And God can make good saints without teaching them theology, feeding them on the fountain of that Life—that objective Fact—of which theology can only say little things here and there. Remember St. Augustine's experience of God saying, "I am the food of the full-grown. Grow and thou shalt feed on Me. Nor shall I be changed into thy substance, but thou shalt be changed into Mine."

And we do this bit by bit by accepting and responding to that which is given. People sometimes say Holy Communion does nothing for them. They are not conscious of new strength and love. Perhaps the answer to that is the answer given Augustine in the invitation of God. None can guess all that this invitation may mean, but we can see in the growth and achievement of the saints something of what is implied in it.

No wonder Augustine thrilled with love and dread when he received that revelation of the destiny of the soul, a destiny which is inexhaustible even as love is inexhaustible. Yet such a destiny will involve suffering under the fierce rays of a light which will sometimes seem more than we can bear. It will bring tension, effort, and purifying pain, for purification from our animal past must be a part of our growth, effected bit by bit as we can bear it.

Another great saint, St. Catherine of Genoa, has said: "The creature is incapable of knowing anything but what God gives it from day to day. If it could know beforehand the successive stages He intends to give it, it would never be quiet." That is a warning by a great saint and expert against looking too far ahead. If we begin to wonder what God is going to give us and where our growth is to end, we shall never be quiet. Our job is to respond bit by bit from where we are now and leave the result. No worry. The worried child or animal never does well. Light, food, air, a demand made on our interest and activity, and our generous response—these are the things that matter.

As the plant grows by simple response to its environment, and not by studying works on botany, so with the soul. All self-occupation checks development. Even with regard to self-improvement, much self-analysis is a mistake. We mortify sins and lower impulses not by ferreting out and repressing them, but by developing and giving priority to contrary qualities and impulses. If we think of and stretch toward what is good and lovely—humility, pity, and patience—we shall bit by bit become less capable of pride, envy, and the rest. This is why meditation on the life and example of our Lord is so valuable a food of the soul. Look all the time at your assigned end, the term and occasion of your growth, shown in Him fully and in the saints in the degree in which they died to themselves and lived towards the Divine Love.

In the prayer of Ruysbroeck which we used to begin, we are taken bit by bit through all the phases of growth, from its rudimentary beginnings in purity of conscience, simplicity, self-control, and kindness, on to purification of thought from every vain imagination, the antecedent required in the giving of the mind to God. Few of us take sins of thought seriously enough, yet they all make paths along which future thought will more and more tend to flow.

Ruysbroeck continues his prayer mentioning the first great mark of spiritual personality: "inwardly abiding in simplicity, in stillness and in utter peace"—that is to say, the perfection of inner poise. It is from that inner stillness, and not from fuss, that power and fervor proceed.

And next Ruysbroeck gives the second mark of spiritual personality: "turning from all things of self into the *freedom* of the Will of God"—not, you observe, in deliberate effort and sacrifice, but in delight and liberation. This means the complete unification of life, the abolishment of all psychic conflicts. All the powers now subserve one interest, and the soul has grown up to find itself at home in the universe. Love, thought, and energy are now aiming one way and are entirely harmonized in God. This is holiness.

Now if we bring together these ideas, we see that they mean that the soul must grow in depth as well as expansive life, its roots plunged more and more deeply into God, that it may the better expand towards human-ity. Only because of this, its deepness, can it maintain this, its expan-siveness, and finally achieve its *own* rightful development which is not necessarily that of any other soul. What is demanded of us is the perfec-tion of our own inherent powers and not conformity to a pattern. Many very different kinds of tools are needed for the completed service of God.

Now you will not achieve this growth by getting inside a comfortable religious system that suits you and looking out over the edge like a cat out of a basket. You may achieve it if you fully accept and fully respond to all the demands, all the graces and tensions, the full rhythm of light and dark which make up the richness of human life, and if you do this in and for Christ in God.

IX

Service

Psalm (not noted)

Hymns and/or the Service of Compline, if evening

Prayers of dedication, offering of life and abilities:

Govern everything by your wisdom, O Lord, so that my soul may always be serving you in the way you will and not as I choose. Let me die to myself so that I may serve you; let me live to you who are life itself. (Teresa of Avila)

Breathe on me Lord, with that breath which infuses energy and kindles fervour. In seeking for fervour, I ask for all that I can need, and all that Thou canst give. In asking for fervour, I am asking for faith, hope, and charity, in their most heavenly exercise; I am asking for that loyal perception of duty which follows on yearning affection; I am asking for sanctity, peace, and joy, all at once. Nothing would be a trouble for me, nothing a difficulty, had I fervour of soul.
Lord, in asking Thee for fervour, I am asking for Thyself, for nothing short of Thee, O my God. Enter my heart and fill it with fervour by filling it with Thee. (John Henry Newman)

We begin our time together with two related statements of St. Augustine: "Love, and do what you like," and "Love cannot be lazy." He did not say: "Love, and do nothing if you prefer it. Just sit on your devotional mat, purring." Real love never did behave so.

We have already spent some time thinking of the real lovers of God, the saints. We have considered their infinite variety of unselfish response and willing surrender to the purpose of the universe. And we have gone on to meditate on the growth needed by us if we are to be capable of this. Now we come to service which, rightly understood, is the object of that growth.

A woman who knew much of the spiritual life lately said to me that she held that it should involve, as its very essence, "torment and effort for the sake of the brethren" *(tormento e travaglia per fratelli)*.* That sounds like a pretty tough ideal, but it is Christ's life, the saint's life, the redemptive life.

If we return to what we said about choosing God, growth and service might be considered as the two aspects, inward and outward, under which the results of that choice, faithfully adhered to, will reveal themselves. Growth means inward purification and expansion; service means outward expression. Both mean life on a new scale, and more abundant life.

We can hardly dare come to Holy Communion unless we are willing to live this life, to offer ourselves to share in the work of Christ and the saints in our tiny way. The object of the sacramental food is to make us "grow up into the fullness of His stature"—and that means to *serve*. This removes the stigma of self-cultivation from those who realize the necessity for growth in order to follow Him who prayed: "For their sakes I sanctify myself."

If you elect for this self-surrender and service, if you join up with the divine activities of the universe, and if you choose God, you are at once plunged into this atmosphere, and it begins to act not only on you but through you. Your contact with other selves is changed because it is no longer self-interested. Your spirit will now touch and modify theirs, perhaps unconsciously. God is now acting through you; you are *serving*. It is true that the majority of us are only raw inbetweeners; the saints alone are fully trained; but the method and its Master are the same.

If we ask what that method is, its right balance seems to be given in Ruysbroeck's prayer:

> Ministering to the world without in love and mercy; inwardly abiding in simplicity, stillness, and utter peace.

That is to say that action and effort go all the way. They are the means, substance, and expression of our life and creative quality; but all this hangs on an inward abiding in peace.

As for our growth, we depend on the given food and God. Still more do we and must we look beyond ourselves to Him in service, "inwardly

---

*This was said to Underhill by Sorella Maria, the Italian Franciscan nun who had established her own tiny community of contemplatives. From that place, the *Refugio*, a society of prayer was begun called the Confraternity of the Spiritual Entente. Their purpose was to pray for unity among all believers and to quietly engage people loyal to all Christian churches to join with them, invisibly, in this effort. Sorella Maria was beloved to Underhill, and they corresponded in Italian for some time. She was one of the few who knew something of the private side of Evelyn Underhill.

abiding in simplicity and stillness." Those qualities permeate right through daily, homely, and professional life, carrying the Eternal through all these because of our daily recourse to and concentration on it. To do this is more and more to transfigure and deify the substance of our temporal life. It is more and more to do the special work of the human soul, linking the worlds of spirit and sense.

Seen on its largest scale in the saints, real growth is towards a life of service penetrated by and utterly united with a life of prayer. Thus it is also a life of peace and power. Of course it is impossible to serve well without perfect contact with those whom we serve. Therefore, those who work for God must attend to Him.

Have you realized the extent to which the Christian life of prayer is also a life of service? Have you recognized the actual, though invisible work done in prayer for God and for souls? Thus intercession, which many people find difficult, is really love acting and serving in the atmosphere of prayer, using for others its spiritual power, reaching out to and affecting other souls within its atmosphere. Such action seems a part of the mysterious economy of the spiritual life. It is a feeble copy of the way in which the divine energy reaches out to act upon us, both secretly within the soul and outwardly by persons and events.

When we think of what the greatest spiritual personality we have ever known did for us in re-harmonizing us, bringing us to God, and compelling us to feel reality, it gives us a hint of the workings of the Spirit in and through human beings. It suggests a new meaning for the word "atonement." Spiritual work costs those who do it much. It is not done at all unless they love God and His deep mysterious interests better than their own and are willing to lose everything for Him, even their own spiritual peace.

We talked first of growth and then of service, but we must not divide them too sharply, for the two go together from the beginning. In a good nursery, children are taught to do little things from the first. Just so, by daily acts of service to God and other souls, we enlarge our souls to receive a love which makes better work possible in the future. It is in thus trying to work for and with Him that we grow; and as we grow, we become more and more capable of continuing.

The growth of spiritual personality, that is to say, our gradual sanctification, is not achieved by some desperate spiritual splash, but by responding without hesitation, as nearly as we can, to the successive impulses we receive from the Supernatural. We may be sure that each time we make a heroic choice for God, we shall be given a further chance of making another later on. Risking suffering and effort for others, the soul stretches until it is able to be filled with the divine will and love. The frictions and tensions of outward life, and our response in active service, are essential to this.

At the heart of all such service must be the Cross. In choosing God, we take sides with a self-giving perfection, a holiness that pours itself out to sinfulness—loving, seeking, and serving the imperfect. In Christ's life we clearly see two phases: first the expansive and happy self-giving of the ministry in teaching and healing; secondly, the inward intensity of self-giving to God for all that which led to Gethsemane and Calvary. The same two-fold response on lower levels is true of all the saints and is a mark of supernatural life in the soul. It involves both suffering and courage through a deliberate "loving of the unlovely into loveableness."

This is the divine method which we are called upon to apply in our own turn. It means the extreme of disinterestedness, that is, of self-concern. When we see it being done, or *feel* it being done, we understand something of the love that the soul is called to—a painful and unlimited sacrifice for apparently unworthy objectives and a steady demand upon industry and courage. We are reminded that all is not right with the world and that the redeeming office of Christ must be shared by His friends.

The sunshine school of piety will not help us here. The time will come when its charmingly optimistic outlook will not work, when God is seen to make the utmost demands of the soul, and the soul is driven to make the utmost demands of Him. It finds itself in a great loneliness but the obligation of service still goes on, or it is beset by old faults it thought it had conquered, a humbling experience which no one escapes. It is then that it is being treated to the food of the full grown.

When the effort and struggle reaches its height, when we are faced with a violent uprush of premature impulse or temptation in ourselves or our neighbors, when the effort to master sin almost chokes us and kills our prayer and our peace, no easy-going religion will do. And when we consider that all other souls are at some stage of this growth and this struggle, then self-giving, even to apparent spiritual loss, does not seem too hard a price for helping them. This alone is seen to be the act of the fellow-worker with God, making life worthwhile.

Now the three-fold Ignatian question: "What have I done for Christ? What am I doing for Christ? And what ought I to do for Christ?" takes on a new intensity. Asked here in God's presence in the silence, it is equivalent to an act of consecration. It is only worth asking when souls are open towards Him. Having asked it with such purity of intention as we are capable of, then that which love makes us really long to do will be right.

Not all are called to the same thing, still less called to do the one thing that they don't like. The variety of equipment and opportunity is infinite.

We are called upon to use the gifts we have and not those we have not. The saints range from Aquinas in the philosopher's chair to Lawrence, the cook, and they warn us not to narrow our conception of service. Someone must give the orders, and someone must attend to the roadmaking, even in the City of God. Some serve by being, as much as by doing. There is a special beauty in the combination of deep spirituality with simple and homely work.

"Who sweeps a room as to Thy laws, makes that and the action fine!" I like to think that when George Herbert wrote that, he was thinking of St. Teresa's Rule—the passage in which she lays down that the prioress shall be the first on the list of those who sweep the house. This gains added meaning when we remember that Teresa was, at that time, herself the prioress and at the very height of her mystical development. So much for the supposed divorce of the active and contemplative life! As she herself said: "They are sisters who must work together if our Lord is to be perfectly served."

The connection between real holiness and homeliness is a very close one. Sanctity comes right down to and through all the simplicities of human life, and indeed would be of no use to us unless it did so. Christ's example warns us against inhuman loftiness. We must fully respond to both sides of reality, and not one alone. When we have done this in the way and proportion right for us, our lives will have the energetic peace of an engine that is running right. If you think you *have* accomplished its smooth running, don't forget that it is up to you to keep that engine in order. Don't over-drive it. Don't behave with feverish fanaticism. Don't forget its fuel and its lubrication. This means that you will need a rule of life which should contain a due balance of prayer and of rest, and should give you food, as well as opportunity for expressing energy and love.

It has been said that "we are not called upon to lay our lives *down*, but to lay them *out* to the best advantage." Although it is easy to overstress this and make it an excuse for utilitarianism, there is a real truth in it. All have access to direct sources of spiritual strength in prayer, quietude, communion, and spiritual reading and will not do their best work without these things.

There is, in *Ferishtah's Fancies*, a story of two camels who were called upon to carry some precious merchandise across the desert. Before they started, they were each introduced to an excellent dinner. The first camel said: "Dinner? Oh no, I won't waste my time on that. I love my master far too well and prefer to serve him without any reward." So he started off, and in the middle of the desert, he collapsed and died. The second camel said: "Dinner! What an excellent idea! I love my master far too well to be taking any chances. I shall eat every scrap, and am very glad that it is tasty as well as nourishing." He made the journey in safety and was called a good and faithful servant at the end.

Now the soul, like that camel, must have its meals if it is going to face the desert. If it were a question of one violent rush for the goal, the dinnerless camel might do it. But it is not. It is a long, monotonous, plodding journey. Exceptional demands bring their own strength with them, and exceptional demands may never come. But ordinary trials, bad roads, and scanty water are a certainty; and we won't meet those conditions properly unless we have had our necessary food.

I seem to see a great many dinnerless Christians about nowadays, yet the spirit of power is something to which every servant has a right. We *must* learn to set up the contacts by which we get at it, and not be disheartened if the training of our attention takes some time. The inner world is not one into which we can plunge suddenly. We must seek, knock patiently and steadily, and educate our souls; and it is a part of service to do this. Indeed, to try to serve at all, without setting up those contacts, is a masterpiece of folly as well as of conceit.

Let us remember that the God to whom we offer our service is a God of truth, of mind, and of will, who makes absolute demands on us in all these departments of life. This God of perfect truth, mind, and will—and of an awe, mystery, and beauty of which we cannot think—is also the God who demands. On one hand, He demands our love and service and on the other, He is the actual source and originator of our ability to love and serve. We can only fully respond to the demand by fully accepting the gift; and to do this is the whole secret of the saints.

X

Concluding Worship

Psalm 121

Hymns: "O Love Who Formed Me to Wear"
"Strengthen for Service, Lord, the Hands"
"Thine Forever, God of Love"

Prayers:

Fill us, we pray, Lord, with your light and life that we may show forth your wondrous glory. Grant that your love may so fill our lives, that we may count nothing too small to do for you, nothing too much to give, and nothing too hard to bear. (Ignatius of Loyola)

Lord Jesus, I give you my hands to do your work.
I give you my feet to go your way.
I give you my eyes to see as you do.
I give you my tongue to speak your words.
I give you my mind that you may think in me.
I give you my spirit that you may pray in me.

Above all,
I give you my heart that you may love in me,
your Father, and all humankind.
I give you my whole self that you may grow in me,
So that it is you, Lord Jesus,
Who live and work and pray in me.

I hand over to your care, Lord,
my soul and body,
my mind and thoughts,
my prayers and my hopes,
my health and my work,
my life and my death,
my parents and my family,
my friends and my neighbors,
my country and all people.

101

Today
and always.   (Lancelot Andrewes)

Concluding Meditation
(with five minute intervals between sections)

1. Let us remember before God these days in which we have sought to be alone with Him, turning from our ordinary interests to His infinite and eternal presence. Remember the desires with which we entered this retreat: to find ourselves in Him . . . Him in ourselves . . . and to sanctify ourselves for the sake of our fellow human beings.

2. Let us consider what sanctity means to us: a steadfast growth of the soul in depth, reality, power, and love.

3. Let us think of that industrious, courageous, generous, self-forgetting love which is the first fruit of the Spirit of Jesus in the soul, and which shows us God in all other souls.

4. Let us think of the joy of our vocation as Christ's servants and the power of joy in winning other souls to Him.

5. Let us think of that unbroken peace of God which is the state of the dedicated will, steadfastly set to love, to work, and to endure.

6. Let us consider our life of communion with God: the growing spirit of prayer and adoration that shall more and more fill our souls and give us even now a share in His eternal life.

7. Let us remember with love and gratitude all our brothers and sisters in Christ, learning from their lovely examples to stretch out our love till it embraces God and the whole world.

8. Let us gather up all we have gained and resolved in this retreat and bring it to Christ for amendment and consecration.

THE END FOR WHICH WE WERE MADE

A retreat given in 1925

St. Ignatius makes the foundation of his exercises one principle. It is that "the human being was created for *this* end: to praise, reverence, and serve the Lord."

The whole of religion is a comment on the Ignatian saying: "I come from God. I belong to God. I am destined for God."

Chapter II: "God"

In retreat we have the great opportunity . . . to ask ourselves the crucial questions of St. Ignatius: "What have I done for Christ? What am I doing? What ought I to do?"

Chapter IV: "Election"

I

Preparation

Preparatory Worship

Hymns: "Come, Thou Holy Paraclete"
"Dear Lord and Father of Mankind"

Prayers:

O Thou in whom all things live, who commandest us to seek Thee, and art ever ready to be found: To know Thee is life, to serve Thee is freedom, to praise Thee is our souls' joy. We bless Thee and adore Thee, we worship Thee and magnify Thee, we give thanks to Thee for Thy great glory; through Jesus Christ our Lord. (St. Augustine)

O Holy Spirit, Love of God, who proceedest from the Almighty Father, and His most Blessed Son, infuse Thy grace most plentifully into my heart. Come Thou and dwell in this soul that longs to be Thy holy Temple. Heal the lurking distempers of my heart; pierce me through with the dart of Thy love. Kindle in me such a holy fire, that it flames out in a bright and devout zeal, and burning up all the dross of sensual affections, may possess and purify my whole spirit, soul, and body. Grant this, O Blessed Spirit, for the sake of Jesus Christ our only Lord and Saviour. (*Treasury of Devotion*)

There's a very old Prayer of the Church still used as part of the preparation of the priest before Holy Communion which says, "Let Thy Good Spirit enter into our hearts." Isn't it with some such prayer as this in our hearts that we come into retreat? The prayer continues, "Thy mystery is exceeding deep." In ordinary life we feel all about us those unplumbed depths. We believe that they are present, even though we haven't *time* to attend to them!

We are seeking to live lives of service to God in the world, lives that only have meaning in reference to His supernatural reality. Yet we get, don't we, so blurred and confused by the strain and detail of these lives, that we tend to forget the great whole—the depth and the height within which our tiny activities proceed? A retreat is an attempt to redirect that balance, to recapture and reinstall the greatest of Christian privileges, the privilege of communion with God.

"Let Thy Good Spirit enter into our hearts." For two whole days, beginning tomorrow, as the quiet hours go by, we are given opportunity of receiving an answer to that prayer, to have such communion with the deep mystery of God as shall please Him and be good for our souls.

"Blessed," says à Kempis, "are the ears which hear God's whisper and listen not unto the whispers of the world." That blessed opportunity is now ours, and for its sake, *silence* is imperative. So tomorrow we shall keep silence, not only in the church, but in the room where we take our meals, and in the garden where we walk and rest. We shall do it for our own sakes and for each other's sakes. We are going to do it in order to listen to God.

We are going to be quiet with One who has everything to tell us and nothing to learn from us. His voice is so still, His deepest contacts so imperceptible, that only in quiet can we perceive them. The Holy Spirit educates us in inner stillness, and it is for lack of this that most spiritual lives are so crude and shallow and vague.

It is commonplace to say that at such quiet times we imitate Christ when He went up alone into the mountain to pray. But let us be sure we carry through that imitation as well as we can, in spirit and in truth. Mere outward solitude and silence is not enough.

Tonight let our preparation for tomorrow be to go with Christ in imagination, to follow Him in one of those times when He was able to withdraw from the bustling crowds, the pressing demands, and the compassionate service which filled His life. What do you suppose those secret hours were like? Don't you think that it was above all with *joy* that He went up into the mountain to be alone with His Father, to give Himself without reserve to adoring communion? There He could be alone with that eternal, living, personal Love, that incomparable Reality from which He came forth to minister and in whose power He did His works of mercy! In those hours there was no room for thought of anything but God.

Our position here is only a faint shadow, an image of that! We've come from the press of completely practical service. We are not to bring with us the problems of that service, nor are we to try to solve them. God is the Solution. Sink then into the ocean of His peace. Do you think that Christ on the mountains of prayer attended to anything but God?

Consider what it would have been like to have been a Disciple, seeing and helping in that ministry and, because you had been taught to love, feeling as though you were shirking your task, not doing all you could. In that very situation, Christ said to you, "Drop all this. Come apart"—and carried you away from healing, consoling, teaching, and all the opportunities of practical Christianity to attend only to God.

Yes, but you *are* a disciple, vowed to a service that tries to carry on His redemptive work, to show forth His praise with lips and lives. But you can't do it unless your souls keep fit and sensitive to God. Today your position is still the same.

In one respect we cannot imitate Christ. We take with us, as He did not, a sense of our sin, our failure, and our unworthiness, and we begin our retreat well if we acknowledge it once and for all. We admit our shabbiness and weakness and our dreadful occupation with ourselves. We confess and have done with it and then turn with complete confidence to God.

Wasn't it this turning in complete confidence to God which nourished and strengthened His soul for work and suffering and made Him the giver of more abundant life? Didn't He turn, in those times apart, from creation to Creator, the source of life and joy? And in this, our example, didn't He teach us to exercise the supreme human privilege: the encounter of our tiny spirits with the infinite Spirit? Doesn't He teach us now to say with Augustine, "Let all creatures keep silent before Thee. Do Thou alone speak unto me!"

How wonderful that our little souls can conceive such a thought as that and make such a claim! But we don't often act up to it. We have the means to turn away from the whole world of things to the deep mystery below things, to "the silence of Eternity interpreted by love." All the rich, incredible variety of nature from Leviathan to the honey bee, all music and language interacting in the life of human societies and their problems, all this and much more is included in the creation of one tiny planet in an uncounted universe.

Your tiny soul and mine, facing all that—all the demands and beauties of the universe—can and does yet say, "Let all this keep silence. Do Thou alone, oh Spirit, speak unto me." We go past everything else to the one thing that gives all of it meaning. Real prayer is just that—prayer in which we lift up our minds to God alone and dwell on the things of God.

In this time set aside, we have the chance to think, to meditate, to feed our souls on spiritual food each in our own way and yet together. It is *not* an opportunity for worrying out problems or currying souls, but for deepening our life in God.

It is not just a bit of our lives that we *call* religious, but our *whole* life. We enter prayer with minds, hearts, and wills, that all these may be submitted to that influence and come out transformed. If this is to happen, it must come through the spirit of proper recollection, dropping all thoughts and interests inconsistent with God, with unlimited confidence in Him, and generous willingness to give in response.

We come, in prayer, to open ourselves to the beauty and mystery of God brought to us in Christ—to learn more, to surrender more, to adore—not to scrape and sandpaper ourselves. When we have been quiet in the Great Presence for a little while, we shall feel quite small and humble. It is far more important to feel small, humble, and happy—as children do—than scraped and raw. Christ never makes people feel raw. Our own inverted egoism and wounded vanity do that.

The machinery of the retreat, the addresses, and services are meant to support the deepening communion. Take from it that which helps you and leave the rest. The results of retreat will come not from what you hear but from *your own meditation*.

As you go out you will be given a paper containing suggestions. The first thing on it will begin: "Think glorious thoughts of God." I hope this motto can stay constantly with us during these two days. *Glorious* thoughts—not anxious ones. Deliberate meditation should be a chief act of retreat, a wonderful education of communion with God.

How do we do it? Look at a passage from the New Testament, at one of the quotes I will be giving you, or at other inspired Christian literature. Place yourself in God's presence. Consider that He says these words to you. Enter the picture which the words paint, and humbly kneel within it. There let His overshadowing love teach you. The Spirit of Christ speaks to you. Open your eyes and look at Him. Open your ears and hear what He says. (We've heard what He says over and over again and missed the heart of it just as we hear great music and miss its heart.)

Consider what is being said to your soul. When your soul is reproved, see what fresh doors open. *Look* at what is put before you. Think it out before God. Thus you correct your faults, strengthen your wills, revive your love, and learn the spirit of the Presence. What you have read or heard you digest in such meditation. Then turn your thoughts and deductions into prayer. Finally *resolve* to act on the light you have received.

The first thought which I requested that you keep in mind comes from Mother Janet Stuart. Think "glorious," not puzzling or utilitarian thoughts, but glorious, life-giving thoughts about God whose splendor all our muddling and imperfections cannot dim. Thus we capture and establish a quiet mind in which we can serve Him best.

Glorious thoughts. It is such a waste of time not to have them! When we see the shadow glory of this world and see that it points beyond itself to more sacred levels, we can hardly help having glorious thoughts! The most wonderful privilege of humanity is to reach out to Eternal Beauty, to expand our souls by the very breath of the Infinite.

How much time do we give this? The conditions in which we serve God with a quiet mind are those to which we will devote the best hours of this retreat, *not* to much self-examination.'

Augustine has told us that in the silence of retreat there shall come the reality, the *fact* of God's silent, unremitting work on us, and that all that matters is that the self yields to His action. Improvement in our work comes from the imprint in our souls and that is the work of God when we are quiet under His Hand. We take from Him the food by which we grow. It is offered; access is direct.

Our religious opportunity is in essence the same as that which gave thrilling joy and beauty, strength and heroism, to the saints. It is still all there. God does not change. Let us think of that when we make our Communion tomorrow, joining our souls at the altar with the heroes of Christianity in the Sacrament of Fellowship.

We, in our littleness and imperfection, are admitted to the same act which was for Terese and others the means of sacred intimation and awe-struck delight. More, when we associate ourselves with the angels, and those beyond us, what opening up of the horizon! It is an opportunity to realize and enjoy our supernatural inheritance in a way made possible to our immature nature.

So we lift our hearts from the ceaseless drive, from petty details, from the misery and pain of human lives gone wrong, from difficulties of our own—from all that—and join in love and adoration of Beauty, Wisdom, and Power, "evermore praising Thee and saying, 'Holy, holy, holy! Lord God Almighty. Heaven and earth are full of thy glory!' "

If even for one day we are able to set our lives to that great melody, we shall have made those lives a bit more real than they were before. And then we will be more able, when our day is over, to serve Him with a quiet mind.

II

God

Preparatory Worship

Psalm 145: "I Will Extol Thee, My God and King"

Hymns: "Love of the Father"
"Immortal, Invisible"

Prayers:

Blessing and honor and thanksgiving and praise, more than we can utter, more than we can conceive, be yours, holy and glorious Trinity, Father, Son, and Holy Spirit, by all angels, all men, all creatures, for ever and ever. (Lancelot Andrewes)

> O Thou who preparest a place for my soul,
> Prepare my soul for that place:
> Prepare it with holiness,
> Prepare it with desire;
> And even while it sojourneth upon earth
> Let it dwell in heaven with Thee
> Beholding the beauty of Thy countenance,
> And the glory of Thy Saints,
> Now and forever.
>
> (Joseph Hall)*

A retreat is our great opportunity to strengthen our attachment and deepen our understanding of the great central truths of religion. Perhaps there is nothing better to begin with and nothing which puts us more directly into the atmosphere of prayer than the cry of St. Francis:

My God and All! What art Thou? What am I?

*Underhill suggests here prayers on pages 35 and 57 of *Mysteries of the Mass in Reasoned Prayers* by William Roche, S.J.

Those words remind us of that which prayer is: the communion between the little creature and that Unchanging Perfection which is the only source of life, power, and joy. What matters first in religion is *God*. So let us begin by trying very humbly to think about Him, in and for Himself and not for our own needs.

St. Ignatius makes the foundation of his exercises one principle. It is that "the human being was created for *this* end: to praise, reverence, and serve the Lord." That sounds all right, but it slips by, like so many religious phrases, almost unchecked. But if we stop and look at it and at the chosen order of his terms, what does it mean?

Praise—Reverence—Service. Our first duty is adoration, then awe, and finally, service. For those three things and nothing else, addressed to God and to no one else, *you*, says Ignatius, were created. Two of the three things for which your soul was made are matters of attitude and relationship. Unless those two are right, the last will not be right. Unless the whole of life is a movement of praise and adoration, unless instinct combines with awe, your work will not be of much value.

And, if that is true, it follows that the Christian revelation, the work done by Christ in our souls, has also as its *main* object the promotion of God's glory. That means the shining out of His reality through our acts. It means increasing our loving adoration, deepening our awe, and expanding our consecration in service. What matters first and last is God. The whole of religion is a comment on the Ignatian saying: "I come from God. I belong to God. I am destined for God."

Attention to God is the primary religious act, and we rightfully begin our retreat by trying very humbly to think about Him. The life of the Christian worker depends for its value on the extent to which it is bathed in that divine light. So here in retreat let it be our first concern. We are here to attend to God, in God, and for God, not for our own needs. He is the first term of all religious life and thought, yet probably the term to which present day Christians give the least undivided attention.

Ignatius asks us for a deeper, more awestruck sense of His richness unsearchable, of His all-penetrating love. Of course we know very little about God. Yet when we consider in prayer His immensity and our tininess, the marvel of what we *do* know and feel becomes greater. We sense, and realize too, its givenness. That rich and loving immensity comes to us from beyond ourselves; it isn't something we have labored to discover or grown up to. The knowledge of God that is deepest, most real, and of which we can least speak is *revealed*. It is the revelation of another world than the human, the natural, or the created. Yet it is a world to which we mysteriously belong.

This awed, adoring sense of the mysteries among which we move, of the tiny bit which at best we ourselves can apprehend of them, must enfold all our prayer and work if we want them to have significance. Just think of the words we address to God, to the Reality of the universe, at the beginning of the Litany: "God–Father–holy, blessed, and glorious Trinity." *What* a summing up of that which has been poured out of the secret fastnesses of the universe into our tiny half-great souls, dwelling on this small inconspicuous planet.

Such thoughts are much needed to restore the sense of proportion in driven lives occupied with the routine teaching of religion or Christian social work. To bring back the atmosphere of eternity, it is a very good thing to say that stupendous prayer and to dwell on it before trying to teach other souls. We should keep in mind the phrases of this wonderful prayer and dwell on them when we are inclined to assume our own importance or magnify our troubles or get smothered in the petty cares and rush of life.

I have heard people who do not realize that dignity and uppishness are not the same thing, object to describing themselves as miserable sinners. Yet looked at carefully, it is not a *very* inappropriate term, even for the best. Miserable means pitiable. Are not we rather pitiful little creatures with our feebleness, our gusty passions and vanities, and our helpless enslavement to unreal things? Indeed we are utterly so if God leaves us to ourselves.

We are so vulnerable, weak, and puzzled by life, so vain about our mental discoveries! But isn't it the mercy of God, the generosity of God, isn't it *this*—enveloping, enabling, and ever using us—that alone makes us worthwhile? And isn't it we who open our gates to receive this unlimited Presence? "Have mercy on us, be generous to us," we pray to this transcendent Spirit of love, life, and holiness. "Come and give to us little half-animals who are yet able to adore and crave for you, what we can never deserve." We call on the generosity of the great toward the humble, a generosity that has all to give and nothing to gain.

These are some of the things humanity is able to think of God! "Holy, blessed, and glorious Trinity"—what does that phrase imply? Surely it means that God is the fountain of all being, the One Reality. Surely it also refers to that strong, heart-breaking, redeeming love in which we know God most clearly. And surely it includes that mysterious, eternal Spirit, within us yet distinct from us, our inspiring supporter. It is the *cause* of our craving for God and the cause of this three-fold revelation of an eternal life, love, and light that are *one*.

So we say, "Holy–blessed–glorious." "Blessed": doesn't that mean perfect in happiness? And "glorious": doesn't that signify perfection in splendor, utterly transcendent, *yet* so near and homely that we can actually ask for its gentle and generous mercy and love? Julian of Norwich wrote so beautifully:

> As the body is clad in the cloth and the flesh in the skin and the bones in the flesh, and the heart in the whole, so are we, soul and body, clad in the Goodness of God and enclosed. Yea, and more homely: for all these may waste and wear away, but the Goodness of God is ever whole.

These are thoughts that tranquilize and humble us, which take us away from the fuss and the clatter of life into strength and the region of peace. They remind us of the words we considered yesterday: "Think glorious thoughts of God." Lose yourselves in them. Then "serve Him with a quiet mind." Dwell on all these a little, and you will find that the Ignatian demand for awe and adoration of God before service is not so hard to accept. Take that as the second part of your meditation.

"Think glorious thoughts of God." Our thoughts of Him are often pitiably thin, narrow, conventional, frequently unconscious. We cease to think of Him in Himself at all. Ourselves, our works, our anxieties slip into the centre of the picture and God becomes merely the source of energy for carrying on our activities. There are a great deal too many who merely utilize prayer. It is done by even the *best* Christians because we are so obsessed by the importance of our work, our friends, and interests. But "your Father knoweth what ye have need of before you ask Him." If we put His worship last and our needs first, all sense of proportion goes. Then instead of the expansion which comes with selfless adoration, our souls contract.

Seek. Find. Knock. Open. We *don't* seek the great spiritual secrets enough. We are to seek God in Himself, He "in whom we live and move and have our being" and from whom we *cannot* depart. With Him we remain partially free, distinct, and capable as we more and more partake of His freedom, growing up into full personhood, becoming tools of His creative and redemptive work.

Now, today, in this retreat, let our ruling thought be of God *in* whom our life abides. He is here, now, in this room, calling you, demanding your complete surrender in order that you may become completed persons. Nothing matters but that demand and your soul's response. The essence of life is that response, whether made in work or in prayer.

Augustine"s great saying is so appropriate here:

> God is the only Reality
> and we are only real
> insofar as we are in Him
> and He in us.

God makes our beatitude *and* our misery according to whether we are in harmony with His mighty will or daring to defy or ignore it. God's will is there: the first concern, the unchanging source of all perfection.

His is a holiness inconceivable, yet a holiness that is love and pours itself out. That holiness is in and through the simplest forms and accidents and makes itself known in the homeliest symbols. It despises *nothing* it has made. Not many of us get through life without despising something, yet every time we do that, we turn from God. You cannot redeem, help, or save anything you despise—*only* that which you love.

God is perfection yearning toward imperfection, not turning from it. He is holy Love that saves and redeems us and compels us in our turn to try and save others. When we see redemption happening or *feel* it happening to ourselves, we understand the love to which the soul is called.

So we are to think of God, but much more—to pray to Him and to feel and know Him as completely present in and with us, determining our reality. We are to think of His life in us as so immeasurably exceeding our own life that it can absorb, transmit, and enter into our lives by all ways and at all times. We are wholly immersed in Him, and the difference between God present and absent is merely a difference in our own awareness.

Let us think of Him too as an ocean of love and life containing us along with all other souls. Thus we throw ourselves more deeply back into Him in prayer. It is thus we reach and touch other souls.

All this is so immensely beyond us as to keep us in a constant attitude of humblest adoration and awe, yet so deeply and closely with us as to invite our clinging trust and loyal love. This is what dry theological terms like "transcendence" and "immanence" mean when we translate them into the language of the heart.

(Read Psalm 139 or 63.)

We don't think of God enough like this, nor do we think of the boundless absurdity of setting up our tiny wills—we, no more than whitebait in the Ocean of Reality—against His overwhelming purpose and power. To grasp something of this, to feel a deepening awe of this realization, is "the fear of the Lord and the beginning of wisdom."

Now thoughts such as these, if they are to be of any use to us, have got to be worked out in our prayer. If God is real, it is the most important fact in our lives, and adoration of Him is the most important fact of our prayer. Only a spiritual disposition which thus puts the whole emphasis on God, perpetually turning to God and losing itself in God, refusing to allow even the most pressing work of this-world problems, even its own sins and failures, to distract from God, is safe. Only this disposition escapes the Scylla of devotion which dwells on its own soul and the Charybdis of practical Christianity which dwells on its work and tries to use God's power for *its* chosen activity.

Neither of these dispositions alone are supernatural. The truly spiritual, consecrated disposition which produces the childlike loveliness of the saints is that which acknowledges that, once we have really given ourselves to God, His action transcends, precedes, and controls our own and goes on all the time, whether we are aware of it or not. The question of what we feel or of what our souls or work seem like to *us* is secondary for us, and if we dwell on it, we will curtail the divine action in us. In so doing, it will spoil our action too.

Therefore the central point governing the work which any soul can do for God *and* other souls is its attitude to Him, its relationship to Him, its self-oblivious adoration.

Now we can gather up the points of our meditation.

We asked ourselves to think glorious thoughts of God. Why? The phrase we began with gives us our answer. "The human being was created for *this* end: to praise, reverence, and serve the Lord God" or, as Ignatius puts it still more vividly:

> I come from God.
> I belong to God.
> I am destined for God.

Oh, Lord, "Whom have I in heaven but Thee? And what is there on earth that I desire beside Thee?" (Ps. 73:25)

III

The Soul

Psalm 139: "O Lord, Thou Hast Searched Me and Known Me"

Hymns: "The King of Love My Shepherd Is"
      "O Master, It Is Good to Be . . . with Thee"

Prayers:

O God, who has chosen the weak things of the world to confound the mighty, do Thou shed forth continual day upon us who watch for Thee; that our lips may praise Thee, our life may bless Thee, and our meditations glorify Thee. (*Sarum Breviary*)

Lord! Give me courage and love to open the door and constrain You to enter, [and to] offer all my resources, whatever the disguise You come in, even before I fully recognize my guest.
    Come in! Enter my small life!
    Lay your sacred hands on all the common things and small interests of that life and bless and change them. Transfigure my small resources, make them sacred. And in them give me Your very Self. (Evelyn Underhill, *Meditations and Prayers*)*

We thought at our last session of the prayer of St. Francis: "My God and All! What art Thou? What am I?" We began with the first of those great questions. Now we come to the second question and the second term of all personal religion: the soul—yours and mine.

What am I? The answer is probably in the words of St. Ignatius which ended our last session together: "I come from God. I belong to God. I am destined for God." These are the things that matter about the soul.

---

*Underhill suggests here the prayer on page 92 of *Mysteries of the Mass in Reasoned Prayers* by William Roche, S.J.

"I come from God." What does it mean when we say that the soul is "made in God's image?" It means first that we are creatures with a little love, will, and freedom. God is and has perfect love, will, and freedom. Our growth in these three is a growth in His image, that is, in holiness. Holiness is no abstract state. It is the full development of the consecrated personality for which the soul was destined.

Consider your situation this afternoon in relation to these three statements of Ignatius. Let us push out and explore all the implications and differences for each one of us. Let us see what each of them means in regard to the intimate communion of personal prayer, and dwell on that a little.

I come from God. I am not just an especially clever animal, the result of natural evolution and part of the physical world. All that is true. But my essential being is an embryonic spiritual personality born of the Spirit of God.

I belong to God, not to myself or society. God's demands override both. Face to face with that—with His absolute personality which is the possesser of my soul—my career, desires, health, and self-chosen work for Him are second in importance. Only in my prayer shall I discover how they are to serve until the end of my life.

I am destined for God, to grow and expand, not after death, but *now,* into a personality fit for His eternal adoration and service. I am here to incarnate, in some degree, his holy purposes. And, to assure us of this, the figure of Christ has completely exemplified it. No one who has loved Him ever had or has a moment's doubt that He came from God and never flickered in his dedication. He belonged utterly to God, and perfectly fulfilled his destiny in His return to God. Thus and thence He has brought God's love and power ever since to human souls. He is our High Priest forever.

Now, as in the great Johannine prayer, Christ still says, "For their sakes I sanctify myself," thus fixing once and for all, corporate with personal holiness. So in our small way, it is not for ourselves that our personal growth and the deepening of our prayer has primary importance, but to make both the self and its prayer more potent vehicles of the creative and saving power of God. They are the raw materials to be turned into the best possible tools for Him. What God demands and His world desparately needs is greater, deeper, more supernatural personalities. Only through such souls is His Spirit poured in its fullness. He comes to men and women *through* men and women.

Is your soul a perfect transmitting instrument? If not, prayer must improve it. The increase in personal sanctity, the capacity of individual souls for God, the enhancement of this in ourselves and others, is the greatest work we can do for the world. The expansion of the supernatural in human life is the coming of the Kingdom of God.

Once we catch the idea of the redeemed soul as a positive energy, a self-giving entity which God can use, our whole orientation changes. The redeemed soul is a crumb of the spiritual universe which by *no* merit whatever of its own has been regenerated and re-formed on the path of Christ and belongs to God to be used by Him.

What is the essential character of this reformation of soul? What can it accomplish? The saints show something of it. They mark the difference between the disguised animal most of us resemble and the spirit acting always under God's impulse and not from self-love. It is a long way between these two points. That space is filled by that gradual process of purification, development, and expansion called "the interior life."

We begin at the baby end; we move, if alive, to the other end because we are destined for God. Outward religion feeds and supports this process. Spiritual literature tells us much of it. It has been writtten by specialists from whom we should humbly learn to "know our own souls." Take such a book as Teresa's *Interior Castle*. Though the divisions may not apply to all of us and only mention some of those among the soul's many mansions, at least such a work brings home the greatness of our unexplored spiritual resources. It demonstrates that most of us *are* content to stay in the scullery all our lives, although gradual stage by stage growth into light and life is possible to us. Teresa describes the expansion of our spiritual resources—in other words, the sanctification of the soul. Her seven mansions will make good subjects for meditation during our retreat.

1. *Self-knowledge*—the humbling sense of where we are, of how little we are, of our own wrongness—*must* be the first step in the soul's expansion. Only the realization of our own inadequacy makes God's action on us possible. We find our place and then acknowledge what we are and that *we* can do nothing about it. In other words, we become humble and contrite of heart and hand ourselves over to the spiritual world.

2. The old earthly standard and the new supernatural standard come into conflict. Temptation and self-interest take on a new meaning because *we* aim at new purity. Most of us go through a stormy time before our life gets arranged around a new centre.

3. Because we realize our personal helplessness we first begin to learn real prayer, and in the power of prayer, the soul becomes capable of renunciation.

4. These twin acts of communion with God and renunciation of self grow and deepen and the soul becomes more and more absorbed in Him.

5. Thus it reaches the pitch of self-forgetfullness in which it *feels* union with God's love and it works in and for Him.

6. Even so, full growth demands more than this. It demands an utter crucifixion of self, even of the spiritual self, the complete purification of *all* but God. Thus in great souls, there is preparation for the next step.

7. The full, mature, spiritual personality radiates love, joy, and peace, and transfers God's redeeming power because it is utterly merged in His light and love.

These stages bring home the gradual growth of the spiritual personality, the achievement of what the human soul was meant to be. But now we have to remember, and great saints always remind us of it, that the test of a soul's *real* growth in holiness is *not* the experience of God given it in prayer, but what it does with and for that experience when out of prayer.

It is very easy for some temperaments to be devotional. It is not easy for any temperament to be consistently loving, humble, and faithful in performing the daily duties of life. And *that,* not any wonderful experience, is St. Teresa's own test of union with God. "We must notice," she says, "whether we make progress or fall back *especially* as regards the love of our neighbour, the desire to be thought least of all (not acquiescence but *desire,* a strong word) and last, how we perform our ordinary everyday duties." Growth in *those* mark growth in the soul's union with God because it can't be done without death to the self. There is nothing in it to feed self-love.

When this self-forgetfullness reaches the level of habit, space left free by such utter self-emptying will be filled by God, and because it is so filled, we shall find Him in the common ways of life. We shall reach the level street of suppleness, going backward and forward between prayer and work and finding our soul's food in both. Because of our loving communion with God, we are able to enrich and accentuate our loving communion with humanity and find Christ not in *one* way, but both. We renounce at our peril either of these movements of soul. Narrow, pious depth is as much to be feared as shallow humanitarian breadth. Only in this double, all-round expansion, finding God both around and above us, does our spiritual life become complete.

See how lovely that is. Remember Augustine saying "The house of my soul is narrow. Do Thou enlarge it!" And God does, under many disguises, sometimes coming in by the senses, sometimes through the invisible gates of prayer, or through human demands. This means that all the deep but vague cravings of our souls for God may be fulfilled and more than fulfilled in ways far above, yet intimately near us. It means that we find Him both by stretching up and by flowing out. He whom the heaven of heavens cannot contain can meet us under simple and pitiful human accidents as St. Francis met God in the leper.

Yet if the soul is to be sufficiently sensitized and wide open to receive Him thus, it must have been deeply cultivated by prayer. We need those times of exclusive attention to God if we are to learn from Him well enough to recognize Him under His creaturely disguises.

There are certain reported sayings of Christ which are unfailing in touching the state of our spiritual dispositions. As long as they are difficult to understand, it seems to me, we have not grown in a true relationship of our souls to God. When we *have* grown in that relationship, their meaning seems obvious. There are three sayings which I would especially like to mention, and those who prefer meditation on Scripture might write them down. They are these:

> Unless you become as little children, you shall not enter into the Kingdom of Heaven. [Matt. 18:3]

> Whosoever will save his life shall lose it, but whosoever will lose his life for my sake, the same shall save it. [Luke 9:24]

> When you shall have done *all* those things which are commanded you, say: "We are unprofitable servants." [Luke 17:10]

These are three dispositions which in their perfection would take us a long way toward sanctity. They are three blows aimed from different directions at pride and self-sufficiency.

Pride is far more stupidity than a sin. It is an inability to grasp the facts, to realize our small creaturely status and helplessness. It is the failure to see that our most magnificent achievements are no more than the success of an ant handling a rather larger bit of straw than that manipulated by another ant. This is why spiritual specialists insist that humility is the same thing as self-knowledge. When you once see the point, you realize something of what your soul is over against: God. *Then* you do:

1. Feel tiny and helpless as a baby. You *do* become a little child and are glad to be so.

2. Become generally aware that self-abandonment, losing your own separate life and point of view, *is* the fullest, richest life.

3. Perceive the painful and obvious fact that performance which others may kindly think is so remarkable in you is really less than nothing at all.

Transforming and uniting the three ways of saying one thing is the one truth of our own nothingness. This is the great awe-inspiring fact which is the heart of religion. It is the fact that *all* rightful energy, all goodness, all prayer is the work of the everywhere present and prevenient God, using us strictly in proportion to the degree of our self-abandonment as His loving tools.

That is literally true. We have *nothing* of ourselves.

Because of the fact of our nothingness and of the literal truth of St. Francis exclaiming, "My God and All!"—that self-sufficiency is the primary wrong relationship of the soul and we can't grow until it is dead. We are hopeless as long as it lasts. It is the thing that shuts the door to God. Sins of the senses, of self-seeking, desire, anger, coveting—all these persistent animal impulses will go on worrying us. We shall do them and be sorry and have to pick ourselves up and try again. But they do not create an impossible situation. They do not kill the child-like relationship with God. Pride does that.

Julian in her wonderful revelation reminds us that there are two ways of looking at the situation of our souls. In God we stand firm, ever kept safe by His love; in ourselves, we are constantly tumbling down. And she says we ought to remember both. One keeps us in peace; the other in humility. The child is still in the nursery even though it sometimes comes down with a bang.

Finally, we see what Christ's incarnate life teaches us of the place of humbleness in the highest, greatest, most God-pervaded life. All through the Gospel we see it, but the Temptation is one of the most revealing episodes.

All three temptations are to pride, the arch sin: from showing what one can do by and for oneself to the personal seizure of abnormal power. The Devil challenged: "If you *are* the son of God, do something startling. Be different from others. Make these stones bread. *Test* your powers. Fling yourself from the pinnacle of the temple. Seize the authority you feel capable of!"

The triumph of Jesus was his refusal of all that, his unwavering dependency on God alone and the deliberate choice of homely and ordinary ways, meekly receiving in prayer and meekly giving in pity and simplicity. In this is the pattern of all souls desiring to work for God. Consider that world dominion were possible. Power so strongly felt might be used to control nature. But the divine transfiguration of soul did not show itself in such a startling manner. Instead it showed itself in quiet wayside acts of compassion and in the lonely nights of secret prayer to God.

IV

Election

Psalm (not noted)

Hymns: "Love Divine, All Loves Excelling"
      "Teach Me, My God and King"

Prayers:

Receive, O Lord, all my freedom, my memory, my understanding, and my will. All that I have or cherish, you have given. I return it all to you that it may be guided by your will. Only your love and grace I ask. With these I am rich and ask for nothing more. (Ignatius of Loyola)

Spirit of Jesus, enlighten my eyes as I dwell with you in the silence, that I may see this choice, the choice which is YOU. And turn my seeing into loving. (Evelyn Underhill. *Meditations and Prayers*)*

Today we have thought chiefly about the two prime factors of religion: God and the soul—the supreme, perfect, unchanging Reality as against the crumb of growing, developing reality which our imperfect, changing selves possess. Perhaps in the silence we have begun to feel the demands made on us by that Eternal Reality which is also Eternal Love. Now we strip off the details of life and get down to the central thing which these details and activities must express: our *vocation* and our *choice*, our *election*, the path of service or self-interest selected by the soul in response to the demands of God.

Vocation is not rare. Everyone has a vocation. It is God's call to the soul, partly disclosed in the gifts He has furnished us with, partly in the

---

*Underhill suggests here the prayer on page 64 of *The Mysteries of the Mass in Reasoned Prayers* by William Roche, S.J.

opportunities that come to it, and partly in the secret inward voice suggesting a special course. Election is the response of the free will to all this.

The Spirit of God indwelling our souls ever presses us to the fulfillment of His purpose. But we have a certain power of resistance, something as it were of our own—our love—which we can either give or withhold. Election for God and the inner life means the free giving of that active love to Him—siding with Him at *all costs*. It is so that we become more and more perfect conductors of His holy energy, spreading His love.

We can either serve God voluntarily as awakened spirits do, or involuntarily as all innocent nature does, or we can rebel against Him and choose sin. Those are the soul's three choices, face to face with the many graded realities of life. We can remain as just decent people in our ordinary natural status: the way of earth. We can choose the supernatural ascent in one form or the other, the hard life of love and prayer: the way of heaven. Or we can choose the infra-natural descent away from God: the way of hell. There they are: respectability, sanctity, and sin. We know which God asks, but which is our election?

None of us here would wish to choose sin, but suppose that nothing but a humble, steady cultivation of inner prayer will save us from choosing respectability? It is very easy for the soul that has felt God's supernatural attraction and has been told to give itself without reserve, to relapse to the natural level again, to gradually slide back from the difficult spiritual life of effort, growth, renunciation, and willed correspondence with Him to the ordinary decent conduct of the average person.

If we let the level of prayer grow slack, we are *certain* to do this. Prayer is the food of persevering election. The intimate, inward prayer of faith and adherence to God in the darkness or the light is one of loyalty, not just a nice feeling. The life of prayer, as St. Francis has told us, consists not in turning the soul into a nicely upholstered little oratory. What Christ asks of us is a roomy workshop, for when He comes into the soul, He comes as a craftsman and brings His tools with Him.

Most people who find that religion has lost its interest for them are found to have slid back. Now in retreat, we have the great opportunity to check this tendency, to brace our wills, to accept our supernatural inheritance, and to ask ourselves the crucial questions of St. Ignatius:

> What have I done for Christ?
> What am I doing?
> What ought I to do?

Now it is clear from these three choices that election is not merely concerned with whether we will or will not live by God's command. That we must try to do if we are Christian at all. But it concerns our whole-hearted response to the further call and counsel, "Follow me"—follow with complete self-forgetfullness, willingness, and delight which alone turns us from slaves of God's purpose, at best bright little animals, into His children and friends.

Consider the story of the rich young man as given in Mark 10. That story is decisive. It isn't against the merely natural, merely humanitarian view of the demands of Christ. All this that Christ commanded, all the moral virtues the young man had persued, but he knew he hadn't done enough. He remained dissatisfied. He had felt the attraction of God, of eternal life, the supernatural craving. For that Jesus loved him and told him that the only possible response to that attraction was complete renunciation, the life of the Cross, the spiritual life. Yet even with all his longing, his thirst for eternity, he couldn't face that. He failed to make the election offered by Christ.

Now a right election is not always, of course, this complete outward renunciation, although it is *always*, I think, toward interior, gradual, self-stripping. It always means surrender and involves such *detachment* from the world as enables us to attend purely to God. But that must be combined with such *attachment* as enables us, with God, to love and try to save the world. It means the surrender to and the acceptance of conditions He gives. Thus it is a letting go of all He takes away.

So our vocation may be, and perhaps usually is, to make the fullest use of our talents and circumstances for God, yet it may cut right across them. It may be a reflection of Christ's life of service and prayer. Like His, it may move towards the destitution of Calvary. Don't let us forget the infinite grades and varieties of souls or suppose that we are all asked for the same thing. Your relation or mine to Almighty God is not necessarily that of any other soul in the whole universe. Your bit of work or mine, however tiny, can't be done by anyone else. Each of you represents one little atom of genuine Christian consciousness and of human matter with which the Holy Spirit works. No one of us can grasp all that is offered to that consciousness or do all that is demanded. The bit we can each grow, do, or respond to is our special job, and election is a whole-hearted accept-ance of this opportunity when God shows it to us.

Thus the right choice, a good election, may in the end turn out to be a career much less apparently spiritual than we expected. This is especially true of those placed in positions of authority, responsible for organizing and directing works undertaken for the service of God. These, in commit-ment to their vocation are often called on to leave God for God. Yet it is true that if they have truly chosen Him they find Him again in another way.

Remember how St. Teresa, hard at work in the convent kitchen, said our Lord walked there among the pots and pans? It reminds us of Brother Lawrence who at last found prayer as easy among the pots and pans as in the sanctuary, knowing he was where he belonged. It is *your* business, Lord, that I am doing, for *your* sake—in the home, in business, in social activities for in You "we live and move and have our being" [Acts 17:28].

Now however various the call of souls and the form of their response to God, a certain characteristic is always present. There is one in particular we might well think of here. When we elect for God, for Christ, we elect for the disciplined life. Our Lord told the deepest of His secrets and offered to share in His cross, only to the Disciples, his little flock. Now a disciple is a disciplined person, and it is to these people that Christ's gifts are still offered. It is to those who abandon softness, waywardness, religious moodiness, and spiritual self-will. It is to those who fully, faithfully, and bravely accept all the various means whereby God disciplines and educates our souls.

It is also to those who don't aim at delightful religious emotions but rather at an increase in the hard, fundamental virtues: humility, endurance, suffering, and love. It is to those who go on steadily with the life of prayer, even when it is hard and unrewarded, who plod on, keeping their rule and doing their job faithfully and saying: "Darkness and light are both alike to Thee" [Ps. 139:12].

It is one thing to come to religion for healing, comfort, and support, as crowds did and do, and quite another to accept the terms on which we are admitted to the company of His fellow workers: the discipline of Christ. But it is to that second group to whom He is united in the sacraments and to whom He especially imparts His joys and peace. Thomas à Kempis is brutally direct when he says:

> Jesus now hath many lovers of His Heavenly Kingdom, but few bearers of His Cross; He hath many that are desirous of consolation, but few of tribulation; He findeth many companions of His table, but few of His abstinence. All desire to rejoice with Him, but few are willing to suffer for His sake. Many follow Jesus unto the breaking of bread, but few unto the drinking of the Cup of His Passion. (ii, 11)

There are only two ultimate religious attitudes for Christians: that which prays for a share in the *benefits* of the Passion and that which asks for the holy privilege of being allowed a *part* in the Passion. The soul can elect to be a beggar or a giver, a delighted acceptor of salvation or a heroic cross-bearer with Christ. But only those who ask for a share in Christ, who can't rest unless they have some tiny part in the struggle against evil and in God's work for souls, know the deepest meaning of His Peace. It doesn't follow that we realize all that is involved in this choice. Most of us must grow a great deal before we have even a glimmer of what Christ really means.

Now we have really gotten down to the heart of election, haven't we? Which is it to be for us—the hard or the soft choice? We can have the soft choice if we like. No one can tell how long is the line of people who say, "Prayer is such a comfort!" and then leave the hard part to Christ and the saints. It is quite possible to get a spiritual Vi-spring* and lie on it. But we can hardly pretend that that is the measure of love and holiness which God asks from any soul.

The central act, the election of the soul that *cares* for God, must be deliberate in arranging itself in one way or another with those who accept the discipline, the yoke, the Christ-appointed means of the soul's growth and testing. It is an alignment with those who don't choose to feel nice in prayer but do choose to be yoke-fellows with Christ, to receive His holy energy and purifying Spirit, to surrender entirely to His service and work with Him for the redemption of the world.

If discipline is an essential part of election, then action of some sort must express that choice. The human soul is a force, an energy, and holiness is the growth of that energy in love and service. "Make my calling and my election sure by good works," says Lancelot Andrewes, speaking for the Lord. Our response to God's call, our choice of Him, isn't made *sure* until it leaves the realm of ideas and enters the realm of action. It isn't sure until we do something about it. This, as St. Peter says, establishes and strengthens us:

> Give diligence to make your calling and election sure, for if you *do* these things, you shall never fall. [2 Pet. 1:10]

The full Christian life, the consecrated life, uses the whole of us and is a life of disciplined action, initiative, courage, and love. Each one choosing it means not just one more grateful recipient of benefits but one more recruit for the ranks. Teresa said that the object of spiritual marriage was "Work, work, work!" making one's call and election sure by good works.

We have probably all noticed again and again how, over the portals of medieval churches, the builders placed two figures, but not quite the figures we might first expect. The two figures represent neither placid holiness nor revelation, but the two aspects of a fighting life! The two

---

*A Vi-spring was an early form of inner-spring mattress.

soldiers are saints: St. George and St. Martin.* All over Europe we find these two as if to remind all of us that the entrance to the eternal mysteries, the deepest communion with God, involves acceptance of that two-fold vocation, that mind which was and is in Christ.

That mind expressed charity in two aspects: the fearless, often lonely attacking of evil and the rescue of souls along with the homely, selfless self-stripping acts of compassion and love. If our calling and election is sure, it will show itself in that courage and initiative on one hand, and that quite homely and practical gentleness and mercy on the other.

The dragon is fought at our own risk. The beggar is kept warm at our own cost. It works out in many different ways. But let us go from here convinced that no life which does not offer us opportunity of that two-fold service of courage and compassion fully answers the demands of Christ.

*St. George (d. 303) is thought to have been a soldier. The legend is that he killed a dragon who could be appeased only by the sacrifice of sheep or human beings. His courage was rewarded by the baptism of 15,000 men.

St. Martin, a soldier who became a conscientious objector, is known for his compassion as one who healed lepers and even raised a dead man. He is said to have cut his cloak in half to clothe a naked begger and then to have later dreamed that Christ appeared wearing the cloak.

V

The Creative Personality

Preparatory Worship

Psalm (not noted)

Hymns: "Praise to the Holiest"
   "Immortal Love"

Prayers:

O Lord, you order and arrange all things for us in your infinite wisdom and love. You know my weakness and every beat and ache of my heart is known to you. Blindly I give myself to your tender loving heart. Only give me grace to think, speak, act, [and] feel according to your loving purpose.
(E. B. Pusey)

Teach us, good Lord, to serve you as you deserve; to give and not to count the cost; to fight and not to heed the wounds; to toil and not to seek for rest; to labor and not to ask for any reward, save that of knowing that we do your will. (Ignatius of Loyola)

We spent the preceding sessions considering our individual situations face to face with the reality of God in whose praise, reverence, and service we find our meaning. We dwelt one by one in God, the soul, and our free, crucial choice. What is the destined result of that choice, of election? Isn't it to be our growth, the flowering of the spiritual personality, the production of the thing destined for God? "The human being was created for this end."

When we elect for God, we envisage the end which is called in the Bible "the fullness of the stature of Christ." This is the creative spiritual personality. We have the germ in us now; what are we to make of it?

As we gather together we are looking toward Christmas. The aim of retreat at this time is the preparation of our souls for the special grace of

128

Christmas and of getting a bit more able to realize it. Advent is a time of expectation, an eager looking out of the natural creature toward the spiritual world. It is a looking out to something that is going to come to us just because we do so long for its advent and can't get it of ourselves. And at the end of looking out, what happens? The work of redemption is set going in sweetness and simplicity and in the most natural of ways.

Remember all that is said in the New Testament about those expecting the kingdom of God? What did they expect? Something vague but tremendous. They had been fed on apocalyptic literature—fluffy, heady stuff. And what they got was just a poor person's baby born under the most unfortunate circumstances. And, in the lovely old story of the infancy, there is the soul's instant recognition of the true reality which broke out at every level: the level of angels, of shepherds, of wise men, and of supernatural intelligence. Even intellectuals are made to see the point and be humble and delighted. Yet that point is expressed in a way that every child can appreciate and that we only realize in all its poignancy when we manage to become little children too.

There is an old ritual of the Catholic Church for Christmas night and Christmas day that brings that home. It is a movement from the great abstract, awe-inspiring sense of God to His self-revelation in simple ways. At midnight, there is the Introit introducing the generation of the eternal Son, the Word. Then the Collect proclaims the shining forth of the mysterious divine light. At dawn, Isaiah 9 is read. The light comes nearer, but it is still a bit abstract and diffuse as we hear: "Today hath a light shined upon us for the Lord is born unto us." But on Christmas day we sing and say, "Unto us a child is born. Sing to the Lord a new song!" There has been a gradual condensation up to the final self-revelation. And in the Preface, the object of the Liturgy is summed up: that having seen God made visible, we may be caught up to the Invisible Love.

How is God made visible? Not with mechanical completeness, but through a growing personality.

There is the first lesson of Advent, one so constantly repeated but seldom fully understood. There is always the naturalness of the supernatural, the fact that the name "Emmanuel" means what it says: "God with us." God gives through nature all the necessities that matter for the transfiguring of the soul. His redemptive energy is most perfectly manifested through human beings.

Now we begin once again our yearly contemplation of what happens between Christmas and Ascension. It is different each time. We cannot grasp the whole. And what we get from it is a rough measure of our spiritual whereabouts. But there are certain constant features: a great strangeness and awe combined with naturalness and simplicity. It covers a span so great that it comes right down to and is taken into our simple lives and goes out beyond even the horizon of the great contemplative saints. And all of it is contained within the limits of personality.

Human personality, something more mysterious than its animal past might suggest, is an embryonic thing, a capsule of the growth and expansion of which Christ is the classic example, an example which the world can't get past. This truth is revealed in the gentlest and humblest way, right down within history, in homely surroundings. A carpenter's baby. Thirty years of obscure village life. Self-identification with the crowd. The refusal of all self-regarding use of spiritual power. Immense compassion. A self-oblivion so perfect we don't notice it. A genial love of all human and natural things. Unflinching acceptance of suffering, failure, and death. Together these were the chief external signs of God's full expression in terms of human personality. If it hadn't happened, we should never have invented it like that. Our highest values couldn't have come to us in a humbler disguise.

This is a reverse of our ordinary human standards, a reverse so crushing, so complete. Attempts to retrace the line of this life on the social chart of the present day are often made. No one likes it. They say that the line of Christ's life is irreversible, but really their sense of discomfort is too intense. It brings two standards vividly before us—not picturesque as in the contrast between the manger and the magi, but stripped of the glamour. It reminds us that the real Incarnation is a bit of uncompromising divine realism and not a lovely mystery play.

It is easy to enjoy Christmas with its live altar as a crib, clean straw, nice furry animals, and its Christmas card atmosphere of sweetness and charm. In the same way, it was easy for the Jews in Christ's time to enjoy temple worship with the Holy of Holies, the Ark, and the Veil: all this undying appeal stimulates and enchants us. But redemption was not worked out in temple worship. It was worked out in ordinary life among the ruck of the sinful, sick, maimed, stupid, and self-interested. It was accomplished through sharing the suffering and injustice of life. There was a temple ritual all ready, but Reality reached and won its creatures by contact through personality, a contact that then and now evades nothing and leaves nothing out.

We are reminded of the nativity legend told by Jules Lemaitre, and of the stunning words: "This really *is* the Messiah." Isn't it true for us too when we see that transcendent human soul knowing its power, yet choosing compassion instead of ambition, when we see human courage and generosity blazing out in the shadow of death, when we feel the human agony and self-abandonment of Christ, that *we* recognize the reality?

Here is the Supernatural, God, seeking us through natural means and known character, through personality. His direct action on the human being is through a human being. His demand on souls is to be so completely surrendered that through them His love and holiness can be expressed.

Now what about us? What about the obligations laid on us? What about the lessons taught us as to our lives, our call to growth in full being, in creative love? Doesn't Christ's life of human compassionate service supported by lonely prayer give us a pattern of humble growth? Doesn't it help us in our response to the two orders of environment? Isn't it a pattern which all Christians must keep their eyes on as they seek to imitate it in thousands of degrees and ways?

The saints, as they drew near to God, tried to imitate that pattern more and more closely, and as they did so, their personalities expanded and shone with love and power. Especially in its most mysterious reaches, in redemptive action on suffering and sin, the saints dimly reproduced and continue to reproduce the life of Christ. Real saints do feel and bear the weight of sins and the suffering of the world. The truth of their lives is not shown in aloof calmness, for they are wounded for our transgressions. When we are fully awake in our souls, we *can* accept redemptive suffering for one another, and they *do*. As saintly souls grow and their real spiritual personality appears, so does their identity with all other souls increase. So does their union with God who never leaves any soul alone. The saints show us throughout history a maturation and transformation of character which we are not able to grasp. Only with their help can we come to understand something about the cross and to realize how little we know of it.

As the saints grow in beauty, they grow in the practice of penance. They feel the weight of sin and redeem it through their creative prayer, their prayers of intercession. The real redeeming saint looks to the outsider more like a publican [a tax collector] than a Pharisee, being so abased and self-identified with sinners. Such a person doesn't stand aside, feeling pure and agreeable to God, but goes right down into the mess and acknowledges his part in it. The edges of the mess are melted off and the saint is now fused with the world which he loves and wants to help. That individual knows that *we* come from God, we belong to God, and we are destined for God!

That seems far beyond us, yet perhaps there are ways in which we too can seek to incarnate love such as this. As Advent shows us, expectation itself is an implicit knowledge of God and a condition of prayer. So too is the trustful craving of the soul for holiness and grace. In the interior life, there is often more sanctifying power in such humble waiting on God than in its vivid realization. The dull shutting of our gates on fresh possibilities thwarts God's action and only contradicts each individual act of faith and self-abandonment. Peaceful self-yielding to the Spirit opens more and more of the gates for the entrance of God into the human soul which in welcome cries, "Behold, the handmaid of the Lord!"

It is not hard for most of us to do active work, but it is hard to maintain that spirit of unflickering self-renunciation and waiting. Yet the Incarnation has taught, and through the saints goes on teaching, that what matters is not what we *do* but is the deepness and self-abnegation with which the serving soul enters the life, movement, and will of God and so can be used for divine purpose. Not the things that Christ did (for He really did very few things over a limited area and numbers of energetic people produce a much longer list of good works) but His attitude and intention compel our response.

It is these things that make work spiritual and only this. We must get rid of the pestilent, deadly notion that the amount of things we get through is the standard. The steadiness with which we radiate God is the standard. Christ did this at dinner parties, on journeys, and with friends as well as in and through healing and preaching. This transfiguration of the ordinary shows us God in the flesh, and it is always this that wins souls.

The moments in Christ's life when the supernatural shone out, most clearly were those when human limits were pressed heavily from the point of view of common sense. An artisan's baby adored by shepherds and magi. A young man coming with the crowd to be baptised by a religious revivalist. A condemned fanatic agonizing between two criminals on a cross. What we contemplate from Advent to Ascension is hardly a speck of triumphal success in *actions,* but it is the spectacle of a triumphant personality over mere events. It is the creative power inherent in the soul.

History supports this and great literature reveals it. In Dante's *Divine Comedy,* what did the love of Beatrice come to, measured in moderate terms of productive social work? What has the *fact* of Beatrice's life, personality, purity, and God's work in Dante's soul through that incarnation of holiness come to in the cumulative power of revealing to countless souls the purpose and demands of divine love? She didn't know she had done it. That is the beauty of the revelation of God through the personal. It doesn't tarnish the humility of those through whom it is made. Real saints never know how much they are doing. What they are doing is continuing the work of incarnation through the perfect self-yielding of the soul to God, making themselves His tools, His channels of revelation to others.

They show us little sudden hints of the wonderful fact of eternal love ever at work in human history, patient with human perversions, endlessly compassionate to human loneliness and sin, gradually penetrating and sanctifying human life, entering, transforming and enlarging the capacity of human character, and making of human spirits, fellow workers with God.

VI

Prayer and Adoration

Preparatory Worship

Magnificat

Psalm 103: "Bless the Lord, O My Soul"

Hymns: "Ye Watchers and Ye Holy Ones"
       "Praise, My Soul, the King of Heaven"
       "O Worship the King"

Prayers regarding God's love, joy, and fervor in communion and service:

O Thou who fillest heaven and earth, ever acting, ever at rest, who art present everywhere and everywhere art wholly present, who art not absent even when afar off, who, with Thy whole being fillest and transcendest all things, who teachest the hearts of the faithful without the din of words; teach us we pray Thee. (St. Augustine)

You, O eternal Trinity, are a deep sea into which, the more I enter, the more I find, and the more I find, the more I seek. . . .
O abyss, O eternal Godhead, O sea profound, what more could you give me than yourself? (St. Catherine of Sienna)

Open Thou my heart for Thy love, keep Thy love in me, prepare me by Thy love for greater fullness of Thy love, until I have reached the fullest measure of Thy love, which Thou, in Thy eternal love, hast willed for me. (E. B. Pusey)

Since we have just been thinking about the saints, it is natural and suitable to pass on to thoughts about prayer, for, along with all the saints we remember, there is a vast company of nameless Christians made completely pleasing to God. They are tender, heroic, merciful, adoring people of prayer.

In our previous sessions, we considered three primary realities: God, the soul, and the soul's choice. The choice, in one form or another, is a choice of a life of communion with God and service of God. Such a life is the life of prayer. But how are we to think of prayer? Surely in the richest way.

All attempts to narrow prayer down to this or that, to emphasize one aspect against another, to understand its richness and variety are fruitless. I've heard people refer to the "need" for prayer as if there is a sort of electrical current which must be employed to move things, to boil the kettle, to do useful work. This would suggest that the holy energy of God is there to do *our* jobs instead of us being there to do *His*. Others say that the loving communion of the Soul with God in prayer is selfish. There are those who contend that to pray *for* something intimates that we can affect the will of God. Then there are some who are captains of real prayer who get distracted because they find their way of praying not like that of others.

Prayer is our *whole life* of communion with God, whether secret or corporate. If one thinks of it like that, one shall get a richer and deeper view of it. We shan't let ourselves be worried by people with special views about it.

Prayer is the whole life of the Soul. It is the life in which one breathes spiritual air, feeds on spiritual food, learns spiritual things, and does spiritual work. It is not one but *all* these things. It is *life*.

Shall this life be less in contrasting variety, richness, intricate beauty, tension, joy, pain, fellowship, and loneliness than is bodily life on earth? All of these are in the life of prayer, and the proportion in which they come to each soul differs.

So too the spiritual lands into which prayer brings us has its mountains, oceans, and plains so rich and great that no one person can explore them appropriately. Still less can anyone live in all of it. We are each to practice prayer according to what God shows us, and we can do that, but we cannot forget the overplus of experience which is not for us but for other souls. As those in quiet inland places may still remember the great movement of the sea, we must try to avoid insularity. It may seem to us that we've been set down, as it were, to grub spiritual potatoes, but from somewhere else they might be seen as very special flowers.

Amidst all the varieties of prayer there are two movements which must, I think, be present in every spiritual life. The love and energy of prayer must be directed on the one hand toward God and on the other toward humanity. In the first movement we turn toward the Supernatural, to God in Himself. In the second movement, we turn with added energy toward the Natural. Prayer, like the whole of human inner life, swings between the unseen and the seen. Both movements are necessary, but the second will only be well done when the first has the central place. Here *lex credendi* is or should be *lex orandi*. [In other words, "what we believe" would be "what we pray." That old Latin saying is, of course, in the reverse order: *"Lex orandi; lex credendi,"* and that means that our belief (and therefore its expression in action) come from our prayer.]

Furthermore, "Thou shalt love the Lord thy God" comes *first* [not only in the Commandments, and not only in action, but in prayer]. This means that adoration, and not intercession or petition, is the very heart of the life of prayer.

Prayer is a supernatural achievement [made possible by God within us] and must be directed to a supernatural end. It must begin, end, and be enclosed in the atmosphere of adoration. It must aim at God, for and in Himself. It too must acknowledge the soul's basic law: "We come from God. We belong to God. We tend toward God."

Perhaps some of us have prayed in the words or spirit of William Law: "May all within me be changed into Thy Holy Spirit and temper." But unless we give time to look at, love, and lose ourselves in contemplation of our path, it is not very likely that prayer will be effective.

Fussy, anxious, exclusively practical, this-world prayer does nothing to enrich Christian character. The reason is quite plain. Prayer is substantially communion with God, and therefore exclusive attention to Him is its first part. We must receive before we can transmit. Our effect as transmitters of His grace and love directly depends on our adoring attention. His spirit is always with us. In the prayer of love, attention, and adoration, we open our doors wide to receive Him. We abase ourselves and acknowledge our nothingness in comparison with his wonder, perfection, and joy. The Soul that has given itself to God becomes part of that Mystical Body in and through which He acts on life. Its destiny is to be a receiver and transmitter of grace.

Is that not practical work? For Christians, is it not the *only* practical work?

But sometimes we are in such a hurry to transmit that we forget that the primary need is to receive in order to nourish our adoring love, our sense of awe, our personal littleness and dependence. Doing this, perpetually turning to Him, adoring Him, losing ourselves in Him, our souls are slowly flooded by His Spirit. Only when our own souls are thus filled to the brim can we presume to offer spiritual gifts to others. When we *are* filled, we shan't be able to help giving.

St. Bernard reminds us that people who are reservoirs are not meant to be canals. The remedy for that sense of impotence, that desperate spiritual exhaustion which religious workers, functioning only as canals, too often know, is an inner life governed not by petition, but by adoring prayer. This is Christ's message and attitude. The very heart of His prayer and doctrine is the presence, the love, the glory of God everywhere awaiting our recognition, knowing our needs before we ask. Christ said little about petition, because he was penetrated by the love and generosity of God.

When we find that demands on us are threats to our inward poise, when we feel signs of starvation and stress, it is time to call a halt and redirect our balance. Then it is imperative to reestablish the fundamental relationship of our souls with Eternal Reality, the home and Father of our spirits. Our hearts shall have no rest save there.

It is only when our hearts are thus at rest in God in peaceful selfless adoration that we can show His attractiveness to others. In the flood-tide of such adoring prayer the soul is carried up to God, is hidden in God. Thus alone can it achieve that utter self-forgetfulness which is the basis of its peace and power. But peace and power can never be ours as long as we make our prayer a means of drawing gifts to ourselves from God instead of an act of self-giving to Him.

From this adoring prayer, this steady concentration on God and joyous self-immolation before Him, springs all other prayerful disposition in our souls. A deep, humble, contrite sense of our unworthiness, gratitude for all that has been given us, learning an increased charity that longs to spend itself on other souls—all these are signs of spiritual vitality, and spiritual vitality depends on the *feeding* of our souls on God. Without that, we can't expect to be strong enough to work for Him.

The full Christian life of prayer swings to and fro between adoration and action. We must be sure that the outward swing toward God is full, generous, unhurried, brimming with joy. Many of us live exacting lives of service full of hard material problems. If we can acquire the determination that *nothing* shall turn us from a steady daily habit of loving adoration, our prayer will be full of loving intimacy and awe. Then we shall have the best of all helps for the maintenance of the soul's energy and peace, and we will serve God with a quiet mind.

This adoring prayer of loving communion with God may take many forms. The point is, we must find the form that suits *us—our* souls— *yours,* not someone else's. Now, at this state of growth, we cannot conceive our prayer in ape fashion. We must not try to imitate that which someone else has told us. Some, who by looking at Christ, meditate on His words and acts, come close to His Spirit and lose themselves in loving worship, entering into ever closer union with Him. Some find in the sacramental life the heart of prayer. Some feel most deeply drawn to self-abasement before the spaceless presence of God. We can't all feel *all* these things.

Our prayer too will change as our souls mature. We must never attempt uniformity. Our task is to act simply, to speak or keep silent as we are impelled. There are little phrases of love and worship, fragments from the Psalms, which often help us to keep our mind pointing in the right way and open up the way for some who find this prayer difficult at first. Think of St. Francis repeating all night: "My God and All!" The perfect prayer of adoration is the humble cry of awed delight. The creature gazes on the Creator and Lord.

Don't all examples and tiresome details fall away and vanish as we dwell on such words? Don't they bring us back to trust that the important thing in prayer is never what we say or ask for, but the way we feel about God?— our attitude?

Complete, loving surrender. You may think that I've insisted unduly on this. It is because I feel that here in current religious life there is a great neglect of humble duty and humble joy. It is this which is responsible for much lack of spiritual depth and power. Adoration, however, is the central service asked by God of human souls. I often think that those who by health, age, and circumstance withdraw from active life, may be so withdrawn (for nothing happens by chance) in order that they may add to the world's gift of adoration—the true music of the spheres.

And isn't this especially true of *sufferers?* We have all seen the peaceful, joyous suffering which witnesses to God—which seems, as it were, to live within Christ and to sing for Christ—just as Francis did! Over against that, what a waste is fretful, melancholic suffering, the suffering that *isn't* prayer, that makes suffering sub-human. Whereas pain, transmuted by adoring love, makes the sufferer superhuman—in a phrase of the mystics, "a partaker of the Divine Nature"—so too, in *our* ordained vocation of prayer and work, the transmuting effect is what counts.

We may not have time for long prayers, though we should make a great effort to set apart *some* regular period of exclusive attention to God. But we *can* form a habit of making short acts of love, adoration, and resignation at odd moments. An important part of education in prayer is to recall us to the atmosphere of Eternity. If we feel slack, dry, or spiritually listless, and all do at times, there is no better way of tuning ourselves up than by deliberately making such acts as these. Such habits will produce a state of mind in which we best use our longer periods of prayer and best maintain the deep serenity of the Child of God through the perpetual strain of pressing practical life.

This deep, self-oblivious, persistent serenity is not those special feelings we may have when praise is the real test of the worth and purity of our prayer. Some people never have those feelings, and its a great reassurance to them to know that they don't matter. St. Teresa reminds us in formidable language that what *does* matter is *never* our special devotional experiences, but always their results: the fruits of prayer.

The Fruits of the Spirit are love, joy, peace, patience, long-suffering, gentleness, goodness, and faith: "the mind that was in Christ." If, in our adoration, we have truly and selflessly poured ourselves out to the Spirit and opened up our souls, that is the temper which will come to dominate our lives: a sweet and humble spirit of acceptance which turns all it touches into gold by bringing it within the radius of God.

VII

Charity

Preparatory Worship

(The usual psalm, hymns, and prayers are not noted by Underhill in this case. Therefore the following editorial suggestions are made.)

Psalm 91 or portions of 107

Hymns: "O Master, Let Me Walk with Thee"
       "We Give Thee But Thine Own"

Prayers:

Set our hearts on fire with love of Thee, O Christ Our God, that in that flame we may love thee with all our hearts, with all our mind, with all our soul, and with all our strength, and our neighbors as ourselves; so that, keeping thy commandments, we may glorify thee, the giver of all good gifts. (An Eastern Orthodox Prayer)

O You who are love, and dwell in love, teach us to be children of love in our actions, thoughts, and words. May we never turn our love away from those who are ignorant of your love. May we be instruments of your mercy reaching out to those in distress and need, giving such an example of your loving concern that all may find unity in the discovery that they are your children. (James Martineau)

We have come to the end of our retreat. Now we glance back at the thoughts we have been trying to carry through it, gathering up those we mean to take away.

We entered our time together determined to bring into God's presence the whole of ourselves: our wills, hearts, and minds and our physical, mental, and spiritual powers and desires. We have remained alone with Him in order that He could purify them. Now, like those initiated into the mysteries who were dipped in the cleansing fountains, we have aspired to come out transfigured and re-energized, not (as they thought) in our *being* (for that sharp change is beyond us), but in our *love* and *desire*.

We acknowledge that our dispositions must be recollected in utter confidence and great generosity. Our recollection is for the purpose of apprehending God; our confidence is in His invitation and love; and generosity is our only appropriate response. With these qualities, we tried to grasp the great Ignatian saying: "The human being was created for this end: to praise, reverence, and serve the Lord." We have realized that any bit of our life and character that does not contribute to that end is not lasting and so, not real.

We have dwelt on the great fundamentals: God, the soul, and our own choice regarding the end for which we were created. We have considered what that choice should mean, choosing the discipline of Christ as our model, and growth in creative personality as our aim, not for our own sakes, but for God's. We have asked ourselves how to pray, reverence, and serve more vividly and fully. We have pondered the ruling attitude of the transfigured personality, the attitude of adoration.

Tomorrow we will be going back into the world. There we will try to improve in that Christian life, that life which ought to seek and spread the incarnation of eternity in space and time. But what about Teresa's tests? Are we taking back a deepened lowliness, a vivid love of our neighbor, and a keen sense of the holy character of our daily work? Are we looking toward perfection in our daily jobs? These are the only proofs by which we truly find and know that God is present in those neighbors and in that daily work.

As we think about the subject of charity, let us remember St. Teresa's test of a healthy life of prayer as making us more lowly, more loving, and more keenly industrious. But these three tests are not only for the outward life of a Christian. We shall find them even more searching if used as tests of the inner life of those who practice prayer. Here they matter most if they are established in the soul, for from there they will soon control individual conduct. It is within prayer itself that these characteristics need to be established. Prayer does and can affect circumstances because a man or woman of prayer is a tool with which God works.

First, let us look at lowliness, the sense of our creaturely status, our own inabilities, and our child-like dependence on God. This is the source of our peace. This is the link with the life of adoration.

Then there are the other two tests—the tests of charity and industry, found on the other side of the life of prayer, the side turned toward the world. Unless we leave the retreat more full of charity, with a wide-spreading, energetic, redeeming love of souls—unless we are more determined to make the daily routine of religion into one of spiritual action—

and unless that routine is so transfigured with God that we must do every bit of it as well as we can, we might as well not have had the retreat.

The point of the third test is guaranteed disinterest in our self-centered selves. If we go on steadily doing what we understand to be both wise and loving without reference to our feelings, we will prove the gentle, unstrained mortification which only the really devoted are likely to accept. The quiet doing of the spiritual job in the sun and in the fog, as well as we can, distinguishes genuine fervor from emotion. That is the discipline which gives backbone to the dedicated life, which ensures the killing of spiritual self-love, and places life within the atmosphere of God. It includes the most unappetizing religious duties as well as the most intimate religious joys.

That life is assured only if controlled by adoration and charity. Real adoration and charity are inseparable because the object of both is God. Where these two reign fully, the life of prayer is lived fully, expanding the soul for God. Adoration is caring for God above all else. Charity is the outward swing of prayer toward the world. It is self-oblivious, embracing and caring for all worldly interests, for God, and for God in the world. It is this point of view which governs the prayer of intercession and is the disposition to which all Christians are called.

So tonight, at the close of our retreat, we think especially of this crowning grace: spiritual charity, sweetening every relationship of life and acting as the soul's self, speaking for other souls in love. Until our prayer flowers thus, we are not real followers of Christ or doing the full work to which the human soul is called. We are stopping halfway.

The call is, by some means, through countless difficulties and opportunities, to be a living tool with which God can work, a supple instrument. This is only possible if we care to transcend ourselves for God's interests in the world and care with Him in His way—generous, self-giving, unclaimful, and infinitely patient—for all in the world. It is to have something of His wide-spreading love and compassion for misery and sin. It is to cooperate with His saving energy.

Such intercession involves real sharing of the world's sorrows and self-giving to need. It is fellow-feeling, not merely being sorry for people, but feeling their pain too. Intercession has hardly begun to prevail and exercise its power until the sin and suffering of others enters deeply into our souls as into the very heart of the Christ. We must even be willing to sacrifice inner peace, to give ourselves for the sins of the world, to risk everything of our own, valuing holiness itself as charity, as an increase in the power of saving love. In this great life-imparting prayer, the true prayer of charity, of Christ's caring love and life for others, the soul really moving

Godward, carries others with it. This is the real difference between Christian saints and those seekers for God in other religions.

Now intercession is charity working on supernatural levels for supernatural ends. And if we are to do it, the one thing which matters is that we should care. We can't help anyone until we do care because it is only by love that Spirit penetrates spirit. Think what is implied in the mystery of intercession: God, Infinite Love, the all-penetrating Spirit of spirits, the ocean in which all are bathed. We are united in Him, but not only so. We are mutually penetrated, spiritually moving and influencing each other in ways yet unguessed, and through it all, molded and directed by God.

In this mysterious interaction of energies called prayer, one tool is put into our hands. Love, will, and desire are three aspects of it. Dynamic love, purged of self-interest, is ours to use on spiritual levels, an engine for working with God on other souls. The saints used it at tremendous cost and with tremendous effect. As their souls expanded and learned adoration, so they went on to the desperate wrestling for souls, exhaustive, creative activity, steady support, redeeming prayer by which human spirits are called to work with God. "God enabled me to agonize in prayer," said the saintly David Brainard.* "My soul was drawn out very much for the world. I grasped for a multitude of souls."

That gives us a sense of unreachable possibilities, doesn't it? Of deep mysterious energies? Of something not quite covered by what is called intercession? It is because of this that Teresa says, if anyone claims union with God and says they are always in peaceful beatitude, she doesn't believe them. Union of the soul with God is in the Cross, in great sorrow for the sin and pain of the world and longs to redeem and heal. Therefore, real supernatural charity has a wide scope and an infinite object. It spreads and spreads with the growing of the soul in love until it embraces the whole world, for its model is God Himself.

We have to grasp that if we are really members of the Body of Christ, His redeeming work in this world will be done through us and largely through our prayer. In prayer we offer ourselves as His tools. He uses us to touch and change the lives of human beings. Remember St. Francis' comment that the soul really given to God will not long remain a cosy little oratory, but is far more likely to become a carpenter's shop.

The call of supernatural charity is not a call to love the nice but the nasty, not the loveable but the unlovely, the hard, the narrow, the embit-

*David Brainard (1718–1747) was an American missionary associated with the Scottish Society for the Propagation of Christian Knowledge (SPCK). His ministry was chiefly among the Seneca and Delaware Indians. Most of what is known about him was made possible through the publication of his diary by Jonathan Edwards in 1749.

tered, and the tiresome who are so much worse! It is a call to love them until you have made them nicer, to love irrespective of merit or personal preference, and to love those who offend our taste.

Intercession *must* be humble. We can't help to redeem what we don't love, where we set up our own standards and are predominantly critical. Think of all the people in the Gospel who would offend our tastes: the stupid, important, over-hasty, self-interested, ungrateful, and those caught up in cheap rationalism; and Martha, Peter, Magdalen, and Thomas. Divine Love goes straight for the undesirable types, meets them on their own ground, reaches them through *their* character, and makes them His friends. The perfect act of intercession was when Perfect Holiness meekly condescended to wash the Disciples' feet.

Suppose God would turn from us every time we offended His standard! Instead of that an unmeasurable generosity seeks us at our worst, ordinary, earthy grubbiness and does for us what we cannot do. And that is a task we in our turn must try to take on, imitating from far off this unfailing patience and longing to save.

Finally, if we are to do such intercessory work, we cannot be swamped by the great ocean of suffering, sin, and need to which we shall be sent. Once again, we *must* maintain and feed the temper of adoration and trusting adherence. This is the state of prayer, and only in this state can we safely dare to seek to touch other souls and affect them. Moreover, the deeper our adoration, our praise, and our reverence, the more we shall want to do that service and the more we try to do it; and then, the more profoundly joyful and the more utterly self-forgetful our adoration will become. There are two kinds of love: the one that goes out of the world to God and the one that goes with Him into the world to redeem it, to enable us to feed and support one another and in the fully developed soul attains the end for which it was made.

If we yearn for both those loves, it means a steady increase in our inward detachment from all personal claims and desires and a constant death to self. Yet side by side, it means a steady growth in loving attachment to all souls worthy and unworthy alike. It means a life in which each soul does, to the utmost of its capacity, praise, reverence, and serve God and in so doing expands and exercises to full creative power that with which it is endowed, growing in love, full being, and real spiritual personality.

INNER GRACE AND OUTWARD SIGN

A retreat given in 1927

All Christians are called to grow and called to the spiritual life, each to the degree and in the way ordained of God. To fulfill His purposes, we need only the equipment He has given and the three graces . . . which Christ, in His life and Passion, showed in their divine splendor: courage, generosity, and patience—all consisting in giving and enduring.

Chapter II: "Courage"

We, . . . as cells of the Body of Christ, are called upon to be . . . channels of His mystical self-imparting. Our lives—gestures, words, and small acts—should be, outward and visable signs of inward spiritual grace. . . . If so, how continuous, faithful, and humbling our communion with Him must be and how alert and ready to find Him we must be in every moment of our lives.

Chapter VI: "Communion"

I

Introduction

We have come together here in this wonderful place* to think in God's presence of the Christian life which we have all undertaken to live. And what is the Christian life? It is simply the life of prayer and consecration, isn't it? Prayer is the life of encounter with God. Consecration is the total dedication of our lives to His interest and will. None dare say we achieve it, yet none dare call themselves Christian unless they are trying to achieve it.

The festival of All Saints is one which reminds us of this truth. For that loving festival is when we especially remember all those joyous, devoted lovers of God who are the pride and glory of the Family of God. Now it has been said that a saint is one who does everything by, for, to, and in God. If we would work toward that goal, all our service must be soaked in prayer.

To live more intently in that direction, to match ourselves against that ideal, to increase our love, awe, and delighted admiration of God, to rekindle penitence, and to allow our humbling sense of failure to give us fresh strength is the object of the time which we are going to pass together. We have cut off, as well as we can, all sources of distraction in order to be still and to know the presence of God, to look and to listen.

The result of this will be a new and more vivid sense of His reality and claim on us. We will be driven to ask two questions which the honest soul, alone with God, is always driven to face. The first is "What am I for?" The second is: "How am I doing my job?" All necessary self-examination is comprised within these two questions.

What am I for? Just what this place which has taken us into its heart is for: to express in my life something of the glory, power, and unchanging beauty of God by my very existence, by my love and my actions. I am here

---

*One of the four places where Underhill gave this 1927 retreat was the crypt of Canterbury Cathedral during St. Lukestide in mid-October. Just two weeks later, she gave it again as a retreat for the Festival of All Saints.

to add to the praise offered by the world, to fit into God's scheme, and to translate something of His spiritual reality into the terms of human life. For this I must accept discipline, submit my will, use my talents, kill all self-interest, and cooperate with my fellow human beings.

I do not exist for myself or for society. I do not exist for the sake of my family or nation. I exist for *God,* for consecration. My service is for *God.*

You know, to be in a place like this and to humbly receive all its lessons, is a complete education in the spiritual life. We need no more than is given here. Here our attention is drawn to the many strains of human energy, both past and present, offered to God in prayer and holiness, effort, suffering, and even martyrdom. We see how each character, however practical, is informed by one purpose: how everything tends, not to human usefulness, but being humanly useful to God's glory. We see how every part is interdependent, each strain doing its special part. And we see how much loving vision and skillful planning, and hard, monotonous labor enters in.

Here the focus is the altar where all else is forgotten in order that ourselves, our souls, and our bodies, may offer sacrificial love and adoration to God. This place is an incarnation of the Holy, a witness to that for which the human soul is really made. It is a material embodiment of spiritual realities. When we ask, "What am I for?" this place gives us the answer: to be a temple of the Holy Spirit in which everything from the most material to the least is dedicated to the purposes of God.

Those purposes of God will, of course, be different for each soul, so the way each soul states and answers the second question will be different. "How am I doing my job?" How far is my particular life so lived in the spirit of prayer that it reflects the values of eternity, promoting the glory of God?

There are two ways in which we can find answers to our questions and guidance when we are alone with God in such a place as this. First, we can consider again His mysteries, rest in them, and humbly bathe our souls in their light. Secondly, in the light of the mysteries of God and His demands and love, we can overhaul our own religious and moral practices in order to discover our slack and disproportionate ways of life. We will be able to see that we have been too busy to attend to the grubby corners of life, that we have broken rules, neglected opportunities, and eluded renunciations. Looking at our own patterns and recognizing them, we can begin to get back into trim.

The first way is objective. It means meditation. The second is subjective. Looking at ourselves means self-examination. Both need to be wrapped in an atmosphere of prayer, of loving, humble dependence on God. It is best that meditation should come first because we don't really see the point of our own shortcomings or achieve true contrition for them except by the light of His mystery and the *contrast* between the perfect model and our own performance.

Therefore one of the ways in which we can best spend our time here is in what St. Ignatius calls *contemplation*. It is a fresh, intentional, and loving gaze at those mysteries of the life of Christ which reveal to us the character of God. God will give us more light through this new living in the Gospel and living toward the Gospel than through any mere dwelling on our own faults and needs.

When we stand, for instance, on the high mountain of the Passion, we look back and see where we began in the valley, so full of humble beauty. Then slowly we climb through the increasing challenges that led to Calvary. The Church turns and looks back at all that. Then it looks forward to a wholly new landscape of opportunities and demands made possible by that which went before. So we, at those times when everything speaks of triumphant life and is so full of the exultant sense of Christ's living Spirit present in our midst, do well to look back and see what this triumph *cost*. Then we can look forward to see how our lives are best lived in Him.

You know the old pictures of the life of Christ or the saints in which you see in one corner a tiny kneeling figure just inside the frame? It is a figure called the "donor," coming from the outer world and humbly gazing at the mystery, utterly absorbed into its atmosphere. We too are gathered from the outer world into this holy place to do just that. We have not come to get information or uplifting from the addresses. We have come to *look*, more deeply and with incredulous awe and love, at some of the things in our religion which we take for granted. We have come to kneel in the atmosphere of the spiritual world, to live and breathe in the presence of Christ, and to look quietly at the eternal truths revealed in Him.

Now however stiff and formal the method of St. Ignatius may be when his *Exercises* are read, when it comes to such meditations as these we cannot improve on them much. You know his routine.

1. Set the scene. Then come with the tiny, devoted follower in the picture, kneel in the corner, and *look*.

2. Face to face with the scene, ask for what you want, whether it be more courage, humility, patience, confidence, peaceful acceptance, generous love, or whatever it may be. It will probably be all of these and much more, but it is best to take one point at a time.

3. Knowing what you want, but in a mood of confident and loving resignation to God, just stay with your eyes, ears, and heart wide open, making such simple acts of love, penitence, and self-offering as rise naturally in your soul.

4. *Then*, when this loving vision is filling you and is beginning to cast its gentle but revealing light on your faults and needs, review your situation in that light. Observe every point at which the picture reproves your conduct and motives as to (a) outward life with others and (b) inward life with God. Finally, gather up the results in humble confident prayer to God, speaking as one friend to another.

St. Ignatius held that it was above all in gazing like this at the scene of Christ's life that the soul became established in the choice of a better life. The making of such a choice is a tremendous thing. Numbers of nice people go on tinkering with religion and enjoying religion for years without ever making that choice.

More and more, through seeing itself in silence over against that supreme example of Christ, the soul is compelled to face all the implications of those two all-embracing questions: "What am I for?" and "How am I doing that for which I was born?" This braces up its will to serve God and shows up its self-esteem and self-interest for the dismal little unrealities they are. It reveals the life of consecration for the noble privilege it is.

Now such a sort of mental prayer is the most searching and purifying of all religious exercises if we use it correctly. It forces the soul to face hard facts: to realize that the full grandeur of religion is not in the consolations it gives us but in all which it demands and evokes from us. Learn what it means to be asked: "Can you drink the cup I drink of?" And learn what it means to respond: "I will take the cup of salvation and call on the Name of the Lord." Whether we meditate on Christ's deeds, His prayers, or His passion, the first thing we realize is that there can be *no* limit to the indebtedness of those who choose God.

In making such meditation we are using history as a channel along which can flow the message and revelation which God has for our souls *now*. The love we find in that history, the life, the demand on human beings doesn't change. It is ceaseless, eternal. We enter the frame of a picture which is always there, and through the things shown us in the picture, receive the changeless light which suffuses it.

All of us know the eternal quality which we feel in great works of art. Yet it is a faint shadow of the eternal quality in God's great revelation to humanity. Never will there be a time when quiet, loving attention to the standards of the Gospel will fail to put us in line with God and establish the continuity between His Spirit and our souls, or give us the chance of fresh discovery of the supernatural treasure hidden in the field. It is an ever renewed opportunity of seeing the Way, of hearing the Truth, and of achieving Life.

What am I for? To glorify God—to praise, reverence, and serve Him.

How am I to do it? By a consecration of my whole life, not just in nice religious surroundings or by well-organized social work, but in the drudgery, the monotony, the rough and tumble of the common life. With the help of imperfect, self-interested, and narrow-minded persons—baffled by hostility and misunderstanding—I am to glorify God in and through all the demands on my love, courage, and patience, all the confusing disillusionments and sufferings that culminate in Gethsemane and the Cross. The saints have always seen in the incidents of Christ's life, the special revelation of the ways in which the soul may achieve God. They have found there, the deepest eternal truths given under historical conditions.

An old book called *The Meditations of St. Bonaventure* says, "When our Lord hung on the Cross He was not idle. He taught great perfection." Really the Cross is a culmination of a series of lessons which stretch from Bethlehem to Calvary. On the way souls are rescued, healed, and purified. This is the way God's work is done.

The Church lives through these lessons each year from Advent to Ascension, but each is so tremendous, each follows the other so quickly, that it is hard to have time to grasp the importance of each. From Whitsuntide to Advent, the Church meditates on these lessons and applies them. This is to be our method now. For a little time, we will be face to face with the central realities of religion. We are to take a look back and try to learn some of the lessons of the great perfection they have taught us.

As we gaze and begin to see that life in proportion, we begin also to get an inkling of what redemption means and the costs that a friend of Christ's, who desires to walk with Him and work for Him, must face. There is something wrong with a world which can only be put right at great cost. Like good material that has been given a wrong twist, a twist felt more in some parts than in others, it is felt especially in human souls. The Incarnation is the immense act of divine love which tries to put the twist right and does so in every soul that fully and willingly accepts the yoke of Christ. The life of consecration means taking, sharing, and offering oneself as a channel of that redeeming love. That is the supreme happiness of the Christian soul.

The saints did that. It is the real means of their labors, renunciations, sufferings, and joys. Everything was given by them to God's purpose. Everything that they were and had was made available for more than themselves. "I see," said Julian, "it is the will of Divine Love that we be on the Cross with Him to take our share in the redemption of the world." However, whether it is in prayer or action, it is not an easy vocation, but it is a glorious one. It takes all that we have. Only a constant recourse to headquarters makes it possible at all.

Days like these of our retreat should be such a resort to headquarters for nourishment and redirection. I think that the real implications of the loving saying: "Come unto me all you that labor and are heavy laden and I shall refresh you" are sometimes lost by us. The exquisite tenderness of the opening words obscures the bracing note on which they end. "I shall *refresh* is nearer the original meaning than "I shall give you *rest*." Christ is saying: "I shall freshen you up for another spell. I shall take away the tired feeling and the strain, but not the work or the weight. I shall give you my yoke to help you bear challenges more steadily and evenly so that they won't seem so crushing. I will feed you, give you the water of life, and make you more adequate to your job."

The words of Christ are not an invitation to holy slackness. They have nothing in common with the maudlin hymn, "Lean Hard!" If you answer Christ's invitation, the room into which you are introduced will not be a room in which to rest. It will be a well-equipped workshop in which we are shown the right use of our muscles and tools, a room where we work side by side with the One of whom it is said that "wherever He comes, he brings His tools with Him."

That refreshing offer of Christ to his laborers is different to each and is done in secret, according to each need. Some of us wish food and some a pause for breath. Some are disheartened and want renewed confidence. Some want a readjustment of the yoke according to the strength needed for a special job. Some want to wash the dust off. Some just want a glance of understanding and love. The invitation to all is just the same: "Come, look, learn. Take My yoke and do it My way." There is no other way to true inward peace.

Today we will try to renew our contact with the Spirit of Christ and in the power of the Spirit to face and answer the two crucial questions with which we began and to learn His difficult lessons. We will try to recapture some of the atmosphere of eternity and reenter the immortal scenes of the Gospel. There, face to face with that vision, we hope to realize the Gospel as putting before us the essence and method of the redemptive work which falls to everyone.

We are called to be the Children of God, yoke-fellows of Christ, and to take a share in the ceaseless burden, the pull, and the effort involved in reharmonizing human life to Him. We have come here to look again at that wonderful vocation, to try to see it in the light of eternity, and to learn what it involves for each of us.

Some will be fulfilled in prayer, some in action, and some in both. Some are called to redemptive suffering, some to an intellectual life, some to very practical and homely labor. It doesn't matter which as long as, in the words of Elizabeth Leseur, we sanctify it by giving it supernatural intent.

And her thought is echoed by William Law. "I know you in my heart!" he cried. "I long for nothing, desire nothing, but that all within me be changed into Thy Holy Spirit and Temper!"

Let us enter into this time of quiet with that same prayer. Let us desire to know the Supernatural more perfectly and fill with God the particular life He calls each of us to lead and the particular service each is able to give. May all within us be changed into His Spirit and temper. That is what we are for, and only by such a consecration can we perform our calling.

II

Courage

"Praise to the Holiest in the Height"
"Who Are These Like Stars Appearing?"
"For All the Saints"

A day like this is an opportunity, isn't it, of getting down to the fundamentals of the Christian life? And that is what we intend to do.

Since it is important not to drift in and out of a retreat, make a plan for the time ahead. Map out tomorrow and the next day into periods of prayer, reading, and meditation. Determine that each address will be followed by a half-hour of quiet assimilation of what God has shown us through the subject dealt with. The schedule which has been given you is only a skeleton timetable. Don't leave the intervening times to chance. On the other hand, you will want to avoid mechanics. It is important not to break off a fruitful time of prayer because it is time to do something else or spoil your spiritual reading by watching the clock. Leave time on the last day to consider and then to write down the fruits of your retreat.

Our purpose here is to become the sort of people God needs as members of the Body of Christ doing His work in the world. We will contemplate the love and Passion of Jesus and the saints in order that *we* may be changed and may more and more become fitting tools for His purpose. So we begin, praying for a spirit of endurance and of courage.

All Christians are called to grow and called to the spiritual life, each to the degree and in the way ordained of God. To fulfill His purposes, we need only the equipment He has given and the three graces on which we will try to meditate today, graces which Christ, in His life and passion, showed in their divine splendor: courage, generosity, and patience, all consisting in giving and enduring, but not in asking.

[Underhill used the following paragraphs in parentheses when giving the retreat to priests and professional religious workers.]

(This is especially important for you. You have offered yourselves for the most sacrificial, most exacting, most Christ-like of all lives—to be the agents of God in His work with the souls of others. It is no one particular talent, it is your whole person that will have to be used in that. The whole of you has got to be His channel and tool. He reaches out through human beings to do His redeeming, saving work on other human beings. You have given yourselves to Him utterly that He may reach out through you.

What qualities do you think you will need most if you are going to make a success of that tremendous vocation? What is most necessary if you are going to be active, disciplined, working pupils of one who saves and redeems by sacrifice, giving of Himself, and in *no* other way? You may or may not have a knowing sense of spiritual things which is called the grace of prayer, or a persuasive way of talking that instills a warm love for Christ. Surely these are great graces and helps, but we don't all have them.

But there are three graces that you *must* have, if you are to be any real use to God. It is these three things that we shall especially think of today. They are three qualities which we always find in all great saints and servants of God, however various they may be in other respects. They are graces which Christ exhibited in divine splendor. In the order in which we will deal with them they are: courage, generosity, and patience.

What does the Christian spiritual life mean? What is consecration? What is prayer? All of them are different aspects of one thing: the loving surrender of the soul to God for all His purposes, a total self-giving that welcomes pain and effort as a privilege shared with Christ. Christianity is a heroism. It wouldn't be worth having if it were not. Heroism requires the ingredients of the devoted life.

It is devotedness which is the main quality of a priest. It is that which makes the priest a channel for God. One's theological college doesn't so much matter. There is room in the Kingdom for a whole paint box of theological colors but not for one self-centered, self-indulgent priest! Isn't it clear that, for such a life, courage, generosity, and patience will be required above all other qualities?)

First let us speak of courage, pluck, real love of the hard to do, a willingness to take risks, to face difficult problems, to suffer, to persevere at whatever cost, to find initiative and zest for overcoming human reluctance, and to accept the austere side of our Christian profession, the fact that it makes absolute demands on us. Christ never minimized the difficulties of being His follower. "Many are called, but few are chosen." "Strive to enter in at the straight gate." "Take up your Cross." Christianity is not a consolation, but a job for people who are whole.

Then there is generosity: unmeasured willingness to give. It is a warm, delightful, instinctive self-spending for God and others. It is the uncalcu-

lated response to *all* that is asked. "Sell all and come and follow me." That
has got to be the disposition of the Christian heart.

Thirdly, there is patience, that self-oblivious tranquility to endure, to
hang on, and to wait. It is tenacious, quiet perseverence in hope, staying
power, "bearing all things." Those who try to work for God need so much
of that!

Now, just see how these three qualities come together and how strong,
steady, and self-giving is the person in whom they rule. "For *this* came I
into the world: to do the will of Him who sent me." That is the stated
purpose of Christ, His saints, and His followers. It points to an utterly
selfless vocation. It means courage, generosity, and patience if the job is to
be done. Of course it is quite easy to dodge such measures and to do good
up to the limit we think reasonable, but the Gospel never countenances
our ideas of reason or any of our half measures.

Christ put a perfectly clear issue before those who offered themselves to
Him, and He illustrated it using choices open to the people of Jerusalem.
He pled for them to stay upon the narrow, stony path that led up to Mt.
Zion rather than to use the broad road downhill that led to Gehenna
where all the refuse of Jerusalem was burned. He said in effect, "What
will you have, an uphill climb or the rubbish heap?" For Christians, there
is no third choice.

Total, glad, fearless acceptance of the steep path—this, not anything
peculiar, is what to follow Christ means, and that is the spiritual life. Your
work for God will succeed in exact proportion to your effort to live that
life.

Then, let us look today at total surrender and total release. Let us look
at involvement in the concept and fact that *only* through such surrender
shall God's redeeming power come into the world and transform lives. We
belong to an heroic religion. It was where the devoted suffered for Christ,
it was where the blood of the martyrs fell, that the Christian church was
founded.

It was founded by supernatural courage, and it still demonstrates
supernatural courage—grit—a true rocky foundation, not sand. Where
the life of Christ is found, there, first to last, is the exhibition of courage in
its calm repudiation of the abnormal, sensational use of power and easy
paths. Courage is steady and persistent in its unpopular choices, its
rejection of compromise, and its tranquil, determined movements towards
suffering and death. Its very essence is summed up in the journey to
Jerusalem which was the prelude to the Passion.

That is the first picture to look at in this meditation. We will look at the
picture given us in Mark 10:32 onward and Luke 14:25 to the end.

Looking intently at them, we will ask for what we want: more courage to face our Christian life and to carry through the job to which God has called us.

It is made clear to us in these passages that this was a deliberate journey for Christ. It is never more clear than when Luke says: "He made his face *rigid* to go to Jerusalem." That is the correct translation of the text. Doesn't it drive home His stern determination to see the job through at all costs? That will is the result of and the reaction to His supreme spiritual experience, for the Transfiguration was the supreme human experience of spiritual things. But Christ turned from that to face and to choose the danger, suffering, and death which He knew His mission involved. He deliberately went *not* to a more ecstatic communion with His Father but to the accomplishment of His Father's will. He went to the agony of Gethsemane and to the spiritual blackness of the Cross.

Has this nothing to teach us in the way of great perfection? In the way of what even our small spiritual experiences and apprehensions ought to do for us? I suggest that such peace and joy as we receive in prayer ought not to make us hang about asking for more like an unsatisfied child. They are given to show us what our privilege is and make us more brave, selfless, and devoted to redemptive work. We always come back to that point. Redemptive love, while it works on us through others, needs us to work on others again.

It may often be your job to sacrifice your own spiritual consolation, perhaps what seems to you your own spiritual advantage, for the good of those you are sent to serve. In doing that, if you do it the right way, you will be drawing near to your Model.

Those who ask for union with God and greater intimacy with God are shown the privilege of being used by God. Therefore, they should ask too for the courage to pay the price. The Gospel shows the kind of price likely to be asked in our imperfect human world: hard work, much misunderstanding, much self-givenness (with perhaps little apparent result), inestimable suffering, and loneliness.

Perhaps what strikes us most as we kneel in the corner of the picture and contemplate that journey to Jerusalem is the intense isolation of the central figure. His consciousness of tragic destiny is not really shared by those who think they love Him best. St. Mark tells us that He went on ahead, and they were amazed. They continued to press on Him their notions of prudence, their little interests and needs.

There is Peter, the fussy, affectionate friend who cannot look beyond safety. There are James and John who cannot forget their own positions and claims. But Christ has the immense self-oblivious detachment which enables Him even in those supreme and awful moments of His mission still to attend with love and patience to trivial things: to heal, to successfully meet each soul on its own ground.

When James and John break in with their self-interested questions, they are dealt with. When the blind man breaks in, he is called to and healed. When Zacchaeus is seen, he too is called although he is someone whom *we* might feel justified in ignoring because we wanted all our strength to face the supreme crisis in our life. Consider the depth of that self-forgetful courage which can thus calmly radiate love and heal and teach as it moves consciously to a terrible death.

Now move on a little and look at another part of the picture, the darkest part. Look at Gethsemane and consider that it has to teach us as to the foundations on which the triumphant life of Easter stands. Realize that every time we say the Lord's Prayer, we ask that God's will be done at *all* costs. Consider that every time we think we are united with the great aspirations of the Communion of Saints, we accept Gethsemane and the utmost demands made on those who offer themselves for the service of God.

The scene in Gethsemane is a clue to the life of consecration. The entire pure action of resignation, of self-giving to the uttermost, of holding nothing back, of conquering the shrinking horror which comes with the first true realization of the Cross: that, for you and me, is the condition of being accepted and used by God for His work. It is the condition of receiving something of that creative and saving power of the Christian life. Alone, facing whatever demands, humiliation, sacrifice, injustice, pain, and loss may be asked of us, we must accept *all* if we are to cooperate with God.

We lose our privileges, our preferences, and our reluctance in the great outline of God's mysterious design. It is because of that agony in which humanity's will was drowned in God's faithful, enduring will that we are here today, and all our brothers and sisters for two thousand years have shared the peace, joy, and power of Christ's redemption. All of us, everyone, is indebted to Gethsemane. All the saints, all "watchers and holy ones," in their joyous and exultant service, drew their life from that hour.

To accept that gift but to shirk from our chance of paying a little of the price (which is uncalculable surrender), is to accept what God gives without counting the cost. Of course we cannot become consecrated by our own wills. However hard we *will* to be His agents, it doesn't come off that way. It only comes by way of surrender of the whole human person to His purposes. And to be able to make that willing surrender, to say "Yes" to God, is the most solemn dynamic of Gethsemane.

It should mean for us the full, firsthand realization that true Christian life is not all beauty and calm. In one form or another, it will involve that awful question, "Can you drink the cup I drink of?" Perhaps it will only be offered us in very unimpressive ways—drop by drop out of a tin mug—the same terrible wine of the surrendered life.

"Many," says Thomas à Kempis, "follow Jesus to the breaking of the bread, but few to drinking the cup of the Passion." But the breaking of the bread goes on, its heavenly gifts being offered to us with free generosity. We forget sometimes that each time we go to commune, we really accept that cup too. A good communion does not merely give us strength, consolation, and peace. It is a mutual exchange. We give ourselves, and in return we receive the Bread of Life *and* the Cup of the Passion. One of these alone is only half the Christian secret.

Each time the cup is offered, a choice comes with it. We can take it with bitterness or with delight. The peculiar mark of the saints is that they always receive it with utmost delight. This is not morbid but real. We see evil in the world opposing perfect holiness, and we know that it can't be vanquished except in the Cross. And the Way of the Cross goes from the contemplative joys of the Transfiguration to the lonely trials of Gethsemane, and then on. It goes on to the ceaseless life of saving, unselfish love to which every Christian is called. It goes on to whatever work of incarnation is needed.

It means, among other things, the willingness to renounce spiritual enjoyments in order to take on ourselves some of the burden of the world's wrongness and put up in our own person with the results. All must suffer. The lesson of Christianity is what can be done with suffering when it is met with self-oblivious courage and faith. Our meditation here should help us to decide where, in our view of the universe, we put that awful fact and how we mean to meet it. Will it be as fellow workers with Christ or as spiritual parasites who shirk the pain and effort of existence and turn religion into a pious dream?

To choose Christ means to choose an heroic course. It means a willingness to suffer for the redemption of the world. You know the story of that wonderful parish priest, the Curé d'Ars, when asked how he effected his wonderful conversions? He replied, "By being very gentle to the sinners and very hard on myself."

Now to choose the heroic course is not so hard when one feels the support of a whole army. Everyone feels brave when singing "Onward Christian Soldiers." But the Gospel is *not* like that. It says that the darkest and most redeeming bits of the soul's life must be seen through alone. It asks some of the courage of the One whose friends did not back Him up in crisis. It asks the courage of the naked will, alone with the will of God. It asks the courage of the lonely soldier in an isolation corner who is yet part of a large army. It asks the courage of the wounded, lying apparently deserted, but still a part of that great army.

It is the courage, too, that gives itself to forlorn hope, that plods on and on with the hard and unpromising job, that has the pluck to go on serving, teaching, and helping other souls, even when its own inner life feels dead and dark (as it must do sometimes), all because we are God's tools and our feelings don't matter that much.

Above all, we have got to have courage with ourselves, with our dark, unattractive natures that oppose all we long to be and do. That means to shoulder the burden of our own psyche's disability—wrong impulses, reluctance, and fears—and to face the instinctive tendencies that seem too strong for us and war against our best minds. So we go on as we must, letting the wheat and the tares grow together to the end, saying within the conflict, "*Thou* understandest my thoughts afar off!" *We* don't understand. But we can go through life with confidence because God understands that obsessive, impulsive difficulty which we *don't* understand. For we know that even through them, He can guide and discipline us.

This is how the saints manifested their courage. Many of them were not at all nice to begin with. But they disregarded their own sense of incompleteness when called by Christ, and responded without hesitation. Paul, Augustine, Angela—what stormy, difficult characters! Yet they had the courage to ignore their natural insufficiencies, trust God, and cooperate with Him.

Likewise, if you and I are to be made by God into people fit for His purposes, it will depend largely on the courage with which we respond to Him. It won't be worked by His action alone. The Holy Spirit isn't like one of those patented cleansers that does our washing while we are asleep! It works through our brave and willing cooperation, our *active* acceptance and use of all the material we are offered, even everything that damages our vanity and opposes our self-will.

If we can't muster enough courage for *that,* how shall we ever go on to the real Christian level and gladly accept undeserved humiliation, pain, and sacrifice for the purifying and redeeming of the world? We have got to go on struggling with and paying the price of our persistent fits of weakness, unspiritual fastidiousness, and hard refusals of love. We have to find the courage to look the situation in the face and go on again after each humiliating fall. We have to find the courage to tackle a job we know needs a strong Christian, though not a shallow Christian, because we *can* do all that through Christ who strengthens us.

Our souls are not made over to God by one mechanical act of conversion, but by the long, unremitting, courageous effort that conversion begins. Bit by bit we are to relate every thought, act, and event to Him until at last He *is* all in all.

Thus far we have tried here to look at and learn a little of what Christian courage is and involves. We have asked ourselves what is meant by those *heroic* Christian virtues which alone successfully oppose sin. Now we come to the depressing part of the meditation when we turn to look at *ourselves* and compare ourselves with the pattern of Christ.

We often feel simply unable to exercise that vigorous and selfless courage of the saints! We look at it in its strength and beauty, but when it comes to the pinch, we can't bring it off. The problem is not in our training. What is it that stops us? Just one thing, isn't it? Self-regard. There is a fear of doing something—of creating a particular impression—of losing someone—of seeming pious, peculiar, or stuffy—of getting "let in for something" or of being hurt. There are doubts as to whether a particular sacrifice would amount to much good—doubts that we can keep up a new rule of life—doubts about the risk worth taking—about the price worth paying—about yielding to our human horror of the austere side of spiritual life—about feeling that Galilee, which is so beautiful and spiritual and makes no excessive demands will do very well for *us,* so why face the grim journey to Jerusalem which is uphill all the way?

Look at all this bit by bit in the light of the Passion and the triumph of Christ, those crowning facts of history. Look at the curve that includes the Upper Room, Gethsemane, Calvary, Easter, and the forty days of radiant self-imparting. How is that curve in line with your own soul's growth? Your idea of your own future? Your vocation? How much courage is mixed with your Christian joy?

Then let us come down to the small things that make up our lives and ask why the opportunity of doing something tiresome was ignored and the trying encounter shirked. Why do we let the feeling grow on us that such and such wasn't our job? Why do we set such high spiritual value on our *own* peace of mind? Why do we forget that God's purposes may sometimes require the sacrifice of that very thing? Why do we instinctively avoid certain situations and certain people? Why do we avoid what perfect love would do because there is no personal reward? Are we quite sure that the will of God is that these things get so conveniently left out of our lives?

We may not be called to heroic action, but we have got to be in training for heroic action; and the training is always offered in the raw material of daily life. A rule of life quite faithfully kept, however boring and inconvenient, is one of the best ways of acquiring *some* spiritual grit.

The final question for us is simple, but very searching. Are we accepting now, with courage and without reserve, everything that our daily life contains? Are we accepting it, never asking for respite, but always for strength?

III

Generosity

Our thoughts were rather on the private side this morning, and I suppose that most of us ended our meditation with our tails between our legs! It seemed as though the demands made were too strenuous for staggering Christians like ourselves who have only begun to wire ourselves up to a courage we are far from feeling! It seems that the problems of the spiritual life are problems of endurance and grit. When obligation and desire don't go together, the human creature always reacts in a poor way. The individual is committed to dealing with a conflict which, if not resolved, will tear him or her to pieces in the end.

We begin with a desire for spiritual comfort, but the central secret of religion is that it *transforms* our desires. From wanting our own well being, in one way or another, it makes us long only to serve and satisfy the will of God. When that transfiguration is effected, courage, grit, falls into place as a necessary condition of doing what we now long to do. It is sweetened, strengthened, and illuminated by the generous love which possesses the soul more and more, as the soul increasingly receives that generous light and warmth of God.

There is nothing harsh, rigorous, or intense about the invitation to generosity. It puts us in line with all the noble aspects of creation: the generous output of sunshine, the uncalculated fertility of the earth, and the great life-giving mantle of air. All these undemanded gifts condition our whole existence and say to us: "Freely you have received; freely give." Creation asks us to join this indiscriminating liberality, to be perfect as the Father is perfect. It puts us in line with one who just did what she could, not what profited her own soul: the woman who gave her last mite—and the woman who broke perfume over Christ's head, washed His feet with her tears, and wiped them with her hair. We are reminded that the attitude of clutching, however spiritual, is never Christian, and that the attitude of giving is always religious because it is an imitation of God.

Generous love is the only kind God wants in us as His servants. It is the only kind that is like His. There are many different feelings, even different religious feelings, lumped together under the word "love." There's the feverish love of the devotee, both real and disguised emotions of egotism, always wanting to enjoy the presence of the Beloved. There is claimful love, always demanding responses. There is narrow love that can't care for or be interested in anything but the one person it loves, and it resents all duties or anything else that comes between. Those sorts won't expand and embrace other souls, make one useful to God, turn anyone into a co-worker with God, or give courage for the dark and lonely bits of the path of life!

There is only one kind that does that, and that is the love that offers itself and all it has in one great spendthrift self-oblivious act of generosity. It even offers the joy of communion with the Beloved. It utterly forgets its own claim and own interests and rights, just giving itself in self-abandoned joy.

It is the love that pours out its precious ointment, then breaks the vase, and gives that too. It is the love that throws in the second mite after the first, that can't rest until it has given all. It is the love that ignores and sets aside personal achievement and appreciation and accepts neglect and even apparent failure with tranquil joy. That is the sort of love that sweetens work, redeems drudgery, and cures discouragement.

It is hardly necessary to talk about courage to a soul like that. "If Thou wilt that I be in the light, blessed be Thou! And if Thou wilt that I be in the dark, blessed be Thou!" That is the very spirit of the saints. That is the sort of love Gertrude More meant when she spoke of a courageous and constant love, not worn out with labors nor daunted with difficulties.*

That unlimited generosity is a fundamental characteristic of God. It is what we mean by grace, His ceaseless, loving self-giving to each of us. That love is the generous, divine sunshine upon which we live. Without that free self-imparting God, that golden shower, you and I and every one are just more or less bright little animals knowing nothing about Him at all. But God loves and gives, and the terms on which we receive are that we should give again, heedless of self-interest and personal consideration.

Generosity is the character above all others which He asks from us. So it has been summed up in its fullest expression and shown to us in the model of Christ. The Gospel begins with "God so loved the world that He *gave,* and it closes on the wonderful note: "Having loved His own, He loved them to the end." It is the story of a ceaseless, unlimited giving that still goes on. And if the call of God to our souls is that we should be remade in His likeness, then it is a call to such a growth in generosity as shall make us able to cooperate with that self-giving act of Christ.

*See prayer on p. 59.

Therefore the subject of our meditation shall be that generosity which God shows us and asks from us. And the first picture we will look at is the picture of the Good Shepherd. We follow St. Ignatius in asking first for what we want: more generous love—for we *can't* have enough. Then we'll take our place again inside the frame of the picture and *look*.

We see the good–beautiful–noble Shepherd. The Greek word carries all those meanings. It is a word which suggests absolute perfection. And next, what is the outstanding characteristic? "The Good Shepherd *gives* His life for the sheep." No one could suppose that the sheep were as valuable as the Shepherd! In ordinary existence, we should call it a terrible waste of a life. But these things are not done on commercial lines, lines of worthwhileness in the supernatural world. Uncalculated, unfailing, generous, self-spending devotion: that is the mark of the Good Shepherd and of *all* who work for God on other souls.

The Good Shepherd not only dies for the sheep; He also lives for them. Imagine that—just for the sheep! He doesn't live to develop His personality, to cultivate His own soul. He gives all His life, with all its varied opportunities and interests, for the sheep. Compare the life of a devoted shepherd in all times and all weathers, tending his flock with all the varied interests and opportunities offered by existence, and see the measure of renunciation hidden in the phrase to which we have given our attention.

Willing, self-oblivious, generous sacrifice for the apparently unworthy is raw material for supernatural transfiguration. This is the mark of real leadership and yet more of real redemptive, willing, loving, sacrifice of infinite worth for the apparently worthless. It seems so wasteful to common sense, but it is the normal method of the saints. There you touch the supernatural. There the human creature really transcends the self and partakes of the nature of Christ. "If any would be first, let him be the servant of all." "I am among you as one who serves." That is the conviction to carry with us when we have to tackle a tiresome or unrewarding job.

Now let us pass on from the great ideal picture of the Good Shepherd and see that generous, compassionate, self-giving love in action in the history of the Passion. Then I think we shall see what St. Ignatius meant when he said that the contemplation of the Passion always gave the soul an inclination to the most perfect things.

Look at the royal generosity with which Christ, faced with a tragic destiny and a horror of suffering and loneliness which are to test His endurance to the ultimate, spends his last hours in deeds of self-giving of a simple kind. He takes a towel and basin of water and kneels humbly to wash the dusty feet of the very men who are going to forsake Him. Then

He takes bread and wine and imparts them to that same weak and faulty collection of men, giving His very life.

"The Good Shepherd gives His life for the sheep." I suppose that those two scenes alone, if we lost the rest of the Gospel, would give us the saving essentials of the Incarnation.

And in the pictures of the hours to come, we see the generosity that keeps compassion burning brightly, not only among the countless claims and demands made upon it, but within the most awful hours of anguish and desolation. We may be sure it was a glance of loving pity that finished Peter and made him go out and weep bitterly. It was generous, selfless compassion that spoke to the daughters of Jerusalem and that won the thief on the cross. In Christ, the horror and hatred of sin which is felt by the Holy, melts into generous pity, and nothing is so supernatural, so destructive of evil as that.

Look at the thief on the cross. There is nothing very splendid or interesting about him. He is an ordinary criminal who got caught, the sort of person who passes through a barrier erected in constructing a street. But the saving energy of Christianity is not directed to interesting sinners but to ordinary sheep. There is no picking and choosing there. The poor publican and the prostitute woman found in adultery were both the sort we see daily in the papers, pitiful exhibitions of human weakness.

Yet on these, the generous compassion of redemptive love shines in its full transfiguring energy. The woman's sins are forgiven. Words are spoken like: "Go, and sin no more." "Today you will be with me in Paradise." Even on the Cross, Christs points beyond mere retribution to a freely, gladly given joy. It is like the laborers in the vineyard who had been taught the same lesson: there are no calculations such as people deserve. We too are called, if we would be perfect, to take this view of human shabbiness and sin.

Generosity means that longing to bring joy, peace, and salvation, not to the loveable but to the unloveable and at one's own cost. It is to bring all this to the people whose views and beliefs we dislike or whose conduct we disapprove. It is to bring it to those who are tiresome, embittered, selfish, degraded, and whose whole being seems twisted out of shape. It means to desire the happiness of people who don't desire it. And it means longing to rescue *these* at our own cost.

Nothing else but such generous love will help them or release them: no justice, no good advice, no teaching or reforming. Nothing but indulgent, uncritical sacrificial love, giving your life in some form, in spite of suffering and renunciation, for the unworthy. To know that is the secret of Christianity, and to *do* it is the secret of sanctity.

Generous love serves and suffers for those from whom it can never hope to receive love, gratitude, or even justice. And in doing that, it shows itself to be the Child of God and enters into the joy and mystery of Christ.

There is a wonderful prayer in Lancelot Andrewes' Morning Office: "Look on me with those eyes of Thine with which Thou didst once look on the Magdalen at the feast, at Peter in the court, and at the thief on the cross."

What was that look? It had to have been a generous, uncritical, and compassionate look. That then is the standard. And how does it tally with our own practice? When we come up against Magdalen, not as an object for philanthropy, not as someone we find in a rescue home,* but as one in our own set, do we meet her half way or not? Which pulls the hardest: generosity or respect?

Then there is Peter. How is our standard of generosity strained when our apparently most devoted friend or co-worker leaves us in the hour of need to save the situation for him or herself?

And there is the thief. What do we do when, in the moment of acute physical and mental anguish that taxes *all* our endurance, an unloving and importunate stranger intrudes on us, begging help?

Have we the self-oblivion that can love to the very end and be generous with compassion in such cases as these? If not, we still fall short of the standard required of the members of the Body of Christ. Ruysbroeck said that "a wide-spreading love to all in common" was the mark of a soul in full union with God, and that is a very costly kind of love to give.

Amiability will not accomplish this. The task needs courage and faith, for it means giving all you have, every scrap, not only what is needed, but the bit you need *not* have given. It means a self-dedication which gladly accepts all the pain and tension a redemptive life must involve. Though you try to rescue or to reform or to serve with kindness, it means the difference between the uncalculable generosity of the Shepherd who gives His whole life versus those prudent measures of self-donation which are careful and safeguarded from serious risk.

Why do we go to Communion unless it is to unite ourselves with the self-giving action of Christ and join ourselves to the Mystical Body through which the love of God acts on human life? We don't go for some private comfort and advantage. That is not Christian. The Gospel contains not one instance in which Christ sought or had a privileged spiritual advantage. We go to Communion to offer ourselves in one generous, unconditional sacrifice to God and to be made a little more fit to mediate His unlimited, generous love to others.

* "Rescue homes" were homes for unwed mothers and unfortunate women who had lost moral reputation.

Now we come to the painful application of these thoughts. How do we stand in respect to the active generosity which God asks of *us*? Are we entirely willing, quick, eager to do or to renounce, to welcome or endure *whatever* God brings out of this retreat for each of us? Certainly there will be something for each, big or little, in relation to Him or to others. Do we set any secret limits to the invasion of His grace? Are we so simple and fully given to God's purposes and service that we are truly indifferent to the means by which He calls us to fulfill our vocation, whether in wealth or poverty, success or drudgery, nice work or nasty, health or weakness, honor or contempt?

The generous soul refuses *nothing* asked by God. It never says, "I couldn't be expected to do *that* or put up with *this*. That is excessive. This is hardly wise." It never deliberately stops short of perfect and says: "Enough!" Its decision is not based on "What ought I to give?" but on "What *can* I give?" It brings us once again face to face with the searching three questions of Ignatius that we have considered in another retreat: "What have I done for Christ? What *am* I doing? What *can* I do?"

IV

Patience

We come to the third of the three great qualities which we have set ourselves to learn from Christ. Patience is the fundamental disposition of the brave and generous soul, yet it is often more difficult for the soul to put in place and keep that quality than to deal with the more active expressions of its love.

Patience is like the steady, even tension of the warp on which the fabric of the spiritual life is woven, the long continuous threads which don't appear on the surface but give it strength and unity and carry equally the light and the dark bits of the pattern, the vivid, significant patches and the long spaces that seem to have no meaning at all until we see the whole design. Without that warp of patience, the woof with its joys and mortifications would have no coherence at all. And when the cloth was finished, it would be shoddy. Very little wear and tear would pull it to bits.

Patience is that aspect of our love that bears evenly all that is uneven. Until it is established, we don't really love. When it is established we not only bear things but accept them with unruffled interior tranquility, for patience "bears the burden without the burden," says à Kempis, "and makes every bitter thing sweet and savory."

When we realize that all forms of *impatience*—anger, resentment, resistance to circumstances, fuss—are ultimately born of self-love and that an impatient person can't put God first, then we see that patience really is the primary virtue.

Its simile is acceptance, and that means the death of self and therefore the death of strain. Strain, which makes half the misery of life, need never happen. Strain is always our own fault. It is always a failure to accept, a stiffening of ourselves against events instead of a supple acceptance of them.

Consider again the warp on the loom. If its tension is right, it accepts without strain all the threads that make the pattern, and an even fabric results. If it is tight and rigid and resistant, the shuttles can't pass easily and the weaving becomes difficult and full of strain.

"Patience," says Ruysbroeck, "is the peaceful, indifferent endurance, for the sake of God, of *all* that can happen." Nothing does so much to deepen and steady the soul's life. Many characteristics have been put forward as the "secret of sanctity," but of course there is no one sort of sanctity, as there is no one type of saint. The secret of sanctity is just perfect, loving, humble correspondence with God wherever you are in whatever He asks you to do.

On the whole, I think the characteristic which impresses me most in the saints I have had the privilege to meet, has been the quiet, genial, unassuming spirit of acceptance in the ups and downs and the suffering of life. In them, there is a complete absence of agitation about our souls or anything else. Like St. Paul, often in conflict within the Christian circle—ill, weary, and over-driven with impossible demands made on them—they are called to bitter and secret conflicts with evil. But underneath, patience is ever there. They are free, fellow workers of One who took the role of Suffering Servant, One who was dumb before His persecutors and acquiescent in spite of mocking and insults, One who was patient under the gradual unfolding of the Father's mysterious will.

When we approach the scene of Calvary, we see how the reasoning, knowing, active side of human nature drops away and there remains an infinite patience and surrender, even in the most terrible confusion and bewilderment, in physical exhaustion, mental desolation, failure, and death. Such patience lies very near the heart of sacrifice.

The lessons of patience are taught not only by the Passion, but by the whole life of Christ. There are so many that they will be different for each soul. As we watch each scene pass before us, we can only respond with the words of St. Ignatius to those who contemplate them: "Look! Gaze! Admire!" So look, you who are His assistants, at the perpetual patience required of One whose whole ministry was among those incapable of comprehending His secret, people who seldom rose above the desire to get healing and comfort for themselves—the crowds sick for sensation, perpetually breaking in on His peace—the foolish questions and cowardice of the disciples. Look at that and then look at our self-important dislike of interruption and our silly or unnecessary demands on our valuable time. Look at His silent endurance of calumny, and feel perhaps just a bit uncomfortable at the memory of our own flow of words in self-explanation and excuse.

Look! Compare what you would risk by patient silence and what Christ endured in silence. Remember how much ignoble fear and lack of generosity contribute to our impatient response to life. How often some of us are afraid that people may think *we* did this or that or planned this or the other. How we dread and resent derision and wither up under critical or sarcastic words! All that looks very cheap in the light of the self-oblivious patience of Christ, that patience, infinitely noble and worthy, which quietly endured the lot of the worthless.

Well, we begin to be ready to accept this idea of patience as the earnest and token of self-oblivion, as the strengthening thread that runs through the supernatural life. And if this is so, we are asking for it in three ways and give it in three ways: in patience toward God, patience toward others, and patience toward ourselves.

Patience toward God is the quiet acceptance of life bit by bit from His hand. It is just letting His molding action work on the soul, whether we see the point of what happens or not. It means patience when He leaves us in the darkness. It is never trying to hurry His pace, never being restive under His hand. You remember that we said that when Christ comes into the soul, He comes as a workman and brings His tools with Him. *He* does chip and shape. *We* impede His action least if we stay quiet, bearing both the sharp blows and persistent sandpaper by which so much of His work on the soul is done, and never seek to anticipate results. When we think how patient God is toward us, it doesn't seem much to ask that we, His tiny creatures, should be patient toward Him and His methods.

We perceive that we will not be perfect servants without patience. But how are we going to increase it in ourselves? What is the raw material? On what is it nourished? Just on the ups and downs of life, on the imperfections of ourselves and others. How do we take these? Look 'round. Do we never appeal for sympathy? Do we never complain to God? Are we hiding pain? Do we simply and generously forget what goes wrong? If we can learn the grateful joy with which the saints took all their trials, we will recognize in them the privilege of suffering with Christ and complete surrender to God.

It has been said that there are three great marks of the soul's love for God. I will list them here. They all require patience.

1. Our entire confidence depends on God. We do not rely on our own endeavors for the spirit to pray, but cast all our care on Him. This is the life of faith.

2. To have hearts not only obedient to His will, but to delight in it as our necessary rule.

3. To practice a joyous resignation to His will in every suffering that comes to us. These testify to our love because they utterly exclude self-interest, whereas the *feeling* of fervor may be disguised self-indulgence.

Patience toward others is bearing even all that is uneven in character, prejudice, and habits. It is "letting the stirrer stir," as à Kempis puts it. It is meeting with equal countenance the nasty and sunny sides of the human person, and the stupid and bitter sides too. It is that same attitude toward people who spoil our work and let us down in the things we most prize. It is equinimity toward the people who offend our taste and rouse our latent fastidiousness, that most unchristian quality which is born of conceit and self and is the death of generous love. It is the same response toward the people who delay and worry us, the people who always ask for a cup of cold water at the wrong time, the stupid, the quarrulous, the obstinate, and the prejudiced. Each of us can fill up more blanks for ourselves!

Perhaps what helps us most here is the remembrance that God comes to us and tests us in and through all these people whom He puts in our way. He dwells within their souls too, and we are being impatient with His dwelling place when we get exasperated with them. All are appointed means whereby we improve our love and service and purify our souls of self-will.

The third type of patience is patience with ourselves. That is perhaps the most important and the least understood. We all realize that we must try to be patient under the action of God's will, in suffering and in bereavement, in trial and in darkness. We know we need to be patient in daily encounters, and we are quite aware that our duty, even if we can't manage it, is to preserve evenness of mind with the unreasonable and the exasperating.

But what about patience with ourselves and our endless tumbles and weaknesses and fallings short—all those things which disgust and humiliate us and for that reason, if we take them patiently, can so effectively purify us from the last crumbs of self-esteem? Considering what we are, so disappointing and feeble, unless we are patient with ourselves, how can we hope to preserve our inward calm? And if we lose that, we lose the presence of that Holy Spirit who is tranquility and peace. With this greater loss, we lose all our chances of usefulness to God.

When Peter's wife's mother lay sick with a fever, Christ came and laid His hands on her and the fever left her. *Then* she rose and ministered to them. We can't do God's work until the fever of impatience has left us. When we have a temper, we fuss; we do not serve. And the germ produced by that fever is disguised self-love. Impatience with ourselves means that that special streptococcie is getting active. However, there is an antitoxin. It is called humiliation. Full humiliation is inseparable from patience. If we are really humble, it doesn't occur to us to mind what happens; we have lost the silly illusions about our own importance and rights.

Let us not go away with the idea that exasperated impatience with our faults and hasty and violent efforts to cure them are penitence. They are nothing of the kind. Real penitence rises from each fall calmly and with courage and goes on again. Because it didn't expect much of itself, it bears evenly its own uneven performance and is content to persevere and leave the outcome to God.

I often think that the spiritual life is very much like gardening, and most of the worst mistakes we make in it, after we have seriously given ourselves to it, are just those mistakes an inexperienced gardener makes. The idea that a good vigorous campaign with a pitch fork is the best way of extirpating tiresome weeds from an herbacious border is the one we most have to unlearn. We plunge in, toss the ground violently in every direction, pluck out the weeds, make a big pile, and retire in a state of moist satisfaction saying we've done a very good morning's work.

But have we? We've disturbed the roots of the best perennials. We've knocked off some shoots. We've grubbed up loads of little modest seedlings springing up in odd corners. And in our hurry, we have broken weeds and left the bottom half of their stems in the ground to start a vigorous life again.

An expert doesn't do it like that. That kind of a gardener drops to the knees with a hand fork and works, bit by bit, being very careful not to disturb the growth of the soul in which God has sown His seeds, where the roots of good and bad quality are planted together. That patient, quiet work is the foundation of a good garden: gently keeping the ground in order, picking off slugs and snails, and tending the plants that will grow. Good gardening is not feverishly sticking in geraniums to get a transient show of bloom.

After all, it is God, not you, who settles what sort of garden it is to be. Your job is strictly confined to making it as good as it can be of its sort. You may want the predominate character to be contemplative and devotional. You would like your soul to grow fragile and beautiful flowers. But perhaps He doesn't want a contemplative just there. It may suit Him better to plant you in potatoes. That is less interesting of course, but just as essential to His plan.

Patience involves a cheerful acceptance of that and settles down to see that the potatoes are as good as you can get them to be. That, not the self-chosen growing of prize chrysanthemums, is the spirit of a good and faithful servant who will be able at the end to repeat the words of the Master: "I have finished the work You gave me to do, not the work I decided to do for You. I do not have the startling achievement my admiring followers expected. But I have worked hard in Your sercret purposes which I have taken bit by bit from your hand. The work has been done in the wet and the cold and the fog, in weakness and exhaustion, steadily, *patiently,* and solely for you. And it has had a mysterious efficacy quite out of proportion to its apparent success."

The Cross, the death of self, enters deeply into such a career. I often think that it will not be the successful and impressive religious person, but the quiet, insignificant workers and sufferers, the obscure, the drudges, and the failures who will be able to say at the end with Christ, "It is finished! It is complete!"

It is those who, by simple faith and patient correspondence with God's requirements given bit by bit, whose quiet homely heroism is so easily ignored and yet so difficult, those who will be able to say: "I, in my tiny way, have glorified You on earth. I have finished the work You gave me to do."

V

Adoration

We have been meditating on three of the qualities most needed by those who desire to lead a creative spiritual life, serving God in the world. They are qualities taught to us by the life of Christ. We have stood and looked back, as we can imagine the Disciples did after the Ascension, trying to remember and to find the full meaning of every incident and saying from those days with Jesus. We have stood with them, gazing at the wonder of those few months which changed them from ordinary, self-interested people into tools and apostles of Christ.

That looking back was, for the early Christians, the seed of the Christian life, and today it is still that seed in our lives. The wonderful and touching exhibition of perfect love in human form is now complete. The end of the golden strand is put into our hands. We turn, looking forward to the future, to going on with the Christian life, and the first thing to consider is what the essence of that life is.

The essence of it is prayer, the relationship between God and the soul. It is a life lived to, for, in, and with God, a life of which every event and opportunity and suffering is seen in relation to God. So as we gather now, we think of the life of prayer which continues in and with Christ and His work on earth and which must be the very heart of life for those who are trying to work for Him.

I am not going to speak of petition, intercession, or penitential prayer, but of those deeper, more central aspects of prayer out of which all these arise.

You know that the saintly M. Olier said that the whole of the life of prayer is contained in three things: adoration, communion, and cooperation—Christ before our eyes, Christ within our hearts, and Christ in our hands. They are three kinds of giving of the soul to God in response to His purposes.

First, there is our humble admiration, our creaturely adoration of His wonder and perfection. It is the first part as well as the very heart of prayer and the essential attitude of the soul looking up to God. Next, there is the

174

loving personal communion with Him found here and now in the soul's secret life. This is the very source of the soul's joy and power. It was these two aspects which St. Augustine realized so clearly when he said, "Thou art more inward than my most inward part and higher than my highest." These aspects are the two roots of the tree of prayer.

Last, there is active self-giving to Him for the redemptive, creative work which he does through the spirit that really prays. This is cooperation, working with God, with Christ, to bring fruit from the tree of prayer.

What a wonderful life this is! And yet it is the life to which every Christian is called.

Because of its cardinal importance and because I don't think we can emphasize it too much, we will dwell now on adoration as, in the widest sense, the supreme duty and delight of the soul.

Adoration is the prayer in which we turn toward the Supernatural—to God Himself, *for* Himself, and for none of His gifts. We bathe our souls in Him, for as St. Augustine said so well: "In His will we find our peace." It is the prayer in which, supremely, we obey the first and great commandment to love the Lord with *all* of the heart, soul, and mind—with all our thought and strength—with ALL, *all,* every bit.

And the second commandment will only be really *well* done where the first has the central place. Lucie-Christine dated the beginning of her spiritual life from the moment when she saw with the eyes of her mind the words, "God only!" These words were to her a light and an attraction and a power. They illuminated and cleared up life for her. They drew her heart to God. They gave her a generous resolve to work for God and the power to do it.

Do these words, "God only," mean anything like that in our lives? Do they give us light and courage and love? If not, the fault *is* with our prayers. We haven't put first things first. We can't hope to get our inner lives in proportion if we leave out adoration. In adoring prayer we are allowed to catch a glimpse of the vast ranges of life, of the beauty and holiness that lie beyond our world. What a privilege, isn't it? Adoration is the very heart of the life of prayer. The "Te Deum" and the "Sanctus" are classic acts of the Christian soul. And they are far more profound expressions of humility than any prayer of contrition can ever be, because in them the self is *entirely* left out.

Prayer is a supernatural activity. It is our conversation with God, the movement out of our little souls toward God. And through its effective overflow into the natural, if we would practice it in spirit and in truth, it must be directed to its supernatural end. It must begin, end, and be enclosed in the atmosphere of self-oblivious worship, pointed towards God in and for Himself.

You know, William Law's beautiful direction of intent: that "all within me be changed into [God's] Holy Spirit and temper." But unless we utterly forget ourselves in looking at, loving, contemplating, and adoring God, not because we want something, not because it does us good, but in Him and for Him alone, it is not very likely that prayer will be given effectiveness. Fussy, anxious, exclusive, practical, this-world prayer does nothing to remodel and enrich Christian character, for it omits the essential first stage. It doesn't carry us toward Him. That exclusive, awed, adoring attention, that realization of His majesty and beauty, must be the first point in this wonderful encounter of our tiny spirits with God.

On such attention depends all our power of receiving anything from Him, and we *must* receive before we can transmit to others. Without that, the prayer of contrition and penitence is impossible, for this arises from the vivid sense of contrast between that Only Perfection and our imperfect, sinful selves. This is why the greatest saints have also been the greatest penitents. It is out of that adoring gaze of the little sinful creature that the entrancing beauty and pathos of Christian prayer is born.

Christian prayer first sets God and soul over against each other—the Infinite Love and finite creature—and then brings them together in closest communion. "Higher than my highest *and* more inward than my most inward." Only those two complementary developments of the life of prayer will make us effective servants of God, of Christ—and we exist for nothing else! The only way to work effectively for God is to do it as an act of adoration to God, however humble it may be, and find the strength for it in prayer.

So you see our Christian effectiveness is directly linked with this adoring attention. God's Spirit is always with us. In adoring prayer, we open our doors wide to receive it, abase ourselves, and acknowledge our nothingness and His wonder, perfection, and joy. The soul which has thus given itself to God becomes part of the Mystical Body through which He acts on life. We are destined to be receivers and transmitters of His grace. But we are often in such a hurry to transmit that we forget the primary need to receive. Receiving means to keep ourselves carefully tuned in, sensitive to the music of eternity.

We can never adore enough, for God's self-imparting through us will be in proportion to our spirit of surrendering adoration. If we want to love and adore more, we must look at Him more. "Angels feed on Thee fully," says the old prayer. Why? Because they are ever beholding His face. "Let the pilgrim . . . feed on Thee according to his measure." How? It is only possible in the same way, by the absorbed gaze of selfless love, by dwelling on His holiness, richness, and generosity over against our tiny souls and the mercy that comes into those tiny souls and uses them.

There are many trains of thought which can help us here and bring us into the mood of adoration. The psalmist cried: "Thy gentleness has made me great!" Let us think of the saints made great by that gentleness, saints who become our companions when we practice adoration. Let us look at that pure joy in God which irradiates all their suffering and labors. Let us think of the whole universe full of His wonder and created for His glory: "Oh, all ye works of the Lord, praise ye the Lord!"

Don't ask for things, don't give superfluous information about your failings and needs. "Your heavenly Father knows what you need." Praise and magnify Him *forever*. These concrete gifts to us of the spiritual world—what the Bible calls the loving kindness of God—will become more real and active to us as we dwell on them. Our spiritual lives are so flat and colorless because we don't know what to look for; we ignore its most priceless gifts. Then let us think of the loving perfection and humility of Christ—God with us, self-given in His beauty, coming to us in communion and in prayer.

These thoughts will color our meditation in which we prepare for adoration and will nourish our worship, love, sense of awe, and of littleness and dependency. Thus, perpetually turning to and adoring Him, losing ourselves in wonder at Him, our souls will slowly be flooded by His spirit. And only when our souls are thus filled to the brim can we presume to offer our spiritual gifts to others.

The remedy for spiritual exhaustion which religious workers know so well is an inner life governed not by petition, but by adoring prayer. This was Christ's message and attitude, the very heart of his own prayer and doctrine: the present love and glory of the Father is everywhere. The glory that was before the world began is *there*, awaiting our delighted recognition. When you have *this*, then you may ask, seek, and knock and all these things shall be added to you.

All that Christ said about petition must be thought of as drenched in this atmosphere of adoring love. When we find demands made on us that threaten our inward poise, when we feel the signs of anxiety, starvation, and stress, it is time to call a halt and redress the balance. Then it is time to think more of the joy and wonder of religion and less of its obligations. It is time to think more of God and less of ourselves. It is time to gaze outward, to remember He is all that matters. Then it is time to go to a lonely hilltop and gaze at the sky full of stars, so that we can come back reharmonized and ready for the tiresome but determined care of the sheep. We need to reestablish the absolutely fundamental relationship of our souls to the Eternal Reality, the home and Father of our spirits. It is really true: "Our hearts shall have no rest save in Thee."

Moreover, it is only when our hearts *are* thus at rest in God, in peaceful, selfless adoration, that we can show His attractiveness to others. In the flood tide of such adoring prayer, the soul is carried up to God and hidden in God. Thus alone can it achieve that utter self-forgetfulness which is the basis of its peace and power and which can never be ours so long as we make our prayer mainly a means of drawing gifts from God instead of an act of utter self-giving *to* Him.

It is from this adoring prayer, this steady, non-utilitarian concentration on God and joyous self-immolation before Him that all the other prayerful dispositions of our souls spring. A deep, humble contrite sense of our own unworthiness, gratitude for all that is given us, and a burning, increasing charity that longs to spend itself on other souls: all these are the signs of spiritual vitality. And spiritual vitality depends on *feeding* our souls on God. Without that, we can't expect to be strong enough to work for Him.

The full Christian life of prayer swings to and fro between adoration and action. Be sure your outward swing to God is full, generous, unhurried, full of awe and joy. We go back from this time of quiet and peace to exacting lives of service full of hard material problems, difficulties, rush, and strain. If we take back the determination that *nothing* shall turn us from a steady, daily habit of adoring prayer, we return with the best of all helps for maintaining the soul's energy and peace. If we train ourselves to think glorious thoughts of God, not worrisome or doubtful thoughts, we shall learn to serve Him with a quiet mind.

Now the adoring prayer may take many forms. The point is that we must find the form that suits *us, our* souls—yours, not someone else's, and *now* at *this* stage of its growth. Then we need to feed and enrich this prayer, this primary sense of God, by reading and meditation.

Spiritual reading is a *regular,* essential part of the life of prayer, and particularly is it the support of adoring prayer. It is important to increase our sense of God's richness and wonder by reading what His great lovers have said about Him. Left to ourselves, our thoughts of Him soon get formal and poverty stricken. We cease to make progress. We settle down into a devotion which is no longer life-giving. The great masters of adoration remind us that it is the loveliest and most loving, but the least conventional, of all religious attitudes. It is full of life, vividness, and variety. It is the spontaneous reaction of the creature to a beauty and splendor beyond our span.

St. Augustine's *Confessions* are full of this sense of adoration. We can hardly learn it better than from him. In fact, the New Testament, à Kempis, and Augustine's *Confessions* make a complete devotional library which the longest life won't exhaust. Think of some of Augustine's great snatches of adoration: "O God my joy, my glory, and my confidence!" "O Beauty so old and so new! Too late have I loved Thee!"

"Highest, best, most mighty—most far and yet most near—fairest and yet strongest—fixed, yet incomprehensible—unchanging, yet the author of all change—never new, never old!" "What can I say, my God, my life, my holy Joy? Or what can anyone say when he speaks of Thee?"

Don't words like that open up the soul's horizons and make us feel that any self-interested, this-world religion, is a very petty, thin sort of thing?

And the same adoring devotion is taught some of us by looking at Christ, meditating on His words and acts, coming close to His Spirit and losing ourselves in loving wonder of Him as others learn by contemplating the spaceless presence of God. We can't all be drawn the same way or practice equal devotion of all types. Christian adoration is rich music. It has many different notes in it. It is enough if we practice simply and faithfully the sort to which we are drawn and never criticize or discredit what others do.

We might well make a far greater effort not to keep such adoring prayer only for set times of prayer, but to weave this added attention into our whole everyday lives so that they are colored with it. We can use little phrases of adoring love, fragments such as the Psalms are full of: "God, Thou are my God!" "Whom have I in heaven but Thee?" "Bless the Lord, O my soul, and all that is within me, bless His holy name!" Phrases such as these, learned, and remembered often, help our mind to keep pointed in the right way. They lift up our hearts above the murky atmosphere we have created to what à Kempis calls "everlasting clearness." And we can remember the perfect prayer of adoration from the lips of St. Francis: "My God and all! What art Thou? And what am I?" It is the humble cry of the awed and delighted creature gazing at its Creator and Lord.

Don't all painful and tiresome details fall away and vanish as we dwell on such words? Many have no time for long prayers, but all should make the effort to set apart some regular period for this adoring attention to God, and *all* without exception can form the habit of making short acts of love and adoration at odd moments.

We know the stream of thought in our minds never stops. In moments of leisure, something will surge into our consciousness, generally a worry, but we *can* so educate ourselves that what surges up will be a loving thought of God and His eternal love, joy, and peace. There are no better thoughts than some of these to restore us to the wonder and mystery and sense of His presence in our lives. And this education and habit will produce the state of mind in which we can best use our long periods of prayer and best maintain the deep serenity of a child of God through the perpetual strain and pressure of practical life.

You may think I have insisted on all this unduly. It is because I feel that in current religious life there is a great neglect of the human duty and joy of selfless adoration. This deficiency is responsible for much lack of spiritual depth and power. *Adoration is the central service asked by God of human souls.* It transfigures work and suffering. It purifies from sin. The moment we turn to adore, we cease to be alone. We share the very life of the angels and take our place in the Communion of Saints.

VI

Communion

In our last session we thought about the first part of the life of prayer, adoration. Now we come to its second part, to communion. And at once the awe, the sense of God, the greatness and otherness which adoring prayer expresses, is tempered by the wonderful sense of intimacy and love.

We also said in the preceding session that when we practice adoration, we enter the Communion of Saints. But who are the saints? All those who were faithful to the life of communion and through it became creative personalities used by God and transfigured by God. It is in gazing at the saints and at their unearthly charm and power, their courage and lowliness, that we learn what the communion of the soul with Christ can mean. For Christ has promised: "Lo, I am with you always." "Where two or three are gathered together, I am in the midst of them." There is the charter of the life of communion.

"He departed from our eyes," says St. Augustine, "that we should return to our own hearts and find Him there. For he departed, and lo! He is here. He would not tarry long with us, yet did He never leave us."

Now communion is a double relationship which gives to us and also asks something of us. Communion with Christ means, in some way, the sharing of His Spirit, realizing that His method of redemptive love, helping and suffering for others, may have to be our way too. Communion doesn't mean only spiritual consolation and support. And devotional fervor and communion are not the same thing. Communion means an entrance into the secret world at the heart of which Christ still stands.

In case we might be tempted to take refuge in the unworthy notion that because He suffered and triumphed for us we might get out of our share in suffering and only have the triumph, saint after saint comes forward to assure us it is not so. They assure us that the suffering which fellowship with Christ includes, means the Way of the Cross. The desolation of Christ is gladly endured with Him. No one can say exactly in what way, but, sooner or later, in some way, it means an inspired life of courage and generosity.

Yet this life is not lived alone, or in our own strength, or for the sake of our own souls. A recent spiritual writer has said: "Christianity means Jesus and all His Christians and the life He lives in, through, and with the whole Mystical Body of dedicated spirits who have emptied themselves to be filled by Him. It means all those who are *in communion* with Him, living the life of prayer."

This vast interpenetrated society of loving spirits "in Christ," all joined together for mutual support in one service, is what we mean by the Communion of Saints. And the realization of that means, once again, the realization that when we pray, we are never solitary. By that one act we enter into the full life of that vast, invisible society, ceaselessly loving and praising God. From the saints Peter and Paul to the last baptised baby, we should never limit Christian fellowship, Christian communion, to those we can touch and see. All of us are interlocked as one body in the Spirit of Christ, and all, as St. Paul said, are fed by Him in the same way. How great a responsibility this places on each of us doesn't it, that we may not damage the body or impede the working of love?

And so the life of communion really means for any one soul, the same as what the Gospel means by "losing life to find it." We lose our narrow, little, individual lives, and find ourselves as cells of the great Mystical Body, filled with His creative life. That ought to mean that in every encounter of the day we should be a vehicle, a channel through which the spirit of Christ reaches out to every soul and situation that we touch.

We cannot live up to such a perfection of communion with Him, but if we remember this, the classic standard will preserve us from the worst deflections and make us ashamed of our self-regard. It acts to stop us from thinking of our prayers and communion in a selfish way, as a means of getting something for ourselves. It reminds us that these mysterious acts involve our total self-consecration to Him to be used as He likes, not as we prefer. The enhancement of life that pours into us is to support us to do *His* work.

It is only by developing this communion that we can arrive at effectual intercession, for intercession is really the application to particular cases of a love and energy derived from God. It is He who reaches out through our prayer to rescue, soothe, and enlighten those for whom we intercede. How can this be until we are in communion with Him?

There is a comparative spiritual continuity between every Christian altar and the Upper Room at Jerusalem. Now do you think that, in the awful hour before Gethsemane, when He gave Himself with self-forgetful generosity to His feeble and bewildered followers, that there was any idea of merely enjoyable, devotional sweetness, merely nice feelings? Let us think of that scene a little, and try to learn from it.

Consider first the solemnity and touching mystery in all that surrounded that scene: the stress, the tension, the foreboding of disaster that must have been in the minds of all who shared in it. Then see the steady, self-oblivious generosity of the One who dominated it. He thinks only of giving all He can to those he is about to leave behind. The standard is thus set for all those in communion with Him.

For a moment, kneel in the corner like a little figure in Fra Angelico's wonderful *Last Supper* and watch the eager figure of Christ as He passes along the rank of disciples, *giving Himself*. Then consider whether your part in the communion of Christ has been loyally performed.

Now of course the great moments of our devotional life are richly blessed, concentrated instances of a give-and-take between Christ and the soul that should go on all the time as a perpetual intimate dependence. But like italicized phrases in a continuous conversation, it does not necessarily follow that they will be the phrases we shall hear most clearly. The conversation takes many different forms and is recognized in many different ways.

The savor of God and the presence of God can come to us in daily events and encounters, in the joys and pains of life. We *can* get the food of eternal life from nibbling the grass at the edge of the dusty road we must travel, or we *can* make the whole of existence more and more a sacrament of communion with God. More than that, we as Christians, cells of the Body of Christ, are called upon to be part, channels, of His mystical self-imparting. Our lives—gestures, words, and small acts—should be outward and visible signs of inward spiritual grace. And if so, how continuous, faithful, and humbling our communion with Him must be and how alert and ready to find Him we must be in every moment of our lives!

To many He does not show himself directly, but reaches us through the press of existence and the souls of other people. Sometimes he wants to get to others through us—through gentleness, patience, and the way we do our work. All these are part of communion. It is not found only in church or in personal revelations. What is called "religious experience" is only one among many ways in which we have communion with God, but it helps the other ways.

When Mary went to the sepulchre on Easter morning, she only found an empty tomb. But when she turned back to ordinary life, Christ met her under the ordinary accidents of existence. Therefore she did not recognize the character of her own experience. She thought He was the gardener. Just so, we, often supposing to find Him in the "religious," seem to find only emptiness; yet He meets us directly in the paths of common life. But if Mary hadn't gone to the tomb, she would have missed the meeting entirely. Just so, the faithful performance of traditional duty, the carrying out of religious routine, though it may seem to result in emptiness, brings us to the spot where the meeting can take place.

That, I think, is especially true of the daily discipline in prayer which many people find so difficult, yet without which our power of spiritual recognition and response would never develop at all. For in that we train our minds to realize the truth of God's mysterious nearness to the soul. We come with effort to the place where we can hope to find Him, and then we turn back to daily life. We find that, "Lo, He is with us always, even unto the end of the world!"

Now that is a little of what this communion with God of our tiny souls ought to come to mean to us. It ought to mean for each a greater and greater certainty of not being just one of a crowd, but also involved in a personal relationship, as a companion to One whose love is so delicate that *nothing* escapes His attention. It is not only when we are saying prayers, but in all our homely jobs—in our work and our worries, in the things we have to bear, in opportunities to do the decent thing—in every one of these He really comes to us.

"How delicately Thou teachest love to me!" said St. Julian of Christ. And as we go on in the spiritual life, we more and more realize the truth of these words. We are taught through the events, vexations, tests, disciplines, and the sudden joys and beauties of every day. All are exquisite adaptations to little human creaturely needs. All are just what is needed to make our souls grow. And all are illuminated if seen in the light of God and realized as lying under the gaze of God.

"Thou, God, seest me." That shouldn't call up the horrid picture of a glaring eye one used to find over the washstand in pious lodges! It should carry a sense of humble delight and make us realize the intimate, incessant awareness, the sheltering, yet strengthening care of a prevenient Love, molding and directing our lives. It should make us realize that there is a Person who most deeply loves us and is watching over us and sheltering us as a mother does—awfully pleased when we do well, very sorry when we have had a bad fall, even though it's our own fault.

You know, the Flemish fifteenth century painters had a secret way of painting the face of Christ in such manner that from whatever angle one saw it, His eyes always looked into one's own. Right or left, far or near, His glance was on all and each. These pictures were called "omnivoyant."

I think those pictures were a wonderful symbol of the essence of the Christian experience. The life of communion means the trusting, delighted meeting of that gaze. Looking back in our turn, from wherever we are—at work, at rest, in company, in solitude, in study, in joy or suffering—all that becomes part of the life of prayer.

This sort of interchange, and not any spiritual selfishness, is what

Lucie-Christine meant when she said that God said to her, "My daughter, for someone that loves Me, there is only Myself and her." That sort of communion is the very life of the saints, the great source of Christian courage, the inciter to generosity, and the teacher of patience and love.

Thus looking back at God, we also learn to share the generous breadth of God's interests and outlook, His wide and pitiful tolerance, His long patience. And we learn to share the exact and detailed care with which that glance enfolds each separate soul along with its peculiar possibilities and needs. "How delicately Thou teachest love to me!"

Now such communion—*all* communion between our souls and God—means meek receptiveness. Holy Communion itself, as the type of all communion, teaches that. Although we have our part to play, it is mainly a duty of response, isn't it? We love because He first loves, and *our* love must essentially be childlike, dependent, receptive.

And what we recognize will change us, whether we like it or not. We can't open ourselves to that influence and remain the same as before. Even practicing the prayer of communion in a small way leaves us different persons. Receiving the supernatural sunshine, we receive not only warmth and light, but the powerful, 'though invisible, chemical rays which will work their mighty changes in our souls. St. John of the Cross tells us that they may burn to heal, relentlessly killing the evil growth and purifying. They may start fresh and even painful development. In the life of communion, we expose ourselves freely to these, and they *will* change us, 'though how, we can't say. That depends on God's will for each soul and that soul's faithfulness, generosity, and courage.

If we read the lives of great Christians from St. Francis to General Booth, what we always read about is people who were very much *changed*. It is not the wonderful things they *did* that matter so much as the different sort of people they became. Developed and undeveloped Christians are just the same. We all begin as infants and have got to grow up. In the life of communion, we get food and help for that process until we become adults who are not hard, uppish, or critical, adults who are a little nearer their Lord, who are willing to suffer and to work unselfishly for the sake of all.

I think we have a wonderful picture of the transfiguration worked by faithful communion, by trying to live all the time with Christ. The soul that puts no limit on its correspondence with Him, through the power and love it develops in His service becomes transfigured. We see the growth of its courage and generosity if we compare our first and last pictures of St. Paul.

In the first picture, St. Paul is intense, cocksure of his own theology, ideas, and position. He assists at the martyrdom of Stephen, because he is sure he is right and Stephen is wrong. His splendid energies are working from their own center; they have not yet been harnessed to the service of light. Then he goes forth to breathe fire against the Christians and to slaughter them. He seems to be strange raw material for a saint!

The second picture is that same St. Paul in prison, writing his little letter to Philemon. How gentle, winning, humble, and drenched in love it is! The great apostle pleads so persuasively for a runaway servant: "Though I am bold enough in Christ to command you to do what is required, for love's sake, I prefer to appeal to you," he says. That is the voice of a pupil of One who taught in action, the royal humility of love, and moved among His most homely and blundering followers as one who served.

Look at the distance in this response alone between Saul the zealot and Paul, the aged apostle. See the narrow, hard intensity of one and the gentle, irradiating generosity of the other. What bridges this difference? It was the life of communion which was made possible by his simple, generous, unconditional act of surrender and consecration, beginning with, "Lord, what wilt Thou have me to do?"* He did not say, "*I* am going to do this for you." There is all the difference in the world between these two.

After that, the life of communion made Paul do some very rough things. He had to go humbly to the people he had persecuted and win their confidence. His capitulation to God began a gradual expanding life of communion, of loving, devoted, arduous, and very costly correspondence. It slowly remade his difficult nature into the image of Christ and enabled one of the most turbulent and stormy spirits ever subjected to Christ to write the great Corinthian chapter on charity. "Where sin abounded, grace," in all its self-oblivious charm and generous courage, did more and more "abound" [Rom. 5:20].

Now this is the end of our thoughts together for this session. I hope that they are thoughts that will help us as we go to Holy Communion. And when you come away from that experience, may it be with fresh strength. May you have a new sense that every scrap of your lives—even when they seem dreadfully hard, seem to have no meaning, and there is not much to look forward to—are yet full of possibilities and worthwhile because we can make them ways of serving God. We can do our ordinary jobs for and in Christ, and so turn them into prayer. To offer every bit of our lives to God, even if it is in boiling potatoes, is to do His work in the world.

Today let us look and wonder at the fullness of life offered to us. Look! Look! For to look and wonder is already an act of communion, provided it is done in the spirit of love.

*Although most current versions of the Bible do not include this question, the Authorized or "King James" Version does include it in Acts 9:6.

VII

Cooperation

In our last meditation we thought a little about communion, and perhaps some of us felt that it represented the utmost that we can hope to reach in interior prayer. But we remember that M. Olier, whom we took as a guide, didn't think so. He said that the third part, to which it led, was what he called "cooperation."

Communion alone can be almost passive and almost individual; cooperation can't be passive or individual. In it we give and use something of our own: our will, initiative, and love. In it, we are co-workers together with God. Our own spiritual interests expand far beyond the area of our own souls and considerations, based on our personal correspondence with God. They do so until they share a little in the general breadth of His interests.

A self-regarding spirituality can persuade itself it lives a life of communion. It can never persuade itself it lives a life of cooperation. But the life of cooperation is the only Christian life. The devotee who is content to be shut up inside his or her own enjoyable, pious practice and nice religious feelings, is the mongrel of the spiritual world. One of his parents may be Spirit, but the other is Self.

What is cooperation? It is complete, active, practical self-giving to God for the purposes of His *redemptive love,* whatever those purposes may be. It is taking the Cross into the very heart of the life of prayer and thus the necessary fulfillment of all *true* communion with Christ. Those two words, "redemption" and "love," sum up the essence of Christianity and the vocation of the Christian saints. One without the other is no good.

Theology has always told us that Christianity is a religion of redemption. Humanitarians say it is a religion of love. They are two sides of one truth. But we don't really glimpse the truth until we put them together and see that it is religion of the sort of love that redeems and the sort of redemption that is only achieved through love.

Further, Christianity is a religion that acknowledges that there is something very wrong with the world and we are invited by God to cooperate with Him in putting it right. Christianity does not only offer redeeming love to each of us, but, as the earnest and token of our redemption, calls us to the high honor of cooperating in its ceaseless work. We, in so far as we are part of the Body of Christ, are each called to take *some* part with Him in the ceaseless work of saving the world, incarnating the Kingdom of God.

As the basis of this last meditation together, I want you to have two passages from one of Cardinal Mercier's pastoral addresses to his people. We couldn't have a better guide than that saintly and heroic spirit whose whole life, intellect, practice, and mysticism was a steady, peaceful, and courageous commitment to promote the interests of God.

In the first passage, he says:

> The interests of a Christian are not a private matter. They are the interests of the whole community. *All* that you do, for good or for evil, either benefits or damages the whole society of souls. . . . The humblest soul of all, by the degree of virtue in which it lives and the work it is called to do in the most obscure situation, makes its contribution to the general sanctification of the Church.

Isn't that a rather serious thought? He says "*all* that you do"—each spiritual movement, each private communion, each tiny act of self-denial, each joyful perception of beauty and holiness, each bit of suffering gladly and promptly accepted, each boring duty eagerly met, each act of self-forgetful love—all these things are doubtless excellent for your own soul, but that is not their real point. The real point, in a Christian, is that they go into the common stock; they are available for the whole world. The Body of Christ, the redeemed organism, depends on the love and sacrifice of *each* of the cells that compose it.

We are never alone, and *nothing* we can do or refuse to do stops with the effect just on ourselves. The simplest prayer, the tiniest act of sacrifice, the humblest act of kindness—is like a pebble thrown into the ocean of divine love. It radiates. It affects the whole community. And so too with every sinful, unloving, despondent, cowardly thought or action that makes us less supple and useful to God—an unhealthy cell in the body checks the flow of grace by reducing our capacity for Him and again, affects the whole community by its failure to cooperate. That, I suppose, is why, in the old forms of the General Confession, the sinner asks pardon not only of God, but of the community, the Church, in the persons of its great souls, Saints Peter and Paul, and all the saints. Pardon is asked for the damage done to corporate life in very personal terms: "my sin, my failure, my shirking of sacrifice."

Mercier's second passage reminds us of the width and variety of opportunity for cooperation with God, saying:

> In your inner life, through an ever closer adherence to the Holy Spirit in the sanctuary of your soul, you can, from within your home circle, in the heart of your country, within the limits of your parish, pass over all earthly frontiers, and by your work, your purity of life, your participation in the common lot of suffering, intensify and extend the Kingdom of Love.

It is done by offering every act, thought, joy, and pain of life to God, thus giving them the quality of prayer. This indeed is the essence of cooperation. It does not mean the showy side of good works. It means the full flowering of the life of prayer: self-givenness in faith and love to the immense, unrealized purposes of Christ, the ceaseless effort of the Holy Spirit working within this recalcitrant world.

Very often it is true in active service, but still more in spiritual service. It means that every one of God's ceaseless, inconspicuous invitations and suggestions to our souls should be met step by step by our willed and costly efforts to respond and work with Him, oblivious to self-interest or any other thing. Always remember that we shall spoil everything by self-chosen activity. His movement must precede our own.

We are like children being taught a job by a loving parent who teaches by allowing us to help with the job. And what is such guidance of a child by a parent worth unless there is an eager, but docile response on the part of the child? The whole value of an interior life depends on this: that no bit of it ever is done alone because we think we know how, but always in response to the gentle guidance and teaching of God.

Look at this principle in the Gospels. How plain Christ makes the priority of the Father's will, waiting in patience for the appointed hour, the fulfillment, not of what He feels He would like to do, but of that which is ordained. What we see in Christ's life is human nature working together with God in such perfect obedience that the line between human and divine melts away. And when St. Athanasius said: "He became man in order that we might become divine," perhaps he was looking forward to such a personal union of will as this, achieved through the faithful imitation of Christ.

So you see, cooperation with God, however small and inconspicuous the job given us, must mean actual self-giving to His purposes, deliberate throwing in of our whole spiritual weight on the side of His redemptive work. It means we must never have a special religion of our own in a corner. However deep our sense of personal communion may be, it is permeated by this sense of being a part of a central organism built of all praying souls whom God desires to *use*.

That will mean an utter death to self, including the spiritual self. And it will mean the Cross set up in the heart of the personality. For this He has picked us up and educated us. We, in so far as we may become sanctified, must follow the great example of Christ. Our sanctification will not be for ourselves alone. God desires to make of our souls a workshop—a real workshop where hard spiritual work is done. What that work will exactly be is a secret hidden in His purpose. What its complete result will be we are not allowed to know.

In the recent Flemish exhibition there was an exquisite drawing by van Eyck of St. Barbara's Tower. It was the magnificent tower of a cathedral, a miracle of detailed work of soaring beauty. And all 'round, filling the middle of the picture, were the tiny figures of the workmen who built it, little undistinguished creatures, cooperating in the myriad kinds of hard, but unexciting labor with their wheelbarrows, scaffolding, trowels and mortar. Out of that the tower rose.

The invisible Church is such a tower, built up by the infinitely small and self-effacing labor of a nameless crowd. It is constructed by the courage, generosity, and patience with which we, the undistinguished mass of souls called to cooperate with God, have each accepted our vocations and responsibilities within His will.

You know, the most ancient of all names for a Christian was *slave*, the slave of Christ. That term emphasized Christ's utter possession of us and our humble and dependent status. The word stands out in the Gospels, in the Parable of the Talents, and so on. To St. Paul, it is deeply important to think of himself as thus enslaved. But the slave doesn't necessarily know the big outline of his master's work. His job is loyal performance of his own bit. Just so, the laborers at St. Barbara's Tower did not conceive the miracle of beauty which was to be created out of their total industry and obedience in the uninspired jobs to which the majority were set.

Well then, what does this mean for us? What are the lessons we are going to take home?

First, as regards ourselves, it means a willing and unhesitating cooperation with God in His ceaseless, steady, purifying action on our own souls, that we may be made perfect tools and kept sharp and bright. It means an incessant war on claimful, possessive, narrow intensity in our religious life. It includes a constant willingness to be the prodigal of time, love, and interest, especially to those to whom we are not naturally drawn. To cooperate with God means sharing His wide, generous self-giving to the world.

Secondly, it means, as regards others, to be willing to collaborate with

Christ as part of his Mystical Body, in His redeeming work. It is a sharing in the pain and conflict, the darkness and mystery of the Cross. We are all connected one with another. The reality of intercession depends on this mysterious truth. God can take our prayer and reach out through it to rescue, enlighten, and soothe.

In the mysterious world of prayer, many victories over evil are won and many rescues from sin are effected by those whose love and courage urge them to offer themselves for this. They become, in the deepest sense, intercessors, continuers of the rescuing work of Christ.

Finally, looking back over the last three aspects of the life of prayer on which we have dwelt, we see what a delicate balance and tension they require of the soul. True, all are different in the degree to which we shall develop them. The prayer of adoration and the prayer of cooperation represent as it were, the Martha and Mary of the interior life. St. Teresa said that if Christ were to be perfectly served, these two sisters must combine. But like other sisters, they don't always get along together. It is above all through the hidden communion with One who bids us to perfect worship and perfect service that we shall learn to adjust their claims.

It is certain that something of adoration, communion, and cooperation must be present in a healthy spiritual life just as in a healthy natural life. We need that wide sense of the great and lovely world over against us with the starry sky rebuking our little personal frettings and self-importance. That over-arching sense must be present in and behind our close and loving communion in our personal relationships and in our self-giving to work and social responsibility. And we must have the Cross before us in our hearts and in our hands. The beauty and the richness of the Christian's life of prayer will be shown above all in the way in which it combines these triune aspects of a full life of devotion and enwraps its communion and its service in the atmosphere of humble and adoring love.

THE CALL OF GOD:

A retreat
based on the visions of Isaiah and St. Francis
given in 1928

Isn't this experience, this rift in the veil, this amazing vision of Reality, of the glory of God, this sense of love and awe awakened—isn't it much the same for Isaiah and Francis? Both have their eyes opened on Reality, the majestic vision of creative will. But the results are not the same. For it is only when the willing sacrifice of the human is seen along with the glory and love of God, as a *part* of His beauty, that we get the proportions of existence right. Then we see how every kind of self-giving for humanity—work, thought, suffering, and sacrifice, whether public or secret— and every kind of worship of God, merge to form one thing, the great *Sanctus* of humanity. . . .

When the holy rift comes into our close knit, everyday existence, when we get a veritable glimpse of God in the natural order, the Spirit of love will come to us bearing the image of a person crucified: an invitation to courage, sacrifice, and love.

Chapter II: "Vision"

193

II

Vision*

Read Isaiah 6:1–8.

We thought last night about the saints and servants of God who are our patterns. Now today we are going to look at the three stages in fitting a human soul for the service of God, preparing it for the particular work it is required to do. And of course there is some particular work which every human soul is required to do for God. For this we came into the world.

Isaiah was called to be a prophet, to spread the news of the relationship of God with human beings. How then was he prepared?

(1) He had an overwhelming vision of Perfect Reality. (2) In its light he saw and acknowledged his own imperfection and weakness. He was cleansed by love, and so made fit for service. (3) Then he heard a call, he was given an opportunity, and, of his own initiative, he responded: "Send me!"

In some way, that process applies to every one of us, however homely and limited the way in which we are required to contribute to the glory of God. The history and literature of enlightenment and transfiguration of the soul show us that when the glory and reality of the Lord is really glimpsed by us, in whatever way it happens, the results are always the same. There is a tremendous sense of our contrasting frailties (what Abbé Huvelin calls "our incurable mediocrity of soul"), then the cleansing power of love responding to our penitence, and finally the impulse to serve.

All the ingredients of holiness are in these three, and we can measure our own spiritual state rather well by them. The same threefold response is asked of us: adoration, penitence, and service, for these are three expressions of the one love of God, each one producing the next. It means looking successfully at how we stand in respect to the three terms of life: God, ourselves, and the world.

*Underhill used chapter I from the preceding retreat as the first chapter for *The Call of God*.

195

If we want to get back into trim, a day like this is above all else an opportunity. And a crucial point for us is the first phase. Let us allow ourselves to be sensitive to the type of experience which Isaiah encountered which is indeed the experience of the saints. If we would come to the sacred place and open ourselves to the holy Presence which is always there, the Spirit of God will do the rest.

This morning, let us think of the first phase of this event which became the foundation of Isaiah's life of service.

Look at him. He has wandered into the temple just as we might wander into St. Paul's Cathedral, perhaps not expecting to get much out of the time spent there. Suddenly he finds himself undergoing a great spiritual experience. He sees, not an impressive religious building, but the glory of the Lord, filling the temple. That which is revealed to him is that which is always there and seldom noticed, although it is the first term of all religion and the only reason that religion exists. It is the all-penetrating, unchanging splendor of the light of God. Then everything else is swept away. There is just a young man there, face to face with overwhelming Reality.

Put in the philosophical slang of the present day, Isaiah had a tremendous experience of value, of quality, not mere quantity. It was an experience of the true spiritual Reality in which we live, move, and have our being. He beheld all that really matters, all that truly *is*: God. The encounter influenced him for life, as a suddenly given glimpse of spiritual truth is apt to do.

What is the first point for us here? Isn't it the imperative need for all valid spiritual action always to begin, not with our own efforts, but with the prevenience of God, the fact that the glory is there? Even now it awaits our recognition and *it* must set the standard for our lives because we belong to God. Adoring prayer is centered on this essential, humbling realization of the actual presence of God.

Let us turn now from Isaiah and look at the type of woman who is part of the Community of the Blessed Virgin Mary. Doesn't her experience teach us the same lesson: the power and presence of God? Remember the angelic greeting of the Annunciation: "Hail Mary, full of grace!" Why? Because the Lord is with you! That presence, that grace, the very life of the Infinite, not of little human creatures, is the source of all that is to happen.

"Blessed art thou!" we say of *ourselves*!—Not for any merit of our own but because the glory of the Lord has fallen upon our temple. And how often it has fallen upon young people! Remember that young girl who was chosen? For each individual, there are always different ways to be a channel of God, but the preparation is much the same. In some way, each person is brought into the presence of God, and every Christian soul is required to be such a channel. We too will only fulfill our vocation if an adoring realization of His presence rules our lives.

Let us be sure we are putting first things first. The most important function of our prayer is to give our soul a glimpse of the holy; then we get the proportions of existence right. We sink into our true background—God; and we see the proportions of our existence in their true environment—God. We no longer see the world as a thing that exists for the sake of our little souls.

"The whole earth is full of Thy glory!"* The sound of that phrase enchants us, but what does it mean? What is the glory of God? Surely not just radiant splendor, a light that never was seen on sea or land. The meaning of the word "glory" is a clear, adoring knowledge. To glorify God means an attitude of soul in which knowledge and adoration are one. When the translators wrote the word, that is what they meant.

The angels song was a manifestation of God's awesome reality, compelling adoration. When it filled the temple it was with music in which notes of certitude and adoration, truth and love were strung together. It conveyed a knowledge full of delight, of joy in God for His own sake. We have to ask ourselves if anything like that—joy in God for His own sake—goes with us in our work and in all the ups and downs of life. For life belongs to God, is destined for God, and is entirely lived in His presence.

Isaiah experienced a clear realization of the fact of God, bringing with it an awestruck delight and harnessing him to the service of Reality. That is always the character of a full religious experience, whatever outward form it takes. Think of Pascal. The essential characteristics of his overpowering, life-giving experience were so much like those of Isaiah's encounter. He called the glory "fire," and exclaimed that it brought him certitude, joy, and peace.

In such high moments we get past the puzzles and conflicts of existence. We don't solve them, but we transcend them. The glory of the Lord fills the temple. We touch something of eternal life. Now it is true that Isaiah saw it only in the temple. He needed the favorable suggestion of a special place, protected from old distractions and images. But the vision of the seraphs was not limited to that space. They cried, saying, "The *whole earth* is full of Thy glory!" *Full.*

The glory of that vision of majesty and love fills not only heaven but earth, the jungle city, the church and market place, the ballroom and the hospital, the most sordid and disheartening spheres of service, the roads humming with traffic and the silent mountains where tiny plants in

*Underhill's notes here actually say: "Heaven and earth." In doing so, she is quoting the *Sanctus* which is based upon Isaiah 6. However Isaiah 6 omits the first two words.

exquisite beauty flower for God. Like those cosmic rays which we now know come from the furthest configurations of space and pass right through the material world, there is no place where it is not. It penetrates you and me. We can't get away from the glory of God.

We are beginning to see what St. Paul meant by being "temples of the Holy Spirit." It is a bold phrase, but it doesn't go beyond the declaration of Isaiah. A soul that really perceives that is driven to its knees in awe, contrition, and joy, isn't it? Consider life and work—one's outlook on the world, souls, and religion, one's habitual condition of mind—from this point of view. Search yourself to ask whether they are quite good enough or quite serene enough for citizens of a world full of God's glory. Then make little lists of sins.

"The chief end of the human being is to praise, reverence, and serve God" whose Spirit fills our temples. "Hail Mary, full of grace. The Lord is with thee" is a statement of fact. All religions throughout history have driven this home: the truth of God's living presence in and with the soul. Each of us is face to face with that tremendous truth. Isaiah's vision is the vision of the glory in which we are always bathed, which penetrates and sustains us. The one and only test of work or the life of prayer is the extent to which they reflect that pure glory of God. How do you feel about that? You know, that is what human beings are meant for. Remember that compelling command? "Be ye holy as I am holy."

Now let us take another point. What does the human creature see when the veil of the spiritual world is lifted? It sees nearest God the living spirits of love, the seraphs. You remember the Hebrew tradition that when angels fell, the seraphs alone were so absorbed in loving God that they never even dreamed of defection. Some of the cherubs, spirits of pure knowledge, fell away, as clever individuals sometimes do. The seraphs (remember, the supreme symbols of humble, adoring love) *might* have been expected, as pure spirits without human limitations, to manifest unlimited vigor in all departments of life, to be engaged in ceaseless busy service, and to gaze without ceasing on the face of God.

But that is not at all true. They have six wings. Two cover their eyes—two, their feet. With two, they fly. Their vision is controlled. Their action is controlled. The picture suggests to us the giving of humble, mortified prayers and disciplined service. It suggests that the only prayers with wings which are fully vigorous are those which are held steady before the face of God. For the seraphs, unlike Isaiah, cannot look at God's glory. They cover their eyes with their wings.

A spiritual vision may seem to be a good and possible prospect to a young prophet beginning his career, but it is full of an unbearable mystery and wonder. It daunts as well as delights the minds which are nearest to

God. When they sing the *Sanctus,* they don't dare to look at that which they adore. The deepest burning love means utter humility.

Sometimes I think that the great interest in spiritual things which many people now regard as hopeful, the modern invitation to "think out" God who is beyond all thought, or get new conclusions of his inconceivable reality, may tend to be something less than reverent. We easily forget that we are daring to argue about a Reality on which the seraphim didn't dare look. We have lost the sense of proportion, of the utter difference in kind between the Infinite and the finite. We have lost the sense of our nothingness and of the merely fragmented glimpses of the majesty of God possible to creatures like ourselves.

Great spiritual literature constantly reminds us that awe and reverence should condition our attitude toward the mystery of God. How unscriptural and unworldly is all shallow familiarity with things of God!

Do you remember how Abbé Huvelin said, "If anyone comes to me and says, 'I have been with God,' I always say, 'How did you feel? Only small, utterly abased? If not, I don't think you would bring in God.' " Surely the first result of true vision is the utter death of self-assurance. There must be the fear and the awe of the Lord which is the beginning of wisdom.

Now let us set another picture by the picture of Isaiah in the temple, a picture from the history of the Christian saints. Look at the experiences of St. Francis on La Verna, the mountain from which he came back to the world marked with the wounds of Christ. Here again it is the real and crucial experience of a real and great man that teaches us. It is something that really happened at a particular moment in history and had permanent and marked results. We think much of St. Francis' wonderful visions of nature and of beauty, of his relationship to all life, to animals, birds, and flowers. But surely what matters about him, as about any great Christian, is the source of all his love and power: his relationship to God.

Look at this picture. Francis is alone, almost instinctively following Christ's example to pray, to enter into a humble communion with God, the inmost Reality of the universe. This is not his initiation into the spiritual life. He is not a budding prophet like Isaiah. But he is already a great man, head of a busy movement of popular teachers. He has gone to pray with a sense of need which sometimes overwhelms spiritual teachers. He has gone to get strength and refreshment for his work, to be alone with that which he loves.

And what happens? There is shown to him, as to Isaiah, a revelation of that which is always there—the glory of God. We see that the two experiences actually relate. The vision which breaks in upon him on that September night is a six-winged seraph flying toward him. It represents for him, as for Isaiah, the spirit of loyal love. But this time it is a Christian vision given to one who begins his career of service in obedience to a voice that speaks for Christ. Something has been added to human knowledge of God since Isaiah saw his awful majesty in the temple. The Franciscan legend puts it in a phrase: "As the seraph drew near St. Francis so that he could see him, Francis saw that the angel bore . . . the image of a man crucified."*

Then what happens? Isaiah's vision is, so to speak, baptised. The love, awe, and ardor of the seraph, the flaming splendor of the Spirit that lives and moves in the divine Presence, is still there. But something else is there too and shared with Francis. It is a mysterious suffering for humanity and the sort of love that involves a willing self-offering to become a part of that suffering. It is summed up for Christians in the Christ. It causes the tragic yet entrancing beauty of the Passion, the beauty of God reconciled to the anguish and sin of the world. That suffering love is at the very heart of spiritual reality.

To see this is to find a much more difficult, a much deeper recognition of the glory of God filling the temple of humanity, isn't it? It means the useful and humble entrance of the love of God into human history in which each Christian soul is called to take a part. It is the veiled, yet truly present glory of the Eternal in intimate union with the love, suffering, and self spending—all the homely and heroic deeds of human beings. It is that same unspeakable mystery upon which we gaze, every time we look at the crucifix.

St. Francis, we are told, was full of amazement and didn't understand the meaning of what he saw. But presently he realized what he was to learn from it. It meant that by the kindling of his mind, not the martyring of his body, he was to be transformed in the image of the Crucified.

The kindling of his mind—our minds glow very dull and smouldering, don't they? The glow and warmth sometimes comes to die out of life. We need to be rekindled by the fire of love, the fire that is part of the glory, in order to be transformed into the image of the Crucified. But what is the image of the Crucified? Isn't it the image of One who knows the very best, can have the very best that spiritual love has to give, that gazes on the whole glory and beauty of God, rather like the seraph always in the presence of the Father, yet will, for the love of God and the sake of others, endure the very worst?

This second picture is one of an unlimited and an unquestioning self-givenness to God for *His* purpose, His children, His world. The sense of solitary mystery, wonder, overpowering presence, and the reality of spir-

---

*For an account of this vision, see "The Life of St. Francis," chap. XIII, in *Bonaventure: The Soul's Journey into God, The Tree of Life, The Life of Francis*, ed. Ewert H. Cousins (New York: Paulist Press, 1978).

itual things is just as great in the experience of Francis as of Isaiah. But now at the heart of this picture, one sees heroic suffering and generous sacrifice for others as the supreme revelation of the love of God. Here is the brightness of His glory and the express image of His person.

How much deeper that goes into our lives, doesn't it? How it swamps all pettiness, all feverish, claimful emotion, all our reluctance to suffer, our nervous fears and calculations about ourselves or those we love! How it takes us right away from our small notions of happiness into something very noble, costly, and creative, and reminds us of how God loves the world!

Isn't this experience, this rift in the veil, this amazing vision of Reality, of the glory of God, this sense of awe and love awakened—isn't it much the same for Isaiah and Francis? Both have their eyes opened on Reality, the majestic vision of creative will. But the results are not the same. For it is only when the willing sacrifice of the human is seen along with the glory and love of God, as a *part* of His beauty, that we get the proportions of existence right. Then we see how every kind of self-giving for humanity—work, thought, suffering, and sacrifice, whether public or secret—and every kind of worship of God merge to form one thing, the great *Sanctus* of humanity.

In the end, we always find what we really love in human beings—their strength, nobility, and beauty on one hand—and their piteousness and need on the other. And through all this is the reality of God revealing Himself through them—in the patterns of poverty, in inarticulate pain, in all the appeals of weakness and the need for our understanding and help. We find it even in sinners and wherever there is freely inviting love—the glory of the Lord filling His little human temples.

Then we must ask: "What do we mean by 'the whole earth is full of His glory?'" It means that every corner is really full of the splendor of God. Isaiah saw in the temple the same vision of majesty and love, and we are set within that in order that we may respond in our own way and be transformed by the kindling of our minds, curing our languor and setting on fire our enthusiasm for Christ. It means the beautiful Whitsunday prayer: "Come Holy Spirit!"

When we get into what seems a dreary or intolerable outlook, "another day just like the rest," when our work seems without result, when we feel we can do little or nothing about the misery and want in the world, when the effort to get all that needs doing done is hopeless, and every little time snatched for prayer is needed for other things, or our love is frustrated, or we are faced with renunciation or humiliating demands on our patience, and we can't stick with it—it does give us courage to realize that it all takes place within the radiance of God's glory.

The vision is really there although our eyes may be covered. The vision is really there, right through and across the mass of petty and unworthy details with which we fill existence. The spirit of love is everywhere without ceasing. "Holy, holy, holy is the Lord!" Then we realize we are amphibious creatures and we must react to two layers of reality: the stress and change of daily existence and the changelessness of God. Only thus can we be fully Christlike, fully alive.

The material of doubleness is just what makes the tension and the discipline of life. I was once present at a Westminster solemn service, and as it ended, a lady in front of me said to her companion, "And now dear, we must go straight to the D and T!"* That's the crucial fact about all human life, isn't it? It can't be maintained all the time at spiritual levels. After a moment of vision, we have got to go to the stores. In the world in which we have got to practice our religion and through which God will purify our souls, the store is just as active a factor as Westminster Abbey and sometimes more spiritually effective. We have got to accept all of the ceaseless stream of natural events, limits, and duties, and through and in them, glory in God and respond to them all, including the invitation of eternal life.

Now let us gather up this meditation, keeping in mind our two pictures: the vision seen by the prophet and by the saint. Let us remember that they are members of our society, and like us, God's servants and messengers. Our outlook can be virtually the same.

When the holy rift comes into our close knit, everyday existence, when we get a veritable glimpse of God in the natural order, the Spirit of love will come to us bearing the image of a person crucified: an invitation to courage, sacrifice, and love. Are we quite willing to accept and respond to that double revelation, to the fact that the crucifixion of the self is essential to the full knowledge and service of God? This means not any self-chosen sacrifice, but the utter self-abandonment to surrender to Christ all that is possible of secret humiliations, apparent unmeasurable suffering, the senseless struggle of monotonous failure, loneliness, and loss—and to bear it all with the wings of loyal love.

So we consider this two-fold level of holiness, the holiness of the Eternal which Isaiah sensed and the holiness of Christ which Francis saw, as substrates of Reality. Its presence is everywhere, mysteriously allied with suffering humanity, and we ask ourselves how we stand in relation to it. How do our main interests, strivings, preoccupations, and worries endure this light? Are we brought by that vision to a glowing acceptance of all

---

*The "D and T" (no longer in existence) was the popular appelation for Derry and Toms, a department store described by former Prayer Group members as a minor, less expensive Harrod's.

that life brings us, or do we instinctively draw away? Are we willing, by the kindling of our minds, to be transformed in that image which is stamped with the character of redeeming love with all its costs?

In light of these considerations we can look at our own positions. We are primarily created and called, not for ourselves, not for the good of our neighbors or the needs of society, but solely "with angels and archangels and all the company of heaven, to laud and magnify His Holy name." We are called to increase that clear, delightful knowing of His being, of that splendor of holiness, that mysterious beauty and wonder which fills the temple of life. That is what we are for.

III

Penitence

Isaiah 6:5–7

We thought in our last session about the first stage in the formation of a servant of God and the glimpse of the divine vision which sets the scene of our spiritual life. Now we go on to the human creature's reaction to that realization of God. "What am I?" said St. Francis, "face to face with Thee, my God and all!" Here is the root of all true penitence.

Real penitence begins in the human creature's glimpse of the holiness of God and the enormous sense of contrast between itself and that which it has seen. Deep penitence is that response of the lover who discovers that something intervenes between the impulse of love initiated by the Spirit of God in his heart and by love's issue in action. We discover that there is something wrong which prevents us from making the perfect response we want to make. For we have seen the Perfect, and like the Psalmist, we want the words of our mouths and the meditations of our hearts to be, in their little way, perfect too. But they are not.

I, the ego, my bodily and sensitive self, I somehow ruin it; I mess it all up. Woe is me, for I am a creature of unclean lips! I am offered the awful privilege of spreading the vision which I know and love in my soul, but something spoils the message every time. My lips are not pure. All the other things those lips say, do, and ask for—all my responses to life, the things that come out of the heart of the human being and have made it unfit for transcendent things, each critical, unloving utterance, each word that falls below the standard of sincerity or is tainted by bitterness or self-love leaves a stain. Faced with the glory of God, all our comments about responsibility to the world—our pessimism, worry, and impatience, our discussion of matters that certainly are not "lovely and of good report," all the virtual insults to God—these appear before the best of us as startlingly distinct.

When God's glory fills the temple and shows us what the Christian life might be, that is, when the first rift in ordinary consciousness comes for us, we're so delighted, so entranced, we think only of what we've been shown and called to do. But presently the sting of our own disharmony, our own sense of importance, kills our joy and our professed surrender. In our homes, wherever they may be—in the spark of our influence, whatever it is—in our first chance of director's work for God—is it easy to hear the song of the adoring seraphs in these?

"I am carnal, sold under sin," said St. Paul in what we think is strong language. But what does it mean exactly? That he felt he had been enslaved by the lower level of life and was living in it all the time. That *is* sin. "Woe is me!" Yet I know and strongly feel now that what religion calls contrition may be a debilitating and objectionable state of mind. We owe some psychological duty to ourselves to keep our tails up at all costs, to be optimistic about ourselves, and keep a lookout for the inferiority complex.

But Isaiah's reaction to reality is the reaction of one destined to spiritual greatness. It was, above all, a sense of inferiority and unworthiness. We needn't suppose him an especially faulty individual. He was probably rather a good young man. We know he had great powers, lofty ideals, a pitying heart, and yet face to face with the unmeasurable glory of God, all that went for nothing at all. The glaring imperfection and the second-rateness of our average human practices was revealed to him. Above all, he felt his powers of expression sullied by the use he made of them. The lips with which he spoke and his spirit which could have fellowship with other spirits—that sacred power of the human being which we take so easily for granted—were unclean when measured against the holiness that filled the temple.

Now I think that we shall all agree that it is what we have done in our relationships with our fellow human beings that has impaired our fitness to be instruments of God. We have all sullied our powers, using them to think, say, put forward, and acquire things below our known standard, which are thus, for us, unclean. In general, what we have done with our average daily life is what becomes our great obstruction when we turn to the spiritual life. What we do, think, and feel outside of prayer is the source of difficult distractions that come between us and vision *in* prayer. No wonder that Christ gave a solemn warning against undisciplined thought and speech.

The Christian life is a whole. You can't fence it off a little, call it spiritual, and do as you would like with the rest. When the glory of the Lord fills the temple, and you see him, and you've failed to work with and for Him in your life, in your home and public interests as well as in your prayer, you understand how Isaiah must have felt.

Put beside this picture of the young prophet convicted of sin, the cheapening of that very gift of speech through which he shall serve God! Compare it to the wonder of the scene in purgatory where Dante, who passed comparatively unmoved through all the circles where the separate moral faults of pride, anger, avarice, and lustful passion were punished and cleansed, met Beatrice in Paradise. "Look well at me, for I am Beatrice!" she cried. That one look did more for Dante than all the previous experience of the horror of sin. It melted the ice around his heart and overwhelmed him with penitence and humbling love.

What was it he saw? It was the beauty of holiness and the awful gap between that vision and his character. He, the great poet and seer, was suddenly shown up to himself. He perceived the narrowness, hardness, and self-will of his soul, a perception many people dodge for years. This was Dante's real purification. The contrast did the same thing for him as for Isaiah. All the sight of sin and its horror—and the further sight of all that the soul must bear to cleanse itself and make it fit for God—and the vision of hell and the vision of purity: none of these could do what the sight of Beatrice did. In her the beauty of holiness was disclosed in a human person. This left him speechless, penitent, and utterly ashamed.

That scene of contrast is an essential point in all purification worthy of the name. Christianity brings that contrast before us in its most heart-searching form. It has been above all the vision of Christ and the simplicity and humility of the saints that has brought self-satisfied piety down with a run and compelled the astonished orthodox Pharisee to take the prayer of the publican on his lips. How bitterly ashamed we shall feel when we see the saints and realize that they had the same stuff of life to deal with as we have! The difference is in what they did with it. Let us mark this as the first point of our meditation.

If the vision of His glory is the first act in God's preparation of our souls for service, and the next is our resultant self-knowledge and our conviction of faultiness, what follows? What follows, if we are honest, is the humiliating discovery that we cannot do very much about it by ourselves. Our hearts cry: "Lord, be merciful unto me! Heal my soul! Send out *Thy* light and *Thy* strength. *Thou* art my help and deliverance."

I cannot by myself handle and purify the confusing energy of my half-evolved nature. I cannot really keep my resolutions, really govern my desires, set my life in order, cleanse my memory of all self-pity and all resentments, or kill self-love, self-interest, and self-will by myself. I acknowledge my need of help far beyond myself.

We are beset in the present day by numerous prescriptions for dealing with our own natures and the natures of those we desire to help. Mental hygiene, practical psychology, character building, and so on, all flatter human nature by suggesting that we need only conduct our own spring cleaning, use our own resolve, trust psychology, and all will be well. It is true that these methods may effect great improvement on the surface, but they can be the root and ground of sin.

See how, when the glory of God fills the temple, we realize that this is not the right way to live and work, that something quite different has to happen? We know then that we need a purifying effect by something not ourselves, done to us, something that points beyond our own moral comfort, mental health, usefulness, or social obligation. We realize that the cure of helplessness that goes with human sin and the first step in recovery is the humble acknowledgment of what it really is. "*Thou* shalt wash me, and I shall be whiter than snow!"

The absolute test of valid religious experience is here in the vivid sense of the need for purification, the sense that something has got to be done *to* us and won't be done until we see our condition as it really is and ask to be cleansed of it. And of course Christianity not only brings into the foreground this need for a redemptive something given to the human being from beyond the world to cleanse and release from the downward pull; it cleanses to possess and regenerate our resources. The fire of love from the altar of the Sacred can touch you and stir you to life again, however dead you feel.

What is the essence of the Good News? Surely in the eyes of Christ it is this, that if you want a fresh start, you can always have it. The Christian life, says Clement, is a perpetual springtime, always ready to produce new, fresh life. The service that has grown weary and slack, the prophet whose spirit is dull from too many earthly contacts, Martha fed up with serving, Mary stale at prayer—all these can be restored to their full power and joy. Think of this. If your inner life has gotten dull and turbid and your standard inclined to fall, know that God is unlimited in regenerating power and active mercy. Point to any stage. "Lo! This has touched thy lips and thine iniquity is *taken away*—all the corrupting effect of use and the deepening discouragement which is a sin against hope, the hard corners of character, the intolerant outlook which is a sin against charity, the torment of unruly desires—all burned away.

All this may sound a bit like a missionary or a service appeal, but in terms of human need, it comes home to each one of us. The inclination to jealousy of which we are somehow ashamed, the standard of worldliness, those dark bits of habit which dog us, the fits of gloom or discouragement or exasperation, and the feverish distracting moments of emotion, indecision, and indolence: all are more familiar than we would like to admit. And what of our hostility, our reluctance to face the difficult, and our passionate and solely self-centered attachments to this or that person, type of work, or point of view? Then there is the fed-up feeling and the nervous, rushed feeling. None of these very well match the seraph's song!

The Gospel says we can be freed from all this if we really want to, if we risk the seraph with the coal of fire, welcome illumination and the suffering that comes with purifying and is of God. If we give this invitation, we must make no stipulation about the response. It *may* be a red-hot coal. There is no effective repentance and no real contrition without courage. We must be willing to endure, without an anesthetic, all that the celestial surgery will do. We needn't suppose Isaiah altogether liked it when he saw the burning coal from the altar of sacrifice coming his way. We needn't think he didn't feel any unpleasant sensations while the coal was doing its cleansing work.

That coal burned away the last taint of self-regard from his mouth, the means of his communion with his fellow human beings. It turned an eloquent young man into a prophet.

That scene of the human creature first shown the glory of God, then seeing with shame and horror itself as it really is, then gladly accepting the painful cleansing administered by love: doesn't that sharply correct any notion we may harbor that religion is a consoling addition to life? Religion's first gift to the human creature is purification for a purpose, and that purification is brought to human beings in and through ordinary life. All sorts of people bring in the red-hot coal, sometimes our nearest and dearest. Children carry it about a great deal. Sometimes someone we've held to be cheap, or someone with whom we've not been at our best, or a victim of poverty or sorrow, or our own quiet selfless suffering will show up our love of comfort, our self-indulgence, or our ingratitude for happiness and ease.

The seraph comes to us where we are, left to our free will. The seraph comes whether we accept this purifying pain in love and joy or shrink from it. It comes whether or not we care enough about being made fit for God to welcome the pain, that is, welcome it in principle. Of course we cannot help an involuntary yelp when we are hurt! Even the most loving dog yelps when given a necessary licking, but it turns and licks the hand that spanked it afterward.

Perhaps we have begun to feel now that a good deal more needs doing to us, even to the best of us, than we had realized at first: things which we aren't quite able to do to ourselves. The standard rises in a most uncomfortable way in the silence of a day like this. We are beginning to see the extent to which we've let our own natural selfish instincts guide our lives. We have seen the subtle ways in which self-love, prudence, and private preferences, tastes, interests, and anxieties have crowded in and spoilt the purity of our response. We have let the natural animal speak through our lips. We have been pulled down over and over again by this-world considerations.

Then comes the bitter realization: "My destruction is coming to me from *myself*." I am to blame for my persistent mediocrity. I *could* have helped my worst deflections. I could have done something about them. I have not done the best possible with the material handed out to me. I have dealt with the things of God at a level below the highest and so entered the sphere of controversy and bitterness. "The good I would do I have not done." My failures are my own fault.

General acknowledgment and not the sort of clumsy psychological analysis sometimes recommended to us in devotional manuals, is surely an essential of Christian contrition. We must acknowledge that there *are* two natures in us and that ages and ages have slid down to the lower choices, have capitulated to impulse, weakness, and earthly points of view. St. Paul is not the only one to have noticed!

There is a wonderful letter of St. Francis de Sales, that prince of Christian psychology, which analyzes such a situation. It reads:

> You say truly, my poor, dear child, that there are two women in you! One is a certain Peronne, who, like her patron, St. Peter, is sensitive, irritable, and apt to depression when crossed. She is a daughter of Eve and therefore constitutionally bad-tempered. The other is a certain Marie who has a very firm and good will, desires to belong wholly to God and be simple and humble and sweet to her neighbor. And the two women are at war. The worthless one is so vigorous that sometimes the good one can barely defend herself. At such moments, the poor thing thinks she is beaten and the bad one has won. But no, indeed, my poor dear Marie, that wicked one is no braver than you, but more self-assertive, perverse, over-reaching, and pig-headed. When you give in and weep, she is delighted because that is always so much time lost.

I think we can all recognize that situation. The truth is that we are always lending our ears and eyes and tongue to Peronne, and the more we give way, the more pushy she grows until we almost reach the point at which Marie can no longer deal with her.

We are, as yet, half-made, and very unstable. The downward pull is ever there. We need to see the Christian way of meeting this situation.

Let us take, as the last picture we look at in this meditation, what is perhaps the most beautiful and touching single scene in the Gospels: that is when Christ washes the disciples' feet. What a contrast to the burning coal held on the lips of the prophet! The humble cleansing of His followers' dusty feet by the very hand of divine Love! There is the difference between the Old Testament and the New. The winning, charming, gentle generosity of Christ's way of dealing with sin and of looking at human nature, is never more exquisitely expressed.

Here is a marvelous, deep, and tender realism, a reverence for the humble material He deals with, a quiet acceptance of facts. There is no savage denunciation of human frailty or demands for the impossible on one hand. There is no silly tall-talk about human nature being so divine on the other hand. Instead, we find a clean, merciful scrubbing of the growing but half-made creature with its earthly side really there and often very primary, and its heavenly side there too. The feet can't help getting dirty because they are involved in life's discipline: we *must* walk in the dust and the mud and not always keep on the carpet, away from the common lot.

Nevertheless, there is no need to take too desperate a view of our condition. "He who has bathed does not need to wash except for his feet, but is clean all over." It is as though He were saying: "The part that has come in contact with the world has gotten very dirty. You go into numerous puddles which might have been avoided with more care. But I'm going to put things right at my own cost." There is no grim, general condemnation here, but a humble, homely cleansing of that which *is* unclean.

Consider the reverence offered toward the humble person which is implied in our Lord's attitude here. What to Him is that collection of imperfect, stupid, unstable followers who, one and all, will lose their nerve and forsake Him when the crisis comes? Here are the children of God, the potential inheritors of heaven, the material from which the Church is to be built. Their blemishes are partial blemishes inherent in their human character. The Lord's aim is to cleanse *that*, not discard them contemptuously or smash them before making them anew.

Peter, impulsive, penitent, utterly disgusted with himself, rushes in and says: "Do me all over! (Change me completely!)" But Christ says, "No, I'll take away the stain of earth from your feet and the rest will do. I want real human beings in their various faulty individualities, not a uniform type, scrubbed to sameness. Offer yourself to be purified for my service. What's necessary will be done to you and not what isn't. Perhaps something such as a quality you consider very regrettable, will be left to worry you and prevent any illusion. I don't undertake to make my agents spick and span about their own degrees of niceness. But the *mud* will go. Those nasty dark marks, those hard lumps, the gritty bits that scratch."

It is those things we come near which we feel are not truly part of our real selves, but which cling on persistently, which *we* can't wash off ourselves. But the patient, gentle, divine action, if we will yield to it, cleanses us in all sorts of simple homely ways. Sometimes it is a hard rub, sometimes soft, repeated touches, but never a giving over until the job is done, unless we draw away.

This blow, that separation, this disappointment, that continued contact with a particularly exasperating person: all these rub us, we think, the wrong way, but they prepare His right way. All this cleanses us, as it were, in spite of ourselves. Through the friction of life and its countless conflicting events and changes, that quiet, patient, purifying action goes on as the humble service of the Spirit of God to His creatures and servants.

The mud often clings and has got to be detached. We, in our restlessness, vary between wanting to draw our feet away and wanting to snatch the towel and finish the job ourselves. But it is the discipline of staying quiet and letting God work that we are asked to bear. Perhaps his action seems so gentle that we are sure all the mud won't come off, or it comes off so slowly we think we will die first! Nevertheless, we profit more from remaining quiet under the divine action than from anxious conflict with our own unruly desires. For only this passive purification which follows on the discovery that we can't do it ourselves, really kills our self-esteem and leaves nothing, not even self-improvement, in which to take pride. And *then* we begin to be fit to speak to other souls of God.

Remember that lovely passage in Julian of Norwich when the spirit of the soul goes to God as a child when it has fallen down and gotten muddy, it "runneth hastily to the mother for help with all its might saying, 'My kind Mother, my gracious Mother, my dear worthy Mother, have mercy on me. I have made myself foul and unlovely to thee, and I may nor can amend it but with thy grace and help.' "

So the Christian vision of the self evokes two movements in us. At first we are impelled to say, "I am a creature of unclean lips, of muddy feet. I have made a mess of myself." That is self-contempt. Then the second movement comes and we cry, "I can't do more about it but you can!" That is self-abandonment. Isn't it worthwhile to have been shown up to ourselves pretty thoroughly, in order to achieve that? The humble, peaceful confidence, and even more, the courage, that can let God work on us—in us—and through us when and how He wills?

Isn't it worth it to have the first-hand knowledge of His entrance right into the human scene, his actual molding, purifying, dynamic presence with us, transcending all we could do for ourselves? "Unless I wash you, you have no part with me," He says. That is the Christian reading of the mystery of redemption.

"We endure His workings beyond our workings," says Ruysbroeck, "and so, enduring Him, we lay hold on Him and are laid hold on by Him." All the saints have gone by that road.

How much more heart-searching is this than Isaiah's vision! All that was meant by the burning coal which the seraph brought from the altar of sacrifice is here given freely with an absolute gentleness. Here is the self-oblivious pattern of One who serves, and pauses on His way to absolve self-given extremes of suffering. Here is One who stoops to cleanse with gentleness and humility the stained feet of those who struggle to follow Him.

IV

Consecration

Isaiah 6:8

Now we reach the final stage for which the vision of God and the contrasting vision of the self have prepared the soul of the prophet: eager, loving consecration. If the Church Fathers were right in dividing love into two classes—desire, as love that wants, and charity, as love that gives—*eros* and *agape*—then the love which the seraph woke in Isaiah was charity.

But which charity? Not just a general amiability and kindness. "Charity suffereth long and is kind, seeketh not its own." Yes, but all these are just the symptoms of a far greater thing. "Charity," said Aquinas, "is friendship with God." There never has been a better definition. If you are absorbed in, for, and with God, and all your acts are dictated by friendship with God, if all you care for are His interests, and you long only to work for His ends, then as you come more and more to share His standpoint and act for His sake, you *will* suffer long and be kind.

We are even charged to "be perfect as He is perfect." Surely that means to be all-round, completed in our love. The saints are, above all else, the friends of God. Their lives are transformed in charity. And so it was with Isaiah. His reaction was a spontaneous gesture of an eager friend who takes the first opportunity to do something for one who is cherished.

"Whom shall we send?" comes the probing question. "Who will go for us?" And Isaiah cries: "*I'll* go! What else is worth doing in comparison?" A daring thing, perhaps, for the little human creature who knows its weakness, to say! It would have been preposterous at the beginning of the story, but it comes out right at the end.

Let us put ourselves in Isaiah's shoes. First, awestruck adoration of God's beauty and then abasement and penitence at our own lack of it. A sudden glimpse of all that lies behind life, the frantic contrasts between the ephemeral imperfect creatures that we are and the majesty and loveliness of God. And then the offering of ourselves after all, such as we are. The divine voice says: "Who shall we send to do our teaching, rescuing,

213

saving work in the world?" And it is the creature who has caught sight of the love and beauty of God and been subdued to the purifying action of God and whose heart is full of penitence and grateful love who answers without making terms or asking questions, "Send me!"

Let us place beside this scene in our meditation that other picture, so full of deep knowledge of souls and of compassion toward our timid, slow-moving human nature. Remember Christ's parable of the laborers in the vineyard? Remember their gradual awakening to the opportunity and meaning of life? Remember how it came for some at the third hour and for others at the sixth, ninth, and even the eleventh hour? But look and see the penetrating love which goes straight to the point, straight to what matters: at least the workers *go of their own accord.*

Their reward was not given for the work which they accomplished. It was given for that awakening of will and love that replies: "Send me!" So here you see we come to human initiative as playing an essential part in the soul's life.

So far we have watched God act on Isaiah's soul. Now, suddenly, we find human freedom brought into the foreground. The next move lies with Isaiah. There has emerged in the temple of life a tiny creature, one special strain of vertebrate with the almost incredible power of saying "yes" or "no" to God. The whole of religion, the whole of sanctity and un-developed spiritual life hinges on this. It is not a forced option but a choice. The choice is not that of a slave, but of a son. The human will is one of the primary realities of the spiritual world. It cannot be used fully except insofar as we offer it. The immense truth of our need of passive surrender to the action of God must never make us forget the completing truth, the part left to individual initiative and will. The will of God surely includes this.

People come to you and say, "How am I to know the will of God?" The answer must be that we know above all by that which in our moments of peace and light He pressures us to do and gives us the opportunity of doing. We learn it by that secret inward push or pull to which we become ever more sensitive with each loyal response to Him. But ordinarily He won't *force* us to do it.

Why do we think that God gave us common sense or the power of choice? Because something in us was not subject to determination. As the poet tries to suggest: I am a bus, not a tram. The sovereign Reality of the universe is felt to say in our souls, not "Go!" but "*Who* will go for us?" "Who will choose to serve the purposes of divine Love? Who is willing to take risks, ignore comfort, and harness initiative to obedience?"

And the questions continue. "Who is willing to bear pain and hardship, endure struggle and frustration, or tolerate the ceaseless drive and anxiety of a monotonous, unrewarding job in and for Me in such a way that it partakes of the creative redeeming power of Christ?" The whole of Christian history consists in the response of adoring souls to that call.

Think of the courage and confidence involved in the call and response of the saints. Consider the element of unexpectedness in their lives. Catherine of Sienna, a girl of sixteen, born into a humble, crowded home, called to be the mother of countless souls and to speak on the basis of equality with the Pope. She died full of joy, worn out by service of God and of souls, and is now recognized universally as a messenger of God.

Think, at the other end of the scale, of Elizabeth Leseur, seldom well, always putting her duty before her religious preference. She was the perfect model of the Christian wife, linked to an unbelieving husband she adored who was only brought to God by reading her journal after her death. Her letters and writings have lit up thousands of lives.

His call is so very simple, but so very exacting. The response is equally clear. "Send me" doesn't exactly mean, "I'm going that way anyhow. Is there anything I can do for you?" It means the delicate balance between freedom and surrender, that self-oblivious zest which is the salt of the Christian life: will and grace acting together on ever higher levels of cooperative action.

We observe that nothing is said to us about what the job is to be. The response is an unconditional one. It says, "Whatever it is and wherever it is, send me and I'll do it. Send me however you like, on foot or in a donkey cart if you can't spare a car. And send me where you like, not where the opportunities are many and the scenery and society are good. Send me to promising or unpromising fields of activity, to apparent failure or apparent success. Only, wherever it is, do help me to keep my head!"

And that unconditional response goes further. "Send me to explore in solitude the deep mysteries of Thy truth or to minister in an insanitary slum. Send me, like Mary Slessor, from the Scottish mill to the African jungle; like Elizabeth Frye from a comfortable country house to win prisoners in the Newgate Jail; or like Henry Martyn from a peaceful life of scholarship to labor, suffer, and die alone in the Far East. Hide me like Julian of Norwich in a little cell by a country church and let my message wait for centuries, if you'd rather, before it makes its effect on the world. Give me, like Elizabeth Leseur, a life consisting of charity in suffering as well as I can and loving as perfectly as I am able; and let the power and witness of such a life and love only begin to show itself in fulness after my death."

There are many who could say, "If it's one of your homely jobs, all the better. Send me to the kitchen or the nursery and let that be a part of feeding and cherishing your lambs and sheep."

The end of such self-giving is simply, "Let all be done your way and at your pace because I love *you* and desire your will to be done. I am your willing tool, your servant, one of the things through which you act on life."

Here is the first standard by which to measure our degree of purification. The complete absence of self-chosen aims. The power of saying at any moment: "Send me!" without adding, "*There*—to do *that*." The perfect surrender of the actively willing creature to perform all tasks in loving subservience to the God who is pure action. The most fruitful line of self-examination is to consider how much of our own preference, prejudice, and how much self-chosen activity remains in our work for God.

The real test of humility is the willingness to risk failure, to take a job with simplicity and let the inferiority complex have a rest. To take it because it and and we are all part of the great movement of divine will. That, not our small, individual success or failure, is the real point. The whistle sounds, and we are next on rank. True, we may feel there's a better taxi between us, but that may be wanted for a better job. Though our gear box isn't all it should be, we've got to start. Carefully driving, we may manage the hills. I don't suppose that Isaiah, after his overwhelming illumination and utter penitence felt peculiarly competent and self-assured. But let all that drop. And let drop all nervous anxiety about our own religious needs and preferences which an ordinary sort of love might show.

"Send me!" It is not so easy to turn away from a temple full of holy glory and go out into the wild where adoration may be difficult and time for visions of God is hard to secure! But Isaiah was quite willing to be off at once. And what can we who follow after say? "Send me from congenial to uncongenial surroundings, from peace to distraction, to a place where the church life is not that to which I am accustomed, where I'll hardly have any time to myself. Or perhaps leave me in a situation where conditions are very difficult, only help me to deal with them in a new way. I make no terms, 'Thy will be done!'"

"I have been given a revealing glimpse of Thy utter beauty and wonder. A coal from the altar of sacrifice has cleansed my lips, and there is *nothing* I am not willing to accept or suffer in order to help the waking of the will or in fulfilling my particular vocation in regard to the whole design."

I sometimes think that history is like a great tapestry, a picture being woven before our eyes. We see the shuttle going to and fro and we observe the changes it makes. Suddenly there are new bits of color here and there, gradually building up new forms, so that we may be inclined to think that the shuttle makes the picture. Sometimes we are even inclined to call the shuttle "chance."

But the shuttle's movement and dependence is in the free and hidden action of the Creative Spirit intervening, initiating, controlling every point, bringing in novelty gradually or suddenly but alone aware of the finished design.

Now *we* are parts of that unfinished, divine history, and questions of where and how we emerge in the pattern are not only questions for our own vocation and our own souls. We are sent to this or that bit of fabric, woven into the background or thrust through that crowded place according to the weaver's requirements because we are wanted just there.

Surely the very essential of a dedicated life is our free acquiescence in this: that simple act of acceptance which combines rightful action with perfect obedience, unquestioning acceptance of a job or of a mission, and the effort to accomplish our assignment. That is what the saints in their beautiful suppleness and selfless love have always realized.

Let us illustrate this by two pictures of supreme obedience which have changed the history of the human race: scenes which have controlled the imagination of Christendom ever since. One is the Annunciation and the other is the agony of Gethsemane. In the beginning there are the words, "Behold, the handmaid of the Lord." In the end, "Not my will but Thine be done."

Let us re-enter the past and see these things happening. Let us see those acts of courage, confidence, true self-oblivion, not mere self-depreciation. Are not they the self-oblivion that gives us the power to go through with our jobs because our own natural dread and weakness is forgotten with the rest? We see in both scenes the overwhelming sense of God's mandate and action. His purpose transcends ours and accomplishes in ways we cannot understand.

Look at the startling character of divine action from the human point of view. See the discrepancy between the initial episode and the final result. First, there is a girl's strange vision and her bewildered acquiescence in her mysterious but tremendous destiny. We hear her words: "I can't understand, but be it unto me according to Thy word." For the handmaid of Creative Love, self-will, self-love, and self-interest are all left out. Then, in the later picture, there is the bitter choice made under the olives of Gethsemane in the words: "If it be possible, let this cup pass from me. Nevertheless, not my will but Thine be done."

Then consider that in the two scenes, we have two supreme examples of the same thing: doors of human love opened to God's supernal action by the pure self-abandonment of the free human will to the purposes of God.

We see the acknowledgment of the priority of His vast design over our small, self-chosen interests, so limitless is the power of generous and unconscious determination to surrender. *Send me:* that is the secret of all the victories the saints have won for God.

Gaze on the two pictures. Live in them with the heart and mind wide open to all they have to teach. They bring, don't they, a solemn sense of tremendous issues involved in the free dealing of God with His creatures through history and human life, through birth and death, courage and suffering, and of our awful responsibility in respect to His call: a realization that our effectiveness as His instruments entirely abides in our free self-givenness to His will. That alone braces and develops us and turns us into creative spiritual personalities.

After all, we instinctively bring up children in just the same way. A wise father doesn't say, "Go and get my glasses!" but "*Who* will go and get my glasses?" Then it's the opportunity to love and enthusiastic initiative that produces the eager rush upstairs and makes joy and service one thing. Even so does God deign to ask service from us and for the same reason: for our sakes, and our growth. The living quality in religion, its power of transforming us, abides entirely in the opportunity of free and willing response.

Once we get down to this simple obligation of response, some of the stock language of our own inner life and prayer begin to clear up for us. The first thing it stops is our persistent tendancy to shirk responsibility, to hang back and attribute this bit of weakness to humility. "Don't send *me* there," we cry. "I should make a mess of it!" On the other hand, we might well add, "I *do* feel good enough to do religious work or speak of religious things. I *do* know enough to guide souls. But *I'm* not strong enough to carry the cross. Someone else had better go." It sounds very humble, but in reality, it is only a disguised form of self-regard, a secret fear of failure or of making a fool of oneself, a fundamental want of trust.

Suppose we just go! Like the travelers on the road to Emmaus, a companion draws near and goes with us. Perhaps our eyes too are unseeing so that we are unable to receive assurance and support. Yet bit by bit as we go steadily on, the meaning of that which we do is revealed. The strength we need for putting the job through is given us from beyond ourselves. We learn precious knowledge in special moments of communion and recognize it in the breaking of bread in the soul. This accompanies every step of the dusty and tiresome journey on which we are sent.

A Christian isn't just a slave, but a partner, and in his or her most bewildering undertaking, never alone. The life of prayer that begins in adoration, is adorned by it, and brings long contrition in its track, will deepen into a wonderful personal communion in which we are fellow workers with a Spirit who never leaves us unfortified. Even when we cannot realize His presence, if we call in a spiritual way, that strengthening power still reaches us by its mere homely channels.

You know the old pictures—the Venetians are very fond of them—of young Tobias sent out from home, as he thought, on a very practical job of collecting a debt, but really as part of the great and hidden plan of God. Tobias thought that the arrangements for the journey were of the most ordinary kind, yet an angel disguised as a servant went with him every step of the way. The picture of Tobias setting out supported by an angel and a dog is a picture of the servant of God sent out to do His holy will. It's a nice picture, I think, with which to end the day. You, like Tobias, may be called to a different and more important mission than you can see. But an invisible companion goes with you. And there is your little, humble relationship with all the natural creatures of God who comfort and support you. We are allowed to see the dog, but not allowed to see the angel. But we are asked to remember that both are there. We are never sent alone.

And another thing. This sense of the priority of God's action and His initiative will tend to cure in us our fussing about our own prayer. When we truly grasp that God is all and does all and that every prayer is just a fragmentary response to His invitation and grace, a response prompted by Him, we shall learn to yield simply and without scruples or argument to our true attraction. Then we can keep quiet and steady on our own devotional path instead of scrutinizing the map for some superior way of reaching what we think is our spiritual goal.

That staying on the path and not sampling someone else's, or stopping and getting worried because the devotional guidebook describes objects of interest we haven't yet seen or hills we have not had to climb is essential to healthy progress. When you say, "Send me," you accept the route along with the errand, don't you? Never mind if it runs between hedges or seems indirect. Reading numbers of contradicting books on prayer each describing one's path but not necessarily yours, is responsible for much fussing which is weakening. What matters, after all, is not whether we use words or not, recite the offices or not, meditate on Christ, contemplate, or practice this method or that, but whether we follow God's leading simply and loyally, responding now as He gives Himself right where we *are*.

The good motorist keeps his eye on the road, not on the horizon. You've given yourself to God to be sent, led, and accompanied along the path which He chose to an end which He ordained. So just deal with the light He gives and another will follow. Don't anticipate. Don't perpetually study, speed on, or wonder whether you can take the next hill in first gear! Meanwhile, you fail to notice a nasty bit of road coming and take it too fast with disastrous results. The useful agent, the good and faithful servant who gets things in good order is one who does the job with discretion and common sense, not in the delirium of feverish activities, forgetting to oil the bearings or letting the engine get too hot. A consecrated life means a moderate, well-arranged life, the right spiritual pace, sufficient spiritual food, patience, staying power, and total devotion to an end which is not your own, remembering those most pertinent words: "I came to do the will of Him who sent me."

Now let us look back on the meditations we have made today. What was the object of the whole Isaiah experience? It was not to dazzle him with the vision of a spiritual reality which his limited human mind could not possibly grasp. Nor was it to make him feel like such an utter worm that he couldn't do anything about it. But, as a balanced response to the vision of God and the vision of self, it was to awaken in his heart the humble flame of divine charity. And charity, as friendship and work, with and for God, is the only reason for doing anything worth doing and the only incentive that lifts us above the craving for personal achievement. Therefore it is the only way in which we can be made and kept fit for the purposes of God as His handmaids, agents, servants, and friends.

V

Members of Christ

Yesterday we thought of the three great movements in the awakening of the soul. First the holy splendor of God is revealed to it, and then its own status over against that splendor becomes plain. Finally the soul is touched by divine mercy and gentleness which asks, in spite of our imperfections, for our willing cooperation.

I suppose that most of us, dwelling on these points as they came home to each of us, were brought down with a run because over against the vision of God came the perception of ourselves as very small and ineffective. But if we would get stuck at this point, we wouldn't have either a very Christian or a very fruitful retreat. I don't wish to end our time together in the state of the revivalist who always wrote after his name the letters L.P.W., meaning the Lord's Poor Worm! That is not the humiliation asked of us. Christian humiliation is not groveling in despair, but joyful in lowliness, saying with St. Paul, "When I am weak, then I am strong." Why? Because the destruction of self-confidence is the gateway to another greater confidence, the confidence that comes from our Christian status, our membership in the Communion of Saints, the Body of Christ.

So we think this morning, since we don't think often enough, of the wonderful state given us as Christians. It is described for us from three angles and three points of view in the catechism. There we are called members of Christ, children of God, and inheritors of the kingdom of heaven. Now that three-fold definition emphasizes, doesn't it, the richness of Christian life and the impossibility of imprisoning it in a formula? It points out its relationship to God, to all other souls, and our celestial citizenship.

What peculiar mark is the link between these three terms, terms of an inexhaustible significance? Isn't it the fact that the emphasis falls each time on something infinitely greater than ourselves? It falls on Christ—on God—on heaven . . . not on us. Not the human being as the crown of creation, but the human being as a faulty, half-realized, half-grown, helpless, imperfect creature, caught up to be made part of a spiritual organ, the Body of Christ, and assured that each of us is the child of a spiritual love, partaking of a spiritual joy. The intimate, cherished presence of the holy God will grow in this spiritual creature that is to be the organ of holy action, the child of His creative love.

We have been shown the vision, given clear self-knowledge, and called to serve. What are the conditions of service?

First let us look carefully at the order of these three designations. Religion individually begins in meditation with the realization: "I am the child of God!" Nothing matters in comparison to that. "*I* am an inheritor of the kingdom of heaven." But that doesn't *merely* mean finding a personal relationship with God in nature or discovering "eternity in a grain of sand" as Blake would say. That's very nice, but it's less than Christian. The Christian is first, a member of Christ, part of a redeemed community devoted to an interest and an action which transcends individuality. That person is not just an individual who is exhilaratingly cherished, but one who shares in and makes up where needed for the suffering and effort, the unmeasured self-giving by which the saving work of Christ is done. That, not personal salvation, is the great privilege of a Christian. That is the thought to take back from this retreat.

What is the first result of realizing that? It redirects us from solitariness and from all risk of spiritual self-centeredness and self-seeking on one hand and despondent thoughts about our own small ineffectual lives on the other. We no longer count for ourselves alone, and our personal failures and successes must not be estimated as if they matter in themselves. We get to know down deep the water-tight compartments which our egoism is always setting up, but we are also given a sense of the vast operation to which our tiny movements contribute.

We realize that God is pure action, the only doer of all good things. Our part is willing, unlimited acquiescence in His free action in and through us. Sometimes that action means pain for us. He seizes and uses us to the limit of our endurance for His hidden ends. And we must suffer or even seem to fail that His purpose may succeed. For members of the mystical Body of Christ, Gethsemane and Calvary remain the classic patterns of the mysterious way in which His will *may* have to be done.

What a new meaning Holy Communion takes on, doesn't it, when we grasp all that is meant by this incorporation, this weaving up of our souls into the actual organ of Christ's action on earth? We are very small and weak by ourselves, but, knit together into the means of God's sacramental action in human life, it becomes literally true that we can "do all things through Christ" who strengthens us.

If we acknowledge this, we have gone a step further in the story of the spiritual life than Isaiah's "Send me!" No longer do we start off to do a job in our own strength, but we may go as part of an organization, supported by a Power and standing for more than ourselves. Our real significance no longer lies merely in ourselves, but in God's action through us. Oh, Lord, "Thy hand upholds me!"

There are two great passages in the New Testament which this whole concept of our corporate state drives home. We might take them in succession as the bases of this meditation. The first of these is St. Paul's great description of the Body of Christ, a description that he felt was so real that he twice used in: in letters to Rome [Rom. 12] and to Corinth 1 Cor. 12]. The other is the Johannine discourse on the mystic Vine [John 15].

St. Paul begins with a mighty vision of the mystical Body of Christ continuing His work in the world of time. He starts on the long journey through human history, that journey which is still being continued in and through ourselves. He speaks of our different duties and faculties, diverse gifts serving one indwelling life, diverse jobs (of teacher, healer, seer, scholar) all wakened by one selfsame Spirit divided proportionately to each person as God wills.

In his vision he sees the Spirit of Christ taking and using, for that one increasing purpose, this brain, that hand, these eyes, this tongue. He uses the keen intellect of the teaching saint, the open soul of a contemplative saint, the great compassionate heart of a philanthropic saint, the mind of a Thomas Aquinas, the spirit of a Francis, the intellectual energy of an Augustine, the courage of a Livingston, the constructive genius of Anselm or Bernard, Damien's love of lepers, Teresa's love of prayer, and the Curé d'Ars' love for ordinary sinful souls. In all these and in countless other obscure members of the one God, the selfsame Spirit is working toward the selfsame end *as He wills.*

With the close union of poetic practice which is so consistent with him, Paul puts his finger on the issue: driving home the lesson of unity in serious words: "For the body is not one member, but many." We are not to expect to be all alike, to envy gifts of others, to worry because they show more spirit or are more useful than ourselves. And the standard of prayer which we can keep or the work for God we can do or the love and sacrifice of which we are capable is strictly limited in kind.

"If the whole body were an eye, where were the hearing?" The choice is not composed of contemplation alone. Mary and Martha are mutually dependent. "The eye cannot say to the hand, 'I have no need of you!' " As one onlooker said in a later form of that story: "It's just as well that Martha *was there* to do the cooking!"

Do your particular job, your particular kind of prayer or service, but never criticize or discredit the other members even though some of them may look queer, have lowly jobs, and their particular activities have no visible results. When it comes to the human body, we now know that the ductless glands are among the most essential parts of the body, although we still are rather in the dark about how their work is done. Yet in the Body of Christ, we find ourselves arrogantly saying that some members make "no contribution to the fellowship." Yet they may be equally possessed by the Spirit and often much more essential than our busy selves in the eyes of God.

As for these people whose obvious faults we are apt to see so uncompromisingly, they are members of Christ just as much as we are. The Body is not exclusively built up of perfect elements with hair and teeth and limbs of the best kind or features of classic purity. If the Body were like that, we shouldn't be in it ourselves! Christ accompanies and weaves into the instrument of His love the imperfect, feeble, unlovely, and undeveloped. But the glory of generous love fills these faulty creatures with its own vitality and transfigures them.

How very poor and unpromising seem some of the agents Christ chose for his ministry! They were chosen by charity, not good taste, yet His standard is presumably higher than ours. Thus we needn't be surprised that He reaches out to us through persons and books we might think rather inadequate. For, if you are the hands through which Christ stretches out to touch, to help another, it is equally true that the other is part of the Body through which He is acting and through which He may reach out to you.

Affecting other souls is not our perquisite or prerogative. We have to be affected in our turn. The privilege of affecting others delights while it humbles us, brings gratitude and a sense of obligation. But being affected by and through others often is more difficult to accept. Gratefulness is required of us rather than lowliness of mind. Nothing is more humbling than the lesson taught to us by persons we are so thoughtlessly inclined to despise or disapprove of. Sometimes they are the jovial, dilatory persons who test our patience by upsetting all our plans. We find ourselves glancing at the eyes of a person whom we didn't treat quite as well as we should, perhaps a person who asked for a cup of cold water at an inconvenient time, or perhaps an elder whom we shocked by our modern superiority to some of their old-fashioned views.

The members of Christ are the lips through which He speaks, the eyes through which He looks into ours, the hands reaching out for the gifts we are supposed to be so glad to offer Him. With infinite patience he uses imperfect material to bring more abundant life into our languid souls.

O Lord, teach us this: the ceaselessness of charity! We fuss so much about our times of prayer and what we do and how to do it, and of course deliberate prayer has great importance, but its chief importance lies in the degree in which it clarifies and simplifies us and in what it trains us to recognize and respond to: the action and the invitation of God come to us in and through the accidents of daily life.

Real prayer constantly restores us to a sense of our real position as cells of an organization dependent for its vitality on the indwelling Spirit of God and bound to a rhythm of life which maintains us in health for His purposes and not our own. Therefore we ought to begin in a profound and peaceful act of surrender to that Spirit, not with any anxious demands or feelings of importance. The sublime and childlike simplicity, which means self-oblivious acquiescence to the part given us to play, is a condition of all spiritual health and effectiveness.

The tendency to discouragement which dogs our over-sensitive, unpeaceful modern minds, however Christianized, the sense of failure, of not doing anything really for God, the fear that if a soul is given you to help you'll make a mess of it—all this comes from forgetting the cardinal principle that we are not free, self-acting creatures. We are not left to ourselves, but we are organs through which God acts. Therefore if we fail in His work, the primary failure is in our relationship with Him.

Had we a deeper sense of the vastness of God's processes and realized what minute crumbs we each are comparatively, we shouldn't feel so upset when we don't seem to accomplish much individually or lack, as we say, "scope." What matters is total love in the actions of the body of which we are a part. It is not the cells which have the most "scope" who are most essential to this, but those which quietly maintain the rhythm of life.

Now it is possible to watch on film the processes of cell-life in tissues out of which the body is built. You see healthy cells go on with their cycle of growing and dividing very calmly and steadily, maintaining the stability and energy proper to their position. Then you see some free cells, unattached, moving with terrific speed, dividing, growing with feverish rapidity, so full of life, so busy, never stopping. They are cells of cancer rushing through the body, starting a vigorous growth which is not subordinated to the body's needs. They have enormous scope and industry, but much disregard for the body as a whole. They are not coordinated and subordinated to the purpose and pace of corporate life. (Some of us have met cells like these on committees.)

A deep entrance in prayer into the total life of the informing Spirit may change the pace and scope of your life, and make what you do more healthy, life giving, and available for the whole. For those surrendered to Christ, sin is mostly what the old writers called "de-ordination," self-actuated action out of touch with the great and calm order of God. It is the meek, the merciful, the poor in spirit, the pure in heart, and not the restful, vigorous, struggling, or contentious who are subdued to the rhythm of the Mystical Body and really form part of its life.

Lastly, let us look at the second New Testament description of corporate Christian life, the great Johanine discourse on the True Vine. Let us *look* at it. We are not looking at the lovely conventional pattern we see in early Christian art, but at a living plant, expressing one specific character of a vine in thousands of different ways. No two leaves or tender branches of fresh green are quite alike. Some are big and others little, but all are alive! Look at the vine's luxuriant growth, order, freedom, and its persistent tendency to grow toward the light. See the close, vital dependency of each branch on the whole. Notice how all parts drink life from one single root thrust deep into the invisible supernatural world. A bit broken off goes on for awhile looking just the same, but gradually its leaves shrivel, its vital processes cease, its strength tends to go limp and shapeless, and it loses all its beauty and vitality. It dies.

Look at the vine's image of vigor and beauty and compare it with a neatly edged, separate life, all on its own, radiating from its own center, more like a mushroom than a bit of the living vine. One might say that the mushroom is not a very "Christian" vegetable! Do you know about the "holy" mushroom? One often sees it used in certain religious rites. Look at it over against the noble, generous, self-giving vine with its many branches, its burden of fruit and its thrust deep into the world of prayer. When you have seen the difference, *then* ask for what you want: a closer, more vital and real incorporation into this divine, self-giving life of the mystical Body of Christ in which each cell forms a part.

Now look at the context in which this meditation is offered to us. Whether the metaphor represents Christ's own words or not, it certainly represents the view taken by those most close to Him in spirit as to the essentials of Christianity. The text of John 15:4 and 5 reads:

Abide in me and I in you. As the branch cannot bear fruit of itself except it abide in the vine; no more can you except you abide in me.

I am the vine; you are the branches. He that abides in me and I in him, the same brings forth much fruit, for without me you can do nothing.

"Abide in me and I in you." These are not consoling religious phrases, but fundamental statements about our life and work, about real relationship in which we, individual human spirits, stand before God. If you have recaptured them here with all they mean, you are going back with fresh strength to the world. For they mean a real life and power, not our own, flooding through us and enabling us so long as we are in communion with Him.

The knife that most surely severs this union is self-occupation. It is all the more insidious because it often takes a pious form. It is expressed as *my* rule of life, *my* problem, *my* sins, *my* communion with God. This separate life with its anxiety must be utterly lost if the life of the whole is to be yours.

The Fourth Gospel omits the institution of the Eucharist, but here, in the fifteenth chapter, the essential characteristics of communion are found. It is done in a way that drives home the fact that the single life of the Vine, the mystical sap that flows in all the branches, is for *one purpose:* to bear fruit. That fruit is the raw material of the wine of eternal life. Yet the grapes, to become wine, must be sacrificed and crushed, devoted without reserve to an end beyond themselves. So here, the Eucharist and Christ are brought together and given under one symbol as the two-fold secret of the Christian life. Only when we accept that position can we be engrafted into the True Vine.

There is nothing more striking in the lives of the saints than the way in which loving communion and redemptive sacrifice go hand in hand, and in this, they are close to the pattern of Christ. Nothing could have been easier for Him than to keep out of harm's way, choose a prudent course, and be satisfied with His own communion with the Father and the instruction of an inner circle of congenial disciples. But He knew that His work could not be done without suffering and self-immolation.

The story of the Passion casts a revealing light on the members of his body. Julian of Norwich comments on it too. "I saw," says Julian, "that it was our Lord's will that we should be in Christ with Him. I saw the privilege of suffering, the possibility of sharing in the eternal redemptive act, irradiating and sublimating the most bitter aspect of our human destiny. I saw the griefs, disillusionments, weaknesses, frustrations, and the helplessness of the human creature on the cross." It is true that things of which she speaks come to all of us, but it is also true that the Christian has an elixir which turns them into gold.

But now let us look for our last picture of St. Paul at the height of his Christian career as he sits dictating the early sections of his second letter to the Christians at Corinth. See how he looks first at his own supernatural spiritual experience, the revelation he cannot tell, and then at that trying, disabling illness which haunts him. He feels, on the whole, that there is more spiritual wealth for him in that illness than in the vision or the ecstasy. Although the illness makes plain his own weakness, it enables him to feel the power of Christ in him as the sole doer of His works.

All of this is very horrible from the point of view of the "Gospel of the Healthy and Efficient Mind" so to speak, but Paul is a witness we have to respect. We have to pay attention when he says: "When I am weak, *then* I am strong. If I *must* glory, I will glory in my infirmity." There's that queer word, "glory," again! Clear adoration, knowledge! It is this that calls to St. Paul the most, through his own weakness. Then it is that he feels most humble and most delighted with his utter dependency on the indwelling life: "I live, yet *not* I!" I exist only to express some small bit of my Lord's characteristics and purpose. For this I must submit to such pruning, purifying, and training of my stems and tendrils as shall fit me for my particular vocation.

Perhaps that may not mean any drastic cutback or any very spectacular sacrifice, but the constant trimming, the little homely disciplines and trials are so much more thorough and mortifying of self-love and self-will. Whatever that pruning may be, I know that the degree of my self-oblivious surrender and docility will be verified and measured by my ultimate vitality and fruitfulness.

VI

Children of God

We thought in our previous time together of our vocation as members of a spiritual society. Now, when we try to look at it with detachment, it seems that a human being's supernatural life always involves a difficult paradox of which that person becomes more and more conscious as the soul matures. From one point of view, each soul supernaturally awakened discovers itself as a cell of that Mystical Body through which the saving, rescuing work of God is done in the world. Yet equally, from another point of view, each discovers itself to be in a close, personal, and unique relationship with its Father. A balance has ever to be struck between our corporate obligation with our responsibility as part of a vast spiritual organism and that personal childlike dependence of the finite on the infinite life which establishes the soul in absolute confidence with God.

"You are of God, little children," we read in I John 4. And it is the steady witness of all deep and experienced religion that human souls are, in some sense, the veritable *children* of God. Religion perceives them as immature, growing spirits derived from Him and not wholly unlike Him. It sees them as able to desire, know, and cooperate with Him, even as possessing some of the freedom which He has absolutely.

The current view of biology is that each human being is the result of natural selection, an organism adapted by countless exquisite devices to maintain its position in the natural world. Idealism says that only the supernatural is real and it is known through our ideas or thoughts; therefore we are important because we are the thinkers.

But for religion, the accounts which are given by science and by philosophy of the nature of the human being, valid as far as they go, miss the real point. That point is the secret link which exists between the human creature and God, the unbreakable link which unites a child and its parent. This link has nothing to do with our feeling, conduct, or belief. It endures through goodness and sinfulness, apathy and fervor. It has to do with the essential nature of the human soul.

That being so, this fundamental spiritual relationship must entail certain spiritual consequences for us. It must govern our status and attitude and condition our religious outlook. And we can get a rough idea of what these consequences may be by the analogy of natural life. Resort to the lessons of the schoolroom may still cast a revealing, if humiliating, light on the conditions of our spiritual childhood.

In the first place, this analogy suggests what our human knowledge of God will be like and what its inevitable limitations must be. We are not to expect to know God in His wholeness as He is or struggle wildly for supernal apprehensions of Him which are utterly beyond the span of our undeveloped minds. We are to know Him in much the same way as a child knows its parent, a way that is intimate, but incomplete, and has in it much homely confidence but little exact knowledge. A child has only a very general idea of its father's character, interests, and activities, but a complete, admiring trust.

Thus it is the child in heart who alone achieves that highest knowledge of God spoken of by St. Thomas, knowledge which consists in "knowing that He far exceeds all that we can think about Him."* And the preposterous modern invitation to "think God out" or "form a concept of Him" which popular books on religion so constantly offer us and which one of the saints bluntly condemns as "ransacking divine majesty" is then realized to be not only fatuous but inconsistent with our true status. That status requires us to be content with that limited, yet deeply personal and most privileged relation which is possible to the child's soul.

Next, our sense of this childlike status involves the realization that this same ineffable God is bringing each one of us up personally, forming and conditioning our souls through the events of our daily life. For the Child of God, everything without exception is a vehicle of grace: every glimpse of mystery or beauty, every encounter with goodness or love, every opportunity for sacrifice, and every pain. The child is educated at home by a secret but absolute action which completely penetrates his or her natural environment. It is the action of a Spirit, subtly molding to the child's needs even the iron sequence of natural law.

We are not left alone in the nursery and things do not happen there by chance. Even though it is not clear to us why we were given that power, the power was forthcoming because it was required. And the very routine of existence, against which we may be tempted to rebel, is seen in the end to be nicely adapted to our needs of growth. Though Providence certainly does not mean exemption from the law of consequence and succession, and the raw material and conflicts of physical life are the same for all, yet

---

*The original of this statement is, of course, by Anselm of Canterbury who wrote in *Proslogium:* "And so, Lord, . . . we believe that Thou art a being than which nothing greater can be conceived.

for the Child of God who accepts that status, that same succession, with all its risks and hardships, becomes the veritable medium of the molding action of Eternal Love.

"We are clad in the goodness of God and enclosed," says Julian of Norwich. That cherishing care of God is for Christians an eternal factor in the universe, and implicit trust in it is the very source of peace.

And just as the best training of a child is done in this ordinary homely life, and the qualities we most desire to produce are first evoked in a small and homely way, so the molding of our souls needs few startling spiritual adventures. "You feel," says Francis de Sales to one of his penitents, "that you would like such a fine mortification! But the finest mortifications aren't the most useful." We are trained through ordinary events and objects, not by peculiar religious experiences. It is better to stay where we are, be gentle and peaceful, and acknowledge that ordinary life. Even the most homely incidents will serve the purposes of God. Our Lord is more likely to come to us in His garden clothes than in robes of glory.

Next, consider the method and aim of this invisible, nurturing love. Its object is the production of personality, a strong, free, disciplined character. As children are gently and steadily trained towards this, so are we in our capacity as Children of the Infinite. And as the parent exposes the child to suitable risks, strains, and choices with his eye on the ideal of maturity, even leaving in the surrounding life certain potentially helpful elements of danger and hardship, so it is true here.

If we use things in unsuitable ways, we learn by taking the consequences: real falls and real stomach aches. If we play with fire, it really burns. No child can be fully trained or rightly developed unless the parent is sufficiently brave and loving to take risks and let it take risks. At every point, God is there, but at every point we are required to use our wills. Spiritual growth is real growth towards the maturity of free creatures; it is not being brought up in an incubator. And holiness isn't a kind of white wash; it is a *growth* in freedom, love, and true being. In the process, we must learn to tread firmly and carefully and to lose our fear of spiritual darkness and our greed for spiritual sweets.

As growth proceeds, we must expect that the lessons, demands, and apparent difficulties will increase. One thing after another, one person after another, is put before us, as it seems, almost casually. We have to be very attentive if we are to recognize in each an opportunity of choice, bracing the will and testing the love and purity of the growing soul. Each period of strain, each trial that seems a bit beyond our strength, is a fresh call to that balanced attitude of courage and dependence, that vigorous surrender of self-will, which is the means of receiving grace into the soul. As the parent desires the child to learn by making choices, so all is not ordered for us; a margin of initiative is always left. Situations arise in which, as we say, we "get no guidance." Our souls could not grow in any other way.

When we do not know what the will of God is, surely His will is that we should do our best and use common sense and initiative as we remain open to His strength and surrendered to His love. If we do, surely He will protect us in the ultimate consequences and as regards what really matters which may not be at all the same as what we think matters.

Our training takes place in a home, not in a special school. In a home, the life is many-leveled. All the children are not of the same age or possess the same gifts or are fed the same way; they are at every stage of capacity and growth. They are doing different lessons and getting different food. Thus we neither need to view with surprised contempt the crude notions of our spiritual juniors, nor expect to be able to do the same work or digest the same meals as our big brothers and sisters, the saints. We are not to fuss, as we sometimes do, about our spiritual diet, but take our cup of devotional milk and water politely, without gazing anxiously at the contents to see whether we have yet been promoted to weak tea! We shall be given what we can digest.

The real child of God learns to be loyal and simple in accepting its own particular place in the family life. It will read the books and take the food suited to its age, and not clamor for jam tart instead of rice pudding, or insist on Shakespeare when only just able to appreciate "Alice." A certain spiritual conceit often enters into the deliberate choice of advanced books or struggles to participate in particular religious experiences. It really isn't for us to say, "I'm getting to be a big girl now." No prayer or reading or experience which does not fulfill St. Teresa's test of leaving us humbler than it found us is likely to be right for our souls. "It is never a good plan," says St. Francis de Sales, "to walk on the tips of either our bodily or spiritual toes." There may be a serious fall if we trip.

Again, a child who has learned some kindness, seeing the teddy bear it has outgrown being given to the baby, does not enlighten the baby as to its previous history and real composition, but leaves baby alone to enjoy his bear. From this we may perhaps learn to treat with a more reverent charity the symbols under which others enjoy God, however immature they may seem. We can perhaps reflect that in the eyes of the angels, the cleverest of us is not very grown-up and, seen in the light of Reality, there is not overmuch difference between the baby's traditional rattle and our most modern mechanical toy.

Last, and most difficult, the status of a child of God must surely mean a share in that wide and unfastidious charity which pours out the gifts of light and love on all creation. The special characteristics of a child of God are utter confidence toward God and utter generosity toward others. These are the two sides of charity.

We look at the first, at the attribute of confidence, of faith transformed by love, and see where, in Christ's own life that confidence led. We see how the perfect simplicity of His relationship with the Father was the real cause and supply of the power, the unearthly authority, the ceaseless self-giving which struck all those who saw Him. How central was that dependent confidence in His teaching! Remember how He reminded His followers: "Your Heavenly Father knows that you have need of these things." He was saying that although our self-chosen wishes might not be fulfilled, the true essentials would not be withheld any more than we would withhold necessities from our children. The cherishing care of God is for Christ an eternal fact in the universe, and implicit confidence in it is surely the very source of peace in the human heart.

We can see, above all, how this confidence supports the suffering of Christ during the Passion. We are shown it by His words: "Even so, Father. . . . So it seemed good in Thy sight. . . . Not my will, but Thine be done. . . ." And we see that the same childlike attitude persisted through the extremes of suffering, humiliation, and conquering the darkness on the Cross. "Father, into Thy hands I commend my spirit" has become to us the classic expression of heroic trust. And yet it is also, as we now know, the prayer which every little Jewish boy was to say when he went to bed. Those were the words that were uttered when the greatest event in the history of humanity took place, an event which seemed like utter disaster, yet even so was met with confident love.

When it seems to us, from our tiny view point, that something atrocious is happening or going to happen, that we can't brook it, that hope is gone—when we are forced to face a position we cannot stick to—then is the time for us as children of God to take Christ's prayer on our lips. "This is our Lord's will," says Julian of Norwich, "that our prayer and our trust be both alike large."

And now let us go back from Christ to the opening act of the Incarnation. Let us look, as we did in a previous session, at the blessed Virgin, standing at the budding point of Christian history. What did the angelic promise mean to her in terms of amazement, fear, misunderstanding, difficulty, and hardship? And how was it received? With perfect selfless confidence. "Behold, the handmaid of the Lord. Be it unto me according to Thy word!"

That response was not with an initial recourse to the inferiority complex: "I'm not good enough! *I* can't carry it through. I can't do this and bear that. There must be some mistake." But with a confidence that kills self-occupation, she replied, "Be it unto me according to Thy word." That childlike simplicity is the first and greatest of God's gifts to the soul. So if the thought of ourselves as members of Christ is expressed more in the prayer of intercession which we pray as our part of the work of the Mystical Body, the thought of the Child of God leads above all to the humble prayer of confident love in which we perpetually renew our dependence and trust.

Now let us look on the other side of that perfection of relationship which is the ideal of the child of God. Towards others, the child must have something of the Father's wide, patient, generous love. Here is material for meditation as found in Matthew 5:45–47. ". . . that you may be the children of your Father who is in heaven: for He makes His sun to rise on the evil and on the good, and sends rain on the just and on the unjust. . . . Be perfect even as your Father who is in heaven is perfect." The children are to be recognized by their share in the perfection of the Father.

"Perfection" is a big word, but here, of course, its meaning is "to be complete." A perfect circle is just a circle redeemed from the breaks, dints, and bulges which would make it not quite a circle. Thus the invitation to perfection asks the child of God to be what human beings are meant to be: all 'round, complete in self-spending and generosity and undistorted by private preference, departmental kindness, sectional religious sympathies and exclusions, canny benevolence, or the subordination of love to the judgments of an over-stimulated moral sense. It means accepting the station of a child of God and accepting His unfastidious and generous point of view.

Anyone can love the loveable. For us to love the unloveable into loveableness is the very method and art of redemption. Conquering unchristianlike tendencies to dwell on what is just and fair is one of our challenges. According to what is just and fair, the Prodigal Son should have had a poor reception. His reason for coming home was not exalted. He was hard up. He couldn't get anything to satisfy his hunger. But the love of God overrides and quietly accepts our shabby reasons for turning to Him. "When he was yet a great way off, his father saw him and had compassion and *ran*." *That* is what sets the family standard.

"You therefore must be perfect as your heavenly Father is perfect." Do you think we *always* quite live up to it? Do we always *run* to those who have treated us as badly as they possibly could? Do we simply forget the question of just deserts? Do we ignore, not merely struggle with the feeling of just resentment? What about that person whom we have not really liked and who turned out just as we expected? And the others whom we trusted absolutely, but who deliberately deceived us? The person who wounds our affection or who delivers stinging blows to our pride? The person whose actions have injured someone whom we love?

We are not living up to our family privilege or sharing in the divine self-givenness of redeeming and creative love until all these bits of natural self-love (which we tend to justify to ourselves) are melted out of us and our statutory rights are forgotten in our passionate desire for the well-being of the other children, both just and unjust.

Now let us gather up this meditation and look back on it. What does it amount to? Surely it is just this: the perfect fulfillment of the two great commandments of confident love toward God and generous love to others. "You are of God, little children" means not only *you*, but *all* the other children too. All that really matters for the full life and health of our spirit is enclosed or implied in those words which contain our deepest obligation and our holiest privilege.

VII

Inheritors of the Kingdom of Heaven

When I was a child, we used to be taught to swim by lying across a chair on our stomachs and exercising our arms and legs in a corresponding way. It used a great deal of energy, but we ended just where we began and quite dry. When at last we *were* put into the sea and found it wet, salty, deep, and with *no* supporting chair under us, that correct series of movements were at first replaced by desperate struggles. But presently we found ourselves using the movements, or something like them, after all. But it was in a much less exact and deliberate way. We were swimming—badly perhaps, but really swimming!

Now many people try to learn mental prayer lying over a chair on dry land. They go through a correct routine, learning from a book, but end up quite dry and just where they began. But real mental prayer isn't just an exercise. It is an entrance into our inheritance which St. Catherine called the Great Pacific Ocean of God. So, to continue our image, the main point is to get into some new water. What one does in it—diving, quietly floating, swimming, going on long excursions, helping others who are learning, or, while we are small, just contentedly paddling—is of secondary importance. All the accumulated knowledge about swimming is of great interest, but, until we are actually *in* the water, we have no right idea what it means.

Real prayer begins with the plunge into the water. Our movements may then be quite incorrect, but they will be real. If we would look on prayer like that, as above all, an act in which we enter and give ourselves, our souls, to our true *Patria*, our ever-waiting inheritance, God "in whom we live and move and have our being," most of the muddles and problems connected with it would disappear. As I John 4 has already told us, "You are of God, little children." This is where we really belong, and if we will only plunge in, we shall find ourselves mysteriously at home.

And this strange home-like feeling kills the dread which might over-

236

come us if we thought of the terrific and unknown depths beneath and the infinite extent of the power and mystery of the ocean into which we have plunged. As it is, a curious blend of confidence and entire abandonment keeps us, because of our very littleness, in peace and joy. So we continue with our limited powers in the limitless love in which we are held. What matters is the ocean, not the particular little movements which we make.

The very essence of all prayer, the very beginning of all spiritual action, is this entrance into the Ocean of the Love of God, this acceptance of our true heritage. Biology says that our primitive ancestors were creatures of the sea, and the reason why the sea so exhilarates us is that antique affinity. The *plasma*, the vital fluid which is the base of our blood, is more like sea water than anything else. It is a strange allegory, not without bearing on the life of the soul and its need of constant re-immersion in its beginning. We are amphibious creatures. We belong *now* to eternity as well as to time. We have an inheritance in the heavens, in the transcendent.

Until we take up mental prayer we are only living half our lives. Look at the frogs on the edge of the pond. They don't seem exactly at home on dry land though they do wonders in leaping about on it. But after a time they start getting dry, and the glory goes. Then we see a sudden leap into the water and soon after, a transformed creature, utterly at home, with free powerful strokes, in a support medium to which it is perfectly attuned. Presently the frog comes out all glistening, refreshed, revitalized. He couldn't give much of an account of what he has *done*. Still less could he define the nature of the water in which he has revised his being, or think out his own peculiar situation, but he has been at home.

Now I feel that prayer turns out to be rather like that for us. "Like a fish in the sea!" said Mechthild of Magdeburg. To that, we are inclined to respond: "Oh yes, she was a saint, very beautiful, very spiritual—but its not for *me*!" But it is *your* Patria she is describing. You are an inheritor of the kingdom of heaven. You are just letting one side of your life atrophy if you don't use your heritage. Its more keenly appreciated, more expected, more like a shout of joy for the saints, but the world of which they speak is ours too.

Remember Paul's words: "Whether . . . life or death or things present or things to come: all are yours and you are Christ's and Christ is God's" [1 Cor. 3:22]. St. Paul added those strange words as he spoke to a very mixed lot of converts whom he had just described as spiritual infants, not to specialists initiated into the contemplative life. We enter heaven, which is reality, when we give ourselves courageously to God, enter His life, and participate in His creation with selfless joy. And our Christian prerogative is to *do* this, not some day, but *now*.

"If children, then heirs," writes Paul in the eighth chapter to the

Romans. We are children of a double order and *ought* to expect, as natural and spiritual creatures, another life to live here and now. We can remember and resort to that eternal love which never leaves us, enter and re-enter that ocean, and carry its refreshment through our days and weeks. Christianity emphasizes our heavenly inheritance, asks us to attend to it, and dwells on it. A time like we have had here reminds us of how real it is and should send us back with determination to maintain a better balance between our visible and invisible lives.

Now let us look at another point under another set of images. Like heirs of a great estate which we have inherited, we have responsibilities as well as possessions. We have to deal with the estate and administer it as well as enjoy it. We must make room for it in our lives. Often the tiresome feature about an inheritance is that it may not be what *we* would have chosen or what we think we would want. It may force us to change our whole way of life and sacrifice ourselves to the amusements and comforts of others.

You know what it is if you live in a small flat and suddenly hear that you've inherited all of the family silver. Every cupboard is already stuffed, although not with valuable things. Somehow you *can't* empty them. The new things arrive, but a worrysome confusion of strewn paper fills every corner and stops all sorts of enjoyment and enrichment.

That situation is reproduced in most people's pile of affirmative claims. To us it is suddenly said: "The kingdom is yours! Take up your inheritance." But there is no room in our lives for it. Instead, there is an awful sense of muddle and a strange perception that it is a practical truth that we *can't* serve God and mammon, that insatiable greed for riches. We must either put our new treasures in the bank, get no use of them, or move to suitable premises where there is enough space, light, and air. We must move away from the laborsome tiny flat in the spiritual suburbs to which we have clung so tenaciously, those suburbs which are neither town nor country. What a wretched sort of life for those who have inherited the kingdom of heaven, who actually "*have* a building of God, a house not made with hands, eternal in the heavens" but yet whose family only lives in it on weekends!

It is vitally important to adapt yourself to that inheritance *now* and live in it *now*. It will be your particular house in the heavens, not someone else's. It is not made to a fixed design. Heaven is not a building estate. Our inheritance *is* in heaven, but that doesn't include all this in it. We get what suits *our* souls, as much garden as we can cultivate.

Look at all the grades and kinds of blessedness in Paradise in which Dante found the spirits living. Each had its own place, its own beatitude, its own relationship to God and to each other. *That* was heaven. There was no claimfulness, no aspiring after things which belong to others with fuller knowledge, purer love of God, or more of a gift of prayer. For some, the Beatific Vision is only as strong as moonlight; others dwell in a heaven of sunlight. But all is heaven because all is within the will of God.

I think that we haven't dealt with the reality of our inheritance because our vision lacks the certitude, splendor, and fullness of the saints. We get what we can deal with: perhaps a cottage, perhaps a farm, perhaps a great industry, perhaps a steady, moderate income coming in bit by bit. Its enriching influence may enter our lives almost unconsciously.

Look at the dividends that are paid directly into our bank! We never see them. We don't feel especially rich spiritually. We don't realize our good fortune until one day we need a lump sum. The pinch comes, the need arises, and then we think we'll have to face the bankruptcy of our peace and happiness. Suffering drains our resources bit by bit or another human creature applies for spiritual food and supplies and it doesn't seem to us that we *can* have anything to give them. Then, to our real surprise, our check is honored. We find we do possess something absolutely solid which we ourselves couldn't possibly have saved in virtue of taking up our Christian heritage.

That heritage comes to us from many sources. It may have been handed down from our historical past. The saints have bequeathed to us, as members of their family, their experiences, their hoard of spiritual treasures, their tools and the secrets of their craftsmanship. We ought to take all that too and use it. It comes through them from God.

We have an inheritance that comes down all those channels which are another level of life, experience, joy, and obligation. They are not mere pleasantness, comfort, or security, but a sharing in the things of God and the deep reality of Christ. Thus pain, struggle, darkness, and sacrifice may be the price of our heritage. The heir to a great property often goes from a life of sleek comfort to one burdened with care. We all share the family obligation of self-giving and self-forgetfulness.

When we speak of our Lord as the Word, what do we mean but that He is in Himself the declaration, the perfect utterance of God's thought? The kingdom of heaven, which is our inheritance, draws near where the mysterious Presence draws near. It comes quite as often, I should think *more* often, in times of suffering, grief, loneliness, disillusionment, and frustrated effort with their opportunities of heroic acceptance. In this life, the inheritance of the kingdom given to us is not just a dwelling place of peace and assurance, but one in the center of which the Cross still stands. It is like one of those lands one sees in Tyrol where the cross of Calvary stands against the eternal snows.

Consider where we stand collectively or individually. We are here, now, in this place, at a particular point in history, occupying a specific position in the unfolding purpose of God. That purpose moves like a great and steady tide in and through His creation. It may seem in its depth and mystery to swamp you and me. It may work out in terms which seem to be failure or frustration for *us*. Nevertheless, in that will is our peace, our joy, and our inheritance of heaven so long as we let our own wills go with it, lose ourselves in it, and are immersed in it. Misery, bitterness, and *real* failure only come when we try to go the other way. "Sink thou into thy nothingness," said Eckhart, "and all things shall be thine."

"Where we *are*," say the mystics, "is heaven and hell. We do not have to go far to find them." Whatever will I have, heaven means self-loss in the purposes of God, becoming a tiny channel for the expression of His love. Hell means the self-centered struggle to express my own personal aims, a struggle which shuts the door on God and seals up my soul against the golden shower.

"Paradise is no other thing than God Himself," said another mystic, "for no other thing is Paradise than to see God. And this the soul knows in truth at all times when she is unencumbered of herself." So you see, our inheritance of heaven, eternal life, the life of prayer, the full, all 'round development of our Christian vocation means just this: the secure possession and enjoyment of God in proportion as we are unencumbered of ourselves. It does not mean to be clear of jobs, troubles, or sufferings, but merely to be clear of self-regard in every form. We are not self-made, but we are inheritors. What a difference! There is nothing of the self-made person about the saint. There is no grim struggle for their own success. So, too, everything worth having is given to us—not fought for or earned. Thus it may include things we would never have chosen. It may take a form we would never have guessed. Yet is it given by love, and when received by love it brings us to God. That is heaven: the love, joy, and peace of the Spirit harnessed, humbled, and unencumbered of itself.

I am not going to prolong this last meditation. In these last hours of retreat we most fruitfully spend our time in silence. I don't wish to give new thoughts and suggestions, but rather to gather up anything we have gained. What have we done? What have we thought about the greatness and richness of our spiritual inheritance, the life of prayer in which our souls can have communion with God? What are the unearthly riches He pours down on us and the humble acts of adoration, friendship, and collaboration with which we can respond? What matters first of all, may not be a very showy or a very religious sort of thing.

Oh Lord, *Thou* art my heritage, the companion of my pilgrimage. All that can matter in my life, whether big or little, is what you do through me.

God is the soul's country. Real prayer must always bring us to that.

Indexes

INDEX OF PERSONS

241

INDEX OF SUBJECTS
("def." = definition)